# ATLANTIC STUDIES ON SOCIETY IN CHANGE

Editor-in-Chief, Béla K. Király

Associate Editor-in-Chief, Peter Pastor

No. 65

# TOWNS IN MEDIEVAL HUNGARY

Edited by
LÁSZLÓ GEREVICH

Social Science Monographs, Boulder, Colorado
Atlantic Research and Publications, Highland Lakes, New Jersey

Distributed by Columbia University Press
1990

EAST EUROPEAN MONOGRAPHS No. CCXCVII

Translated by
T. SZENDREI

English text revised by
P. C. McCULLOCH

JOINT PUBLICATION WITH AKADÉMIAI KIADÓ, BUDAPEST 1990

ISBN 0-88033-194-I

Printed in Hungary
by Akadémiai Kiadó és Nyomda Vállalat

# PREFACE TO THE SERIES

The present volume is a component of a series that, when completed, will constitute a comprehensive survey of the many aspects of East Central European society.

These volumes deal with the peoples whose homelands lie between the Germans to the West, the Russians to the East and North, and the Mediterranean and Adriatic Seas to the South. They constitute a particular civilization, one that is at once an integral part of Europe, yet substantially different from the West. The area is characterized by rich variety in language, religion, and government. The study of this complex subject demands a multidisciplinary approach and, accordingly, our contributors represent several academic disciplines. They have been drawn from universities and other scholarly institutions in the United States, Western Europe, as well as East Central Europe.

The Editor-in-Chief, of course, takes full responsibility for ensuring the comprehensiveness, cohesion, internal balance, and scholarly quality of the series he has launched. I cheerfully accept this responsibility and intend this work to be neither a justification nor a condemnation of the policies, attitudes, and activities of any of the persons involved. At the same time, because the contributors represent so many different disciplines, interpretations, and schools of thought, our policy in this, as in past and future volumes, is to present their contributions without modification. Finally, the Editor-in-Chief wishes to thank the Soros Foundation in New York for the financial support of the series.

Budapest, 1990. August 20.                                              BÉLA K. KIRÁLY

# CONTENTS

6

# INTRODUCTION

There are few fields of historical studies that express 'development' in a more spectacular or dramatic form than urban studies that have only recently caught the interest of most historians.

The cultural achievements and historic fate of medieval Hungary was by and large determined by the fact that during the Roman Imperial period this region lay on the periphery of classical culture and Roman power, and formed one of its most important border zones (the Danubian *limes*); the border zone-like nature of this region can also be noted in Charlemagne's eastern aspirations. Its dividing role was dual: it separated the Romanised south and west from the Barbarian north and the alien, nomadic east. The Hungarian Kingdom united the Barbarian and Romanised regions and overcame the divergences in geographic landscapes and cultural levels between the various regions of the Middle Danube region which prevented the emergence of a uniform imperium or kingdom until the close of the lst millennium.

The history of the first few centuries of the Hungarian state was at first decisively influenced by this situation: for it was to this region that nomadic peoples migrated from the east, and it was this area where the political aspirations of eastern and western Christianity, and of the German and Slav peoples clashed. The emerging Hungarian state overcame these divergences, and there evolved a strong state that gradually reached cultural uniformity on the fringes of medieval Western Europe. However, this peripheral state at all times preserved the vestiges of its diverse cultural components that were, for example, reflected by regionally differing settlement systems and settlement forms. This is most clearly illustrated by the regionally differing town types that, in a sense, only became uniform following the arrival of western *hospites* in the 11th–12th centuries. The towns founded by the *hospites* often preserved influences of the area whence they migrated.

One of the most intriguing problems is posed by Transdanubia—the most developed region that bears most resemblances to Western Europe—, namely, whether in spite of the longeval Barbarian rule there remained any strands linking it to the Roman period beside the antique ruins. It is an undisputed fact that urbanisation disseminated from this region both formally and legally. The first capitals and larger towns emerged along the Danube, in the best fortified parts of the former Danubian *limes*. At the same time, the Danube acted as a link to the west. Towns were dotted along the river at the intersection of major routes and river fords; these towns, that were more or less similar in plan, could all boast ferries, marketplaces, coves of tributaries, winter harbours of warm springs, towers protecting the harbour *(portus)* and a citadel of sorts. The towns of Pozsony (Bratislava), Győr, Visegrád, Vác, Esztergom and Buda virtually all shared the same topographic plan and perfected a characteristic outlay whose parallels can be quoted from the Upper Danube region. However, this had slightly different implications for Hungary: the Danube was an artery linking this peripheral region to the west without which this region would never have grown into a powerful medieval state that was for centuries able to check the forces attacking Europe at her most vulnerable point. It would appear that this area, girded by high mountains, can be considered as a corridor between the northern Germanic and Slavic plainland, and the Mediterranean Balkans embracing a Byzantine culture; and even though it differed from both, it nonetheless acted as a kind of corridor for migrating peoples and various cultural influences, through which peoples migrated mainly from the east— even though the opposite can also be quoted: the Celts, whose hillforts and oppida in Esztergom and Buda predate the Roman towns there. Esztergom, Óbuda (Old Buda) and Buda were capitals of the country from the 11th century.

Spectacular results have been achieved in the excavation of royal castles and palaces. In Esztergom the excavations were begun in the 1930s; at Óbuda at the dawn of the 20th century; in Buda in the mid-1940s. The latter investigations covered the entire area of Castle Hill, whilst in Óbuda the one-time royal castle and its fortifications were uncovered during the 1960s and the 1970s. The excavations at Sopron, Kőszeg, Székesfehérvár, Veszprém and Pécs have considerably broadened our perspectives, even though the full evaluation of excavation results is not yet available. The various excavation reports and publications would fill a library and even a brief survey would exceed the scope and objective of this volume, since it was thought that this compendium of studies should cover the cultural context and historic importance of the different — but nonetheless highly developed — towns and town groups of Hungary.

The problems concerning the role of previous urban agglomeration, in other words, Romanisation need also be clarified in the case of Pannonian and Danubian towns. The plan of the former Roman town is known in the case of all Pannonian and Danubian towns; moreover, Roman watchtowers and cemeteries have been uncovered in their vicinity. Nonetheless, there is hardly any evidence for the survival of the antique population and their culture, or for the continuous, uninterrupted occupation of these towns, the only possible exception being Fenékpuszta. There is no forthcoming solution to this problem yet in spite of the fact that the plan of the earlier Roman and the later medieval town generally coincides and that the Roman buildings were reused, rebuilt or renewed; their stones were often used in the construction of 11th–13th century buildings when the Roman quarries had not yet been reopened or re-exploited.

The survival of the population and its links with the Roman town is illustrated by the report on the excavations at Győr. The full evaluation of the investigations at Óbuda had not been completed at the time of the brief preliminary report submitted for this volume. The Roman towns were considerably larger than the later medieval towns, as for example at Óbuda, where not only the remains of buildings, but also sections of the town walls were reused as in other parts of the former *Imperium Romanum*. However, they no longer fulfilled their former role since in the early Middle Ages it was the Barbarian overlords of provincial estates that wielded power instead of the large towns representing state power. The bloodstained drama of transformation, first acted out in Pannonia, was not mitigated by the mediation of the Church that played an active role in the transformation of the classical heritage. Interestingly enough, it is on Pannonian territory that the emergence of medieval towns adopted from the west can be noted

from the beginning of the 2nd millennium. In contrast to antique towns, the royal ones, such as county seats, wedged inbetween the estates of feudal power, began their production and trade in a more protected position, and also their gradual development towards democracy, a development that made full use of the organisational and cultural possibilities offered by the Church in the establishment of new towns.

It can be demonstrated for the major Danubian towns and also for towns lying in other regions of Hungary that the royal and ecclesiastic town parts (Esztergom, Győr and Óbuda) frequently lay beside each other, often in the same castle (Esztergom, Veszprém and Győr). However, their decline appears to have been unarrestable if from royal suzerainty they passed into the hands of a feudal owner such as the Church (Esztergom, Óbuda).

A network of major towns, reminiscent of the Danubian ones, bordered the Great Hungarian Plain in the uplands along the road leading northeast. It would appear that the nature, layout and architecture of a given town was to a large extent influenced by the region in which it lay. Thus, for instance, the south German influence was extremely strong in western Pannonia, whilst in the towns of Northern Hungary a Slavic–German influence reminiscent of the eastern towns of the Holy Roman Empire can be noted.

The Southern Hungarian towns that came under the influence of Byzantium at an early date are among the least known in terms of archaeological research. They emerged under extremely contrasting influences in focal points of roads leading to the Balkans, Northern Italy and the coastland. These towns developed along different lines than the western ones and, similarly to the towns of the Great Hungarian Plain, they did not have a castle that elsewhere played a decisive role in the emergence of towns.

It is to be hoped that the studies collected in the present volume will offer new insights into the colourful picture of medieval Hungarian towns, into their history and controversial situation arising from their peripheral location.

# THE SETTLEMENT HISTORY OF GYŐR (ARRABONA)
# IN THE ROMAN PERIOD AND IN THE MIDDLE AGES

## D. Gabler–E. Szőnyi–P. Tomka

### ARRABONA DURING THE ROMAN CONQUEST

Imperial Rome, after subduing the territory of present-day Transdanubia during the reign of Augustus,[1] took possession of the strategic points along the Danube under Claudius (and in some places, somewhat earlier).[2] One of the first steps in the Roman military occupation was the strengthening of the hold over the fords and main intersection at the mouth of the river Rába. Recent research has revealed that the military occupation of Arrabona may have taken place soon after the establishment of the legionary fortress at Carnuntum, the first *limes* fortress of the Romans.[3]

The Late Iron Age settlement layer cut through by L. Barkóczi during the excavations at Káptalan hill in the area of the Roman fort[4] led earlier researchers to assume that the Celts had perhaps used the Győr basin as a military stronghold, realizing its strategic significance. Accordingly, the defence of the fords at Káptalan hill beyond the river (the new town) had long been considered an unavoidable necessity for effective military organization.[5]

That many of the Roman *limes* settlements had been built in the vicinity of, or even on top of, the earlier Celtic hillforts is well documented. The strategic fortifications inherited by the Romans were either reoccupied (like Acumincum–Stari Slankamen,[6] Lugio–Dunaszek-

cső[7] or Solva–Esztergom[8]), or were destroyed and replaced by an auxiliary garrison designed for exercising control over the population settled on the plain (Hainburg–Carnuntum,[9] Wien–Leopoldsberg–Vindobona camp,[10] Buda–Gellérthegy,[11] Aquincum and Albertfalva, and Ostffyasszonyfa[12]–Bassania–Sárvár in the heart of the province, along the military routes).

However tempting it may be to assume a strategic continuity in Győr, i.e. to infer certain Celtic predecessors at the fort at Káptalan hill, the available evidence firmly contradicts these assumptions. Firstly, no Celtic artefacts were identified among the finds brought to light by the excavations conducted in 1955,[13] and thus the pottery could not be related definitely to early, middle or late Celtic types or to the wares of the Roman Imperial period. Secondly, the more extensive excava-

[1] For the history of Pannonia during the reign of Augustus, cf. A. Mócsy: Illyricum északi határa Claudius előtt (Die Nordgrenze Illyricums vor Claudius). *ArchÉrt* 106 (1979) 177–186.

[2] For details of the occupation under Claudius, cf. L. Barkóczi: *Intercisa II*. ArchHung 36. Budapest (1957) 449; J. Fitz: Die Eroberung Pannoniens. *ANRW* II. 6. Berlin (1977) 552–556.

[3] Cf. M. Grünewald: Zur Frühzeit des römischen Carnuntum. *AnzÖAW* 116 (1979) 1–8.

[4] Borbiró–Valló (1956) 127–130, offers a brief account of the excavations.

[5] A. Uzsoki: Győr településtörténete az őskorban (The prehistoric settlement history of Győr). *Győr. Várostörténeti Tanulmányok*. Ed. by L. Dávid–A. Lengyel–L. Z. Szabó. Győr (1971) 14.

[6] D. Dimitrijević: Recherches de Musée National de Zemun

sur le limes romain. *Starinar* 7–8 (1956–1957) 307–308; D. Dimitrijević: Spätlatenèzeitliche oppida in Jugoslawien. *Arch Rozhl* 23 (1971) 567–587.

[7] É. F. Petress: The Late Pre-Roman Age in Hungary with Special Reference to Oppida. *Oppida: The Beginnings of Urbanization in Barbarian Europe*. Ed. by B. Cunliffe and T. Rowley. BAR International Series II. 11. Oxford (1976) 59; for the Dunaszekcső camp, cf. F. Fülep: Lugio. *Der römische Limes in Ungarn*. IKMK A. 22. Székesfehérvár (1976) 113.

[8] É. F. Petress, *op. cit.*, 54; *MRT* 5, 78; Soproni (1978) 16–21.

[9] H. Mitscha-Märheim: Die vorgeschichtliche Wallburg auf dem Braunsberg bei Hainburg. *Mitteilungen des Vereins der Freunde Carnuntums* 3 (1950) 2–7.

[10] R. Pittioni: Ein spätkeltischer Töpferofenfund von Wien III. *Jahresbericht des Vereins für Landeskunde von Niederösterreich und Wien* 28 (1939–1943) 1–9; H. Kerchler: Das Brandgräberfeld der jüngeren Urnenfelderkultur auf dem Leopoldsberg Wien. *ArchAustr* 31 (1962) 49ff, 70ff; L. Franz–A. Neumann: *Lexikon Ur- und frühgeschichtlicher Fundstätten Österreichs*. Vienna (1965) 204.

[11] É. B. Bónis: *Die spätkeltische Siedlung Gellérthegy–Tabán in Budapest*. ArchHung 47. Budapest (1969).

[12] M. Károlyi: Őskori településtörténet (Prehistoric settlement history). *Sárvár monográfiája*. Ed. by F. Horváth. Szombathely (1978) 63; T. Buócz: Római kor (The Roman Period). *ibid.*, 67–76.

[13] Borbiró-Valló (1956) 131.

tions carried out later—in 1969,[14] 1974 and 1978, led by E. Szőnyi and P. Tomka—likewise did not uncover Celtic layers on Káptalan hill. The majority of Celtic cemeteries and stray finds known from the environs of Győr can definitely be assigned to the early or middle La Tène period; few finds from the La Tène D period, that immediately preceded the Roman Age, have been reported from among these.[15] This can probably be attributed to the Dacian wars in the mid-1st century B. C. and the military campaigns of Boirebistas which, according to contemporary sources, had resulted in the depopulation of the area to an extent which prompted the sources to refer to the area simply as *deserta Boiorum*.[16] A more exact understanding of the settlement patterns in the Rába region would be gained through further archaeological excavations; the suggestion that Arrabona had earlier been a centre of the Eravisci also remains to be proved.[17]

Roman inscriptions found in Arrabona and its immediate vicinity do not provide evidence for presuming a dense native population in the area. However, the same does not apply to the comparable objects coming from the western territories of the Boii or the area settled by the Eravisci. The natives named in the inscriptions (Siscianus, Colapianus, Breucus) were South Pannonian in origin, who reached the *castellum* on the river Rába as soldiers of the *ala Pannoniorum* stationed in Arrabona.[18] That no native names or persons could be identified in the area may be related either to the small number of the original settlers or to their quick assimilation.[19] The burial customs of the natives did not include the erection of tombstones, therefore no inscriptions or sculptural relics were recovered from their traditional burials. However, the hand-made pottery found in the earliest layers of the Roman Imperial period are clearly indicative of the presence of the natives in the area. (Quite a number of hand-made native pottery was brought to light during the excavation in 1978 from the earliest

layer of Káptalan hill.) The fill of a small semi-subterranean hut also yielded amphora sherds and Tiberian sigillata wares. Iron Age pottery types were not recovered from the deposits dating from the mid-1st century or later. Stray specimens of hand-made vessels have also come to light in the *vicus*. Some of the inhumation graves in the Kálvária Street cemetery, dating from the turn of the 1st–2nd centuries, can be linked to the tradition-bound native population who, similarly to certain groups of the Eravisci, had preserved the tradition of simple inhumation.[20] However, the artefacts buried together with the deceased were for the most part Roman, with only a few winged brooches (Flügelfibel) of Noricum–Pannonia, indicating the survival of the traditional native costume.[21]

Recently the idea has been put forward that the rivers Rába and Marcal marked the eastern boundaries of Noricum annexed by the Romans in 16 B. C., and the military forts at Arrabona and, presumably, also at Sárvár were marked out for defending the eastern frontiers of the occupied province.[22]

In our opinion the camps at Arrabona and Sárvár, the latter presumably dating from the first half of the 1st century, should be considered parts of the boundary routes (called *limes* during the reign of the Julius–Claudius dynasty[23]), supplying and covering the advanced camps, rather than parts of a *limes* system (frontier, defence line) created only in later times. The strategy employed in the conquest under Augustus and Tiberius precludes the possibility of presuming linear frontier defences—comparable to those in later times—along the rivers Danube or Rába. On the other hand, we have every reason to believe that the route between Savaria and the mouth of the river Rába supplying Arrabona was fortified with strong posts and bases built at more or less regular intervals at fords and strategic points, similarly to the strongholds, forts and strategic veterans' settlements built to defend the Amber Road supplying Carnuntum, which was occupied between 35–40 A. D.[24] The early finds (pottery, coins, glass) and the observations made during the excavations suggested similar forts or bases near Sárvár (Bassiana) and Árpás (Mursella).[25]

[14] K. Kozák–A. Uzsoki: A győri székesegyház feltárása (Les fouilles exécutées dans la cathédrale de Győr). *Arrabona* 12 (1970) 111–159.

[15] Cf. A. Uzsoki: Győr településtörténete az őskorban (The prehistoric settlement history of Győr). *Győr. Várostörténeti tanulmányok*. Ed. by L. Dávid–A. Lengyel–L. Z. Szabó. Győr (1971) 14–16. The La Tène Period finds from the environs of Győr were analysed by E. Jerem. She found that artefacts that could be assigned to the Late Celtic period were very scarce in the Győr assemblage.

[16] Pliny, *Nat.hist.* III. 146. Cf. A. Alföldi: Zur Geschichte des Karpatenbeckens in 1. Jh. v. Chr. *Ostmitteleuropäische Bibliothek* 37 (1942) 6; A. Mócsy: Pannonia. *PWRE*, Suppl. IX (1962) 529; M. Szabó: *A kelták nyomában Magyarországon (Heritage of the Celts in Hungary)*. Budapest (1971) 18.

[17] J. Fitz: Arrabona, Arabo, Aravisci. *Alba Regia* 4–5 (1963–1964 [1965]) 255.

[18] *CIL* III 4377 = *RIU* 256 (Breucus), *CIL* III 4373 = *RIU* 259 (Siscianus), *CIL* III 4372 = *RIU* 255 (Colapianus); cf. A. Mócsy: *Die Bevölkerung Pannoniens bis zu den Markomannenkriegen*. Budapest (1959) 243.

[19] Z. Farkas–D. Gabler: *Corpus Signorum Imperii Romani II. Die Skulpturen des Stadtgebietes Scarbantia und der westpannonischen Limesstrecke Ad Flexum–Arrabona (Kom. Győr-Sopron)*. Budapest (in print).

[20] E. Szőnyi: A győri Kálvária utcai római temető csontvázas sírjai (Inhumation burials in the Kálvária Street Roman Cemetery in Győr). *Arrabona* 16 (1974) 30.

[21] *Ibid.*, Fig. 6.

[22] E.g. *J. Fitz:* Die Eroberung Pannoniens. *ANRW* II. 6. Berlin (1977) 555, note 51, and E. Tóth: Epigraphisches aus Savaria. *Alba Regia* 13 (1972) [1974]) 301.

[23] G. Forni: Limes. *Dizionario Epigr.* Vol. 4. Fasc. 34, 1080; A. Piganol: La notion de limes. *Quintus Congressus Internationalis Limitis Romani Studiosorum*. Arheološki Radovi i Rasprave 3. Zagreb (1963) 119–122; H. Schönberger: Der römische Limes in Deutschland. Begriff und Funktion. *Forschungs- und Sitzungsbericht 48. Historische Raumforschung 7. Grenzbildende Faktoren in der Geschichte*. Hannover (1969) 14.

[24] D. Gabler: Pannonia megszállásának néhány kérdése a terra sigilláták tükrében (Die Besitznahme Pannoniens im Spiegel der Sigillaten). *ArchÉrt* 106 (1979) 199–216.

[25] Cf. E. Tóth: A Savaria–Bassiana útvonal (The Savaria–Bassiana route). *ArchÉrt* 104 (1977) 65 ff. The excavations at

## ARRABONA IN THE 1ST CENTURY.
## THE EARLY *ALA* CAMP AND SETTLEMENT

The first garrison of the fort built in the 1st century near the strategic point of the mouth of the river Rába, consisted of light cavalry (the same can be said of the camps at Aquincum, Vindobona and, presumably, also Brigetio). During the reign of Claudius (and possibly also in the preceding years) the fords were defended by the troops of the *ala Pannoniorum*, commanded there from the Peresznye camp on the Amber Road. In the mid-1st century these troops were replaced by the *ala I Augusta Ituraeorum*.[26] The earliest fort of the *ala* is assumed to have stood on Káptalan hill. Although its exact dimensions are unknown, the area of the 1st century *quingenaria* fort must have been considerably smaller than that of the *ala milliariae* built at a later date. The layer containing the remains of the first camp was cut through by L. Barkóczi in 1955; the 1974, 1976 and 1978 campaigns[27] brought to light some of the buildings and their remains.[28] Conforming to the architecture of this period, the earliest *castellums* were all earth-timber forts. On the plot of a late 17th century store-house (3 Martinovics Square) and the basement of the neighbouring building (1–2 Martinovics Square) there were uncovered foundation trenches and postholes of timber barracks, timber-framed houses, as well as burnt daub fragments. These timber buildings were probably rebuilt on several occasions during the 1st century, as suggested by the intersecting foundation trenches uncovered on the site. Regrettably enough, it is extremely difficult to establish the chronological sequence of these rebuildings, since the layer containing these structures was too thin to provide a firm basis for applying archaeological methods. The earliest artefacts—some of which were recovered in secondary position from later constructions—included types definitely antedat-

ing the reign of Claudius. These finds, current in the last phases of the merchants' settlement at Magdalensberg (before A. D. 45, i.e. under Tiberius), include Hofheim 1 and Hofheim 5 type North Italian sigillata;[29] hemispherical rough cast cups, vessels with appliqué decoration and dark-grey, thin-walled, 'Gitterbecher' types.[30] Thus the excavations conducted at the fort definitely supported the results obtained during the excavation of the adjoining civilian settlement (*vicus*) and of the investigations carried out in Széchenyi Square in 1968–1969,[31] as well as the earlier analyses of the inscriptions, the tombstone sculptures and the pottery too.[32] Arrabona was presumably occupied in the second half of the 30s or in the early 40s A. D.; accordingly, this Claudian fort must have been erected earlier than the fortifications on the Danubian *limes*, the occupation of which may be related to the events around A. D. 50, i.e. with the fall of Vannius' vassal kingdom.[33]

The buildings of the *vicus* attached to the earliest fort of an *ala* have come to light in an approximately 10×25 m area in Széchenyi Square. Most of the buildings were timber-framed constructions with foundations and thin wooden walls. The walls were daubed with clay, and were occasionally also painted (as suggested by the wall-plaster fragments recovered in the lowest layer). Since the layer of the timber constructions yielded no tiles, the houses were presumably covered with shingles or reeds.[34]

The observations concerning the date of the erection of the fort made at the settlement were supported by the coins found in the earliest burials of the Homokgödör cemetery (the area demarcated by the plant of the Győr Carriage and Waggon Works, the Danube, the Budai and Vas Gereben Streets). The cemetery flanked the road leading to Brigetio along a 300–350 m long section. The observations made in this area suggest that the first burials can be dated to the mid-1st century.[35] The *vicus* was presumably smaller in the 1st century than in the 2nd–3rd centuries—this may be inferred from the cremation burial found in Ujkapu Street, close to the Danube[36] (indicating that the early wing of the cemetery may have lain much closer to the camp),[37] and also from the fact that some of the tombstones that date to the middle third of the 1st century had come to light in an area still closer to the fort. It would appear that the tombstones had not been far removed from their original findspot even if they were later reused in the construction of Late Roman graves or smaller houses. (Obviously, this does not apply to the tombstones found

Árpás, led by E. T. Szőnyi, were started in 1973. Since then, a number of early Italian sigillata, glass and other artefacts have come to light. Considering these finds, the suggestion that in the 1st century Mursella was a simple *vicus* of the local population is hardly tenable. Its strategic location (a crossing place on a main road) and its distance from Arrabona and Bassiana do not support this assumption.

[26] For the early occupation of Arrabona, cf. A. Radnóti–L. Barkóczi: The Distribution of Troops in Pannonia Inferior. *ActaArchHung* 1 (1951) 209; A. Mócsy: Pannonia. *PWRE*, Suppl. IX (1962) 619; D. Gabler: Arrabona. *PRWE*, Suppl. XII (1970) 91–92. The camp of the *ala Pannoniorum* was thought to have been at Gyalóka, the findspot of the inscriptions *CIL* III 4227, 4228. However, these inscriptions definitely come from Peresznye. Cf. D. Gabler: Römerzeitliche Villa in Szakony–Békástó. *MittArchInst* 2 (1971) 57; Z. Farkas–D. Gabler: *Corpus Signorum Imperii Romani II. Die Skulpturen des Stadtgebietes Scarbantia und der westpannonischen Limesstrecke Ad Flexum–Arrabona*. Budapest (in print).

[27] For the earlier observations on the camp, cp. E. Lovas: I risultati degli studi archeologici su Arrabona e dintorni. Le ricerche di archeologia romana nell'Ungheria dopo la guerra. *Bolletino Assoziazione Internazionale Studi Mediterranei* 2 (1931) 3; Borbiró–Valló (1956) 127.

[28] E. T. Szőnyi–P. Tomka: Győr, Martinovics tér 3. *ArchÉrt* 106 (1979) 279.

[29] Szőke–Szőnyi–Tomka (1976) 109.

[30] E. Schindler-Kaudelka: *Die dünnwandige Gebrauchskeramik vom Magdalensberg.* Kärntner Museumsschriften 58. Klagenfurt (1975) forms 95, 115, 120.

[31] Gabler (1971a) 16.

[32] D. Gabler: Arrabona legkorábbi sigillátái (The earliest sigillatas of Arrabona). *Arrabona* 9 (1967) 25, 49–50.

[33] Mócsy (1974) 48–50.

[34] Gabler (1971a) 10.

[35] Szőnyi (1976) 31–32.

[36] Lovas (1942) 14.

[37] D. Gabler: Arrabona legkorábbi sigillátái (The earliest sigillatas of Arrabona). *Arrabona* 9 (1967) 22–23.

built into the wall of the cathedral. These stones were in all probability transported to the site from distant territories.) The road was probably flanked by a thin strip of the cemetery as implied by an observation made in 1977 in the plot of the house at 59, Rákóczi Street.[38] Early Roman pottery vessels, deposited as grave goods, were displaced from their original position by agricultural work and were found in a black humus layer under the remains of an Árpádian Age settlement.

The transfer of the *ala I Augusta Ituraeorum sagittariorum* to Intercisa may have taken place at about A. D. 92.[39] The artefacts found at the site provide evidence for a longer stationing of this troop in Arrabona. This suggestion is especially significant in the light of an earlier suggestion that the military unit *cohors I Noricorum equitata*,[40] recorded by contemporary inscriptions, had been stationed in Győr. According to the practice of the period, the commander of this troop, P. Volcatius Primus, was also the head of the *civitas Boiorum* and the *civitas Azaliorum,* the administrative units of the natives set up by the Romans and vested with limited autonomy. The fort of this unit had earlier been located to Arrabona on the assumption that the Rába delta, which at the same time separated the two *civitates,* may have been ideal for keeping both areas under military control. However, no inscription recording the *cohors I Noricorum* has yet come to light in Győr. The layers dating from the Flavian age found in Széchenyi Square had earlier been linked to the stationing of the unit in Győr. But the years after A. D. 73, the time of Vespasian and Domitian, saw large-scale building activity along the Danubian *limes* in Pannonia[41] (the timber barracks and the wattle-and-daub constructions of the earth-timber fort on Káptalan hill may also have been repaired and rebuilt within the framework of this programme), and thus there is little conclusive evidence for directly associating these layers with the stationing of the *cohors I Noricorum equitata* there. The marked increase in the number of goods imported to the camp during the last years of the 1st century[42] does not expressively indicate the stationing of a new military unit since this tendency was typical of almost all the camps throughout the province.

That the Flavian layers have survived in Széchenyi Square, in the territory of the *vicus,* is mainly due to the fact that this low-lying area had to be filled in repeatedly; the layers dating to the turn of the 1st–2nd centuries were found 1–1.5 m above the Claudian levels. During the reign of the Flavian dynasty the settlement presumably extended over a larger area; this is indicated by the fact that in the Kálvária Street cemetery, the other large

necropolis in present-day Győr,[43] the first burials can be dated to the reign of Domitian. The artefacts recovered from the settlement and the cemeteries all indicate a considerable increase in the degree of supply to these areas.

ARRABONA IN THE FIRST HALF
OF THE 2ND CENTURY.
THE FORT AND *VICUS* OF THE *ALA I ULPIA
CONTARIORUM MILLIARIA*

The transfer of a new military unit to Arrabona in the first decades of the 2nd century brought about considerable changes in the life of the settlement.[44] The *ala I Ulpia contariorum milliaria,* formed under Trajan, was presumably commanded there to replace the *ala I Hispanorum Aravacorum,* stationed in the town until the end of the 1st century.[45] The 1000-strong cavalry, replacing the 500 soldiers of the departing unit, may have had important military assignments, similar to those in the Marcomann wars. The fort of Arrabona was the garrison of the most efficient auxiliary unit in Pannonia Superior, i.e. in the western half of Pannonia that had been divided into two parts by Trajan. Obviously, a number of new buildings had to be erected in the *castellum* of the departing *ala quingenaria* to accommodate the redoubled troops. Thus the earlier earth-timber fort was gradually replaced by stone structures. In the course of the reconstructions, paved roads were built in the camp in the first half of the 2nd century. The fragmentary tiles bearing the inscriptions ...*P CON*.. and *AL I V*... must have been used in their constructions. However, the excavated area was too small to provide evidence as to the date of these stone structures, and therefore they could not be ascribed definitely to either Trajan's or Hadrian's reign. The stone structures in the legionary fortress at Carnuntum were erected under Trajan,[46] whilst those along the Pannonian section of the *limes* date from the reign of Hadrian and Antoninus Pius. In Arrabona, the first stone structures may have been built simultaneously with the arrival of the new *milliaria* unit as part of the special defensive measures. The excavations carried out on Káptalan hill in 1978 furnished proof that the latest timber structures had still been in use by the time the first stone buildings were erected: the walls of the first stone structure were built in line with the earlier foundation trenches. Thus it can be ascertained that the *ala I Ulpia contariorum milliaria* moved into a 1st century structure which, on

[38] E. T. Szőnyi: Győr–Rákóczi út 59. ArchÉrt 105 (1978) 284.

[39] B. Lőrincz: *Pannonische Stempelziegel II. Limes-Strecke Vetus Salina–Intercisa.* DissArch II. 7. Budapest (1978) 23.

[40] J. Fitz: Der Besuch des Septimius Severus in Pannonia. *ActaArchHung* 10 (1959) 240; K. Wachtel: Kritisches und ergänzendes zu neuen Inschriften aus Mainz. *Historia* 15 (1966) 247; Gabler–Lőrincz (1977) 145, note 11.

[41] Gabler–Lőrincz (1977) 150.

[42] D. Gabler: Arrabona legkorábbi sigillátái (The earliest sigillatas of Arrabona). *Arrabona* 9 (1967) 50.

[43] E. T. Szőnyi: A győri Kálvária utcai római temető hamvasztásos sírjai (The cremation graves of the Roman cemetery of Győr–Kálvária Street). *Arrabona* 15 (1973) 43–44.

[44] J. Fitz: A Military History of Pannonia from the Marcomann Wars to the Death of Alexander Severus (180–235). *Acta ArchHung* 13 (1962) 42; A. Mócsy: Pannonia. *PWRE,* Suppl. IX (1962) 619.

[45] E. Birley: Alae and cohortes milliariae. *Corolla memoriae E. Swoboda dedicata.* Graz (1966) 56, 60.

[46] H. Stiglitz–M. Kandler–W. Jobst: Carnuntum. *ANRW* II. 6. Berlin (1977) 659.

the evidence of the uncovered buildings and roads, had survived well into the Roman Imperial period.[47]

The stone structures found in Széchenyi Square apparently date from the age of Hadrian. (The stone structures in the fort and the *vicus* do not necessarily date to the same period. The building techniques used in the spontaneous settlement surrounding the camp must have lagged well behind that of the official military installations.) The excavations in the *vicus* at Arrabona have revealed that the first buildings with stone foundations date to the early 2nd century. Their internal walls, and also some of the outer walls, were built of sun-dried bricks. This building technique was still frequent during the 2nd century in the Pannonian towns of Roman rank.[48]

The stone structures and the Late Roman wall in the fort were built conforming to the *cardo-decumanus* system, i.e. their orientation deviated from the north–south and east–west direction by about 14°. This degree of deviation also served as the starting point in the reconstruction of the 2nd–3rd century *castellum*. (The earlier attempts by D. Gabler were based on the orientation of the buildings found in Széchenyi Square, which differed slightly from that of the structures in the fort.) The section of street contemporaneous with the stone structures uncovered by L. Barkóczi can probably be identified with the *via praetoria*.[49] Three rooms were found in each of the two stone buildings uncovered in 1978 and were assigned to the period of the stone structures. A 6 metre wide paved street separated the two buildings. Their dimensions and ornamental design (wall paintings with floral decoration during the latest phase) seems to imply that the said buildings can hardly be considered to have been barracks. Most probably they represent parts of one of the central buildings of the camp. The excavations have brought to light only a quarter of both buildings; only after the completion of the excavation, when the foundations for a building to be erected over the excavation site were laid, did it become clear that the excavated remains had probably been the southern outer rooms of the complex. The excavators also uncovered the remains of a street intersection. The part of a stone wall brought to light by a small trench in 1974[50] was later identified as being part of the southern outer wall of the eastern building unearthed in 1978.

In reconstructing the position and dimensions of the walls an engraving by Domenico Zeno, showing the 13th century walls, proved very useful. The only long and straight wall section with a projecting gate in the middle can be identified with the eastern wall. The vicinity of the gate has yielded a number of Roman stones with inscriptions. These stones may have found their way into the building of the capitular library during a presumed rebuilding (perhaps in the course of walling up the gate in the Late Roman period.) The gate shown in the engraving may have stood on the site of the library. The eastern wall of the medieval castle had perhaps been influenced by its Roman predecessor. D. Gabler had earlier suggested that this wall section was built on Roman foundations.[51] Recent excavations, however, have challenged the validity of this suggestion, and now the relationship between the medieval and Roman buildings and walls are considered less close and direct. The Roman constructions influenced the medieval structures only indirectly.

The northern wall of the 13th century fort is not shown in Domenico Zeno's engraving. This wall may presumably be identified with the buttressed wall and its continuation shown on Nicolò Aginelli's map. D. Gabler considers the building of the latter wall to have been influenced by the northern outer wall of the Roman fort, and he also thought that the internal tower at the intersection with the buttressed section had been erected near a Late Roman horseshoe-shaped internal tower (earlier he considered these structures to have had Roman footings). The area of the fort presumably extended as far as the river Rába in the west. Since no Roman layers came to light during the 1960 excavation of the keep at Püspökvár,[52] we may confidently assume that the area of the camp did not extend to this region. According to a 19th century source, the southern wall of the fort was uncovered at the southern foot of Káptalan hill; regrettably enough, the lack of a detailed report and a plan hinders the determination of its exact location. Some of the ruins mentioned in a source dating from 1534 may in all probability be also considered Roman structures (*a parte meridionali versus pontem territorio publico seu fundamento structurae antiquorum gentilium dirute adiacentem*),[53] since the expression "structures of the ancient nations", referring to the 16th century structures outside the wall of the fort near the Rába bridge, can hardly be associated with medieval walls.

The fort of the *ala I Ulpia Contariorum milliaria* described above, and reconstructed primarily on the evidence furnished by the excavations in 1978 (led by E. Szőnyi and P. Tomka),[54] may have extended over a

[47] E. Szőnyi–P. Tomka: Győr–Martinovics tér 3. *ArchÉrt* 106 (1979) 279.

[48] E.g. T. Szentléleky, excavation report in *ArchÉrt* 92 (1965) 237; *ArchÉrt* 96 (1969) 257 (Savaria); T. Nagy: Perióduskutatások az aquincumi polgárváros területén (Erforschung der Perioden im Zentralgebiet der Zivilstadt von Aquincum). *BudRég* 21 (1964) 15; J. Fitz: The excavations in Gorsium. *Acta ArchHung* 24 (1972) 14; J. Fitz: *Gorsium–Herculia*. Székesfehérvár (1976) 37; Mócsy (1974) 166.

[49] Borbíró–Valló (1956) 132.

[50] Szőke–Szőnyi–Tomka (1976) 108.

[51] For a detailed report, cf. D. Gabler: Untersuchungen am oberpannonischen Donaulimes. *Studien zu den Militärgrenzen Roms II. Vorträge des 10. Internationalen Limeskongresses in der Germania Inferior.* Ed. by W. Horn. Bonn–Köln (1977) 305; For Domenico Zeno's engraving, cf. J. Pfannl: Régi ábrázolások Győr városáról (The town of Győr in old pictures). *Győri Szemle* 1 (1930); L. Gazdag: Győr város térképei (Maps of Győr). *Arrabona* 7 (1965) 301.

[52] K. Kozák–A. Uzsoki: Régészeti és műemléki kutatás a győri Püspökvárban (Archäologische und Kunstdenkmalforschung in der Bischofsburg in Győr). *Arrabona* 4 (1962) 60.

[53] *Litt. Capituli Jaur. ddto Festi assumpt.b.Virg. anno 153.*

[54] E. Szőnyi–P. Tomka: Győr–Martinovics tér 3. *ArchÉrt* 106 (1979) 279.

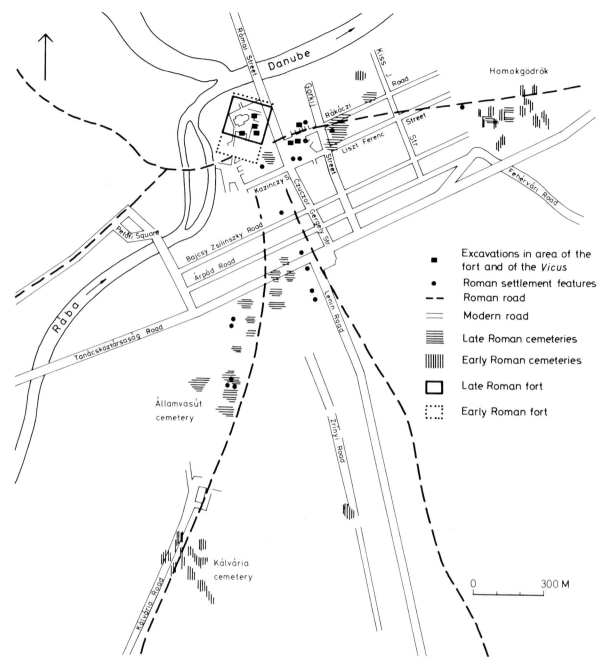

Fig. 1. The topography of Győr (Arrabona) in the Roman Age.

**Legend:**
- ■ Excavations in area of the fort and of the *Vicus*
- ● Roman settlement features
- – – – Roman road
- ═ Modern road
- ≣ Late Roman cemeteries
- ‖‖‖ Early Roman cemeteries
- ▭ Late Roman fort
- ⬚ Early Roman fort

0     300 M

220–230 m×150 m area (Fig. 1). (The earlier reconstruction by D. Gabler was an area of 217 m×135 m.) Accordingly, the southern corner of the fort may have reached as far as the line of the present-day Szabadsajtó Street, south of the line of Alkotmány Street. The fort thus reconstructed was obviously smaller than, for example, the *ala milliaria* camp at Stanwix.[55] Of the *castellum*s in Pannonia, the one at Vindobona, dating from the era of Domitian, is unknown to us, while the one at Albertfalva (even though this fort could hardly

have been *ala milliaria* camp), covering a 210 m×186 m area,[56] was larger than the Győr castellum, but this may not be considered an exception since all the forts in this region were smaller in area compared with structures in

[55] R. G. Collingwood–I. Richmond: *The Archaeology of Roman Britain*. London (1969) 26.

[56] T. Nagy: Az Albertfalva Hunyadi János úti római település (The Roman Settlement in Hunyadi János Street, Albertfalva). *Budapest Műemlékei* II. Ed. by F. Pogány (1962) 519–523; T. Nagy: Drei Jahre Limesforschungen in Ungarn. *Actes du IX<sup>e</sup> Congrès International d'Études sur les Frontières Romaines*. Ed. by M. Pippidi. Bucuresti–Köln–Wien (1974) 27–37; T. Nagy: Albertfalva. *Der römische Limes in Ungarn*. Ed. by J. Fitz. IKMK A. 22. Székesfehérvár (1976) 91.

Raetia–Germania or in Britain. The closest parallel to the Győr *castellum* is the fort at Almásfüzitő[57] (203 m× 166 m), although these dimensions may correspond better to the camp with stone structures. The fort of the *ala I Batavorum milliaria*, stationed there during the first half of the 2nd century, may well have been larger in area. The circular building discovered near the Rába bridge in the last century was interpreted as being the remains of an *amphitheatrum* by J. Czech. The suggestion that it was the Late Roman, fan-shaped angle tower of the fort which had earlier been considered as an *amphitheatrum* was first raised by D. Gabler.[58] The results of the recent excavations, however, challenge this interpretation; the corner of the Late Roman fort must definitely have been located somewhere to the north of the Rába bridge.

A systematic arrangement of the buildings, conforming to the roads leading out from the fort, could be established on the evidence of the structures—datable to the first half of the 2nd century—unearthed on the territory of the *vicus*. This arrangement is still unparallelled in the settlements adjoining the auxiliary camps in Pannonia. Small houses of similar dimensions, as have been excavated, were typical of the *vici*—the first larger structures appeared only in the late 2nd century. The *vicus* at Arrabona may be considered exceptional in this respect as well: a large building there can be dated to the first half of the 2nd century (its southern outer wall could be traced along a 17.5 m section, but its dimensions have still not been established). It would appear that this period saw the emergence of a systematically arranged settlement with large-sized, properly built, *villa*-like structures and a steadily developing industry. Indicative of the latter were the kilns and the lumps of slag, from bronze working, found in the area. The faulty and semi-finished artefacts among the bronze objects *(opus interrasile)* found at Arrabona may well be considered indicative of a local workshop, and the artefacts found in the area of the Kálvária cemetery are thought to be products of a local glass industry by L. Barkóczi.[59] The developed agricultural activity of the *vicus* (baker's ovens, millstones), and also the smithies, may have catered for the garrison, while the tradesmen of Arrabona may have been responsible for the provision of the cavalry troops (repairing of arms, shodding, etc.).

As a matter of course, the increasing numbers in the garrison attracted more and more tradesmen and merchants to the settlement, thus increasing the population of the *vicus*.

This trend is also reflected by the sudden qualitative and quantitative changes observed in the material brought to light in the cemeteries. It is by no means coincidental that the more intensive use of the Homokgödör cemetery[60] as a burial ground started at the beginning of the 2nd century. Most of the burials there, and also in the Kálvária cemetery, datable by the coins found in the graves, can be assigned to the age of Trajan and Hadrian.[61] These apparently indicate a more extensive currency system and trade in the period.

The earliest burials unearthed in Zrínyi Street in Nádorváros,[62] along the road leading to Sopianae, can be dated to the turn of the 1st–2nd centuries or to the beginning of the 2nd century. Some of the cemeteries and burial groups located far from the centre of the ancient settlement may be associated with the neighbouring small settlements, rather than with Arrabona. A small *villa*-like settlement of this kind was located in the northern part of Kálvária Street in, or in the immediate vicinity of, the area where L. Barkóczi's 1954 excavation brought to light a group of Late Roman burials. The artefacts found in the area (sherds of *mortaria*, storage jars, amphorae) were definitely indicative of a settlement. A suggested settlement therefore of the 2nd century[63] would have provided the quernstones used for covering the graves in the Kálvária cemetery. These stones were probably brought to the cemetery from the neighbouring settlement.[64] We had the luck to observe features indicating a Late Roman settlement during gas-pipe laying in the spring of 1980 in Révai Street, in the southernmost part of the present-day centre of the town between the buildings of the City Council and the Post Office. The finds from this clay-lined, burnt pit included animal bones and pottery. The red marbled vessel with impressed and incised decoration found there dates from the 2nd century. Amphora sherds also came to light during excavations in front of the building of the present-day Post Office. Comparable features have also been uncovered some 300 m west of this site. Bulldozers working in the area have turned up the stones and red fresco fragments of a building. No definite date could be ascribed to this building of the Roman Period, although its type and building technique indicate a later date. The above discussed small settlements were all located along the road leading from Arrabona to the south (most probably to Sopianae and Savaria), and they obviously had a great share in supplying the ever increasing population of the settlement.

[57] E. Bíró: Azaum–Almásfüzitő. *Der römische Limes in Ungarn.* Ed. by J. Fitz. IKMK A. 22. Székesfehérvár (1976) 39.

[58] J. Czech: A Győr vidék legrégibb időben és a rómaiak alatt (The environs of Győr in the earliest periods and under the Romans). *Magyar Tudós Társaság Évkönyvei* 1 (1831–1832 [1833]) 336; D. Gabler: Untersuchungen am oberpannonischen Donaulimes. *Studien zu den Militärgrenzen Roms II. Vorträge des 10. Internationalen Limeskongresses in der Germania Inferior.* Ed. by W. Horn. Köln–Bonn (1977) 306.

[59] I. Sellye: Adatok az arrabonai fémművességhez (Beiträge zu der Geschichte des Metallgewerbes in Arrabona). *Arrabona* 12 (1970) 69ff. For the activity of the glassware-makers, cf. L. Barkóczi: Ein Glasstempel aus Aquincum. Verbreitung und Herstellung der Flaschen mit Würfelleib und der rechteckigen Prismenflaschen in Pannonien. *MittArchInst* 6 (1976) 61, 65.

[60] Szőnyi (1976) 31.

[61] E. Szőnyi: A győri Kálvária utcai római temető hamvasztásos sírjai (The cremation graves of the Roman cemetery of Győr–Kálvária Street). *Arrabona* 15 (1973) 43–44.

[62] E. Biró: A Győr–nádorvárosi koracsászárkori sírok (Frühkaiserzeitliche Gräber in Győr–Nádorváros). *ArchÉrt* 88 (1961) 240–247.

[63] Szőnyi (1979) 5–57.

[64] Gabler (1971b) 38.

## ARRABONA FROM THE MARCOMANNIC WARS UNTIL THE EARLY 4TH CENTURY

The Marcomannic–Sarmatian wars of 167–170 left large parts of Arrabona in ruins. The fort, lying at the strategic point where the military road leading to Italy started, was damaged when the advancing Barbarians laid siege to Aquilea, threatening to raid Italy. Several parts of the buildings on Káptalan hill have yielded traces of the Antonine destruction layer. (The debris was then levelled.)

Also indicative of the destruction of the *vicus* was a thick layer of burnt wattle-and-daub and the charred timber remains excavated in Széchenyi Square.

The garrison of Arrabona gave battle in the fiercest clashes of the war, their commanders (including Macrinus Avitus Catonius Vindex or M. Valerius Maximianus)[65] usually emerged victorious, and it cannot have been mere coincidence that after the Marcomannic wars the garrison was awarded the epithet *c.R. (civium Romanorum)*.[66]

Remarkably enough, the latest coins recovered from the Homokgödör cemetery were those of Antoninus Pius, indicating that the area ceased to be used as a burial ground when the Marcomannic wars broke out. However, the 3rd century again saw sporadic burials in the cemetery.[67]

The reconstruction of the fort took place in the last quarter of the 2nd century. It is presumably one of the repeated rebuildings of the stone structures that can be related to the late Antonine–Severan building activities. In the course of these reconstructions, some of the partitioning walls of the eastern building, unearthed in 1978, had been demolished. Some of the rooms were floored with pink, brick-dusted terrazzo. On the evidence of the coins, this floor had been in use throughout the 3rd century. In terms of orientation, the structures found during the excavation of the cathedral fit fully in the system of the other excavated parts of the fort presumably dating from the late 2nd–early 3rd centuries.

Judging by the evidence provided by the excavations in Széchenyi Square, the Severan era had brought prosperity to the *vicus*. The sun-dried brick houses were gradually replaced by stone buildings, with the walls erected with the *opus spicatum* technique. The smaller outhouses, however, were still built of mud-bricks. It would appear that owing to the long period of peace under the Severi and the general economic prosperity of

the province this was the very period when Arrabona was larger than at any other time in its history. The majority of the stone buildings described in 19th or early 20th century sources had probably been inhabited in the late 2nd–3rd centuries. The practice of erecting stone structures was typical particularly of this period. (In the 1st century, and also in the early 2nd, timber-framed structures were more general in the civil settlement. The 4th century, and especially its second half, must be left out of consideration here for certain topographic considerations—see below). In determining the extension of the *vicus* we can rely on the following data: The sources mention walls made of sandstone found south of the camp:

(1) in Kazinczy Street near Lenin Street (formerly Baross Street),
(2) in the area of the office block of the department store built on the western part of the intersection of Lenin Street and Bajcsy-Zsilinszky Street, some 200–250 m from the fort,
(3) and south of the latter site, in the vicinity of the northern side of the former marketplace, in the area between present-day Tanácsköztársaság Street and Árpád Street. This site has yielded remains of the walls of houses destroyed by fire, Roman pottery and bricks used for heating.[68]

On the basis of these finds, J. Czech suggested, as early as 1830, that the Roman settlement lay somewhere in the territory of the marketplace, on the road traversing it.[69] Unfortunately, the majority of the Roman ruins in the area south of Arany János Street and extending almost as far as Tanácsköztársaság Street were destroyed during the digging of a moat in the 16th–17th centuries. The line of the moat is marked by a wide strip of land that yielded no finds whatsoever. The moat contained a number of Roman artefacts.[70] Remains of Roman walls were also found in the northern, southern and western corners of Széchenyi Square to the east, at the corner of the house belonging to the Secondary School of the Benedictine Order, during the building of the foundations of the Rába Cultural Centre (formerly the Lloyd building)—regrettably enough, none of these finds has been properly surveyed—and again in Liszt Ferenc Street, in front of the former County Hall, some 350 m from the fort[71] (Fig. 1). The southeastern section of the 16th–17th century moat runs beyond the outermost row of houses in Újkapu Street–Újvilág Street; the eastern row of houses in Tarcsay Vilmos Street already lies outside the line of the moat.

[65] L. Barkóczi: Die Naristen zur Zeit der Markomannenkriege. *FolArch* 9 (1957) 96; J. Fitz: A longobard-obius betörés i. sz. 166/167-ben (Der Einbruch der Longobarden und Obier in 166/167 u. Z.). *FolArch* 11 (1959) 62; H. J. Kellner: Rätien und die Markommanenkriege. *BVbl* 30 (1965) 171; J. Fitz: Der markomannisch-quadische Angriff gegen Aquileia und Opitergium. *Historia* 15 (1966) 336–367; A. R. Birley: The Invasion of Italy in the Reign of Marcus Aurelius. *Provincialia. Festschrift R. Laur-Belart* (1968) 214–225.

[66] W. Wagner: *Dislokationen der Auxiliarformationen von Augustus bis Gallienus.* Berlin (1938) 32; J. Fitz: A Military History of Pannonia from the Marcomann Wars to the Death of Alexander Severus (180–235). *Acta ArchHung* 13 (1962) 43.

[67] Szőnyi (1976) 31.

[68] Gabler (1971a) 37–43, 47–48.

[69] J. Czech: A Győr vidék a legrégibb időkben és a rómaiak alatt (The environs of Győr in the earliest periods and under the Romans). *Magyar Tudós Társaság Évkönyvei* 1 (1831–1832 [1833]) 336.

[70] For the location of the ditch and the area devoid of archaeological finds, cf. Lovas (1942) 14. For the secondary Roman finds, cf. B. Szőke: Leletmentő ásatás az ún. Teleki laktanya udvarán (Rescue excavations in the yard of the so-called Teleki Barracks). *Arrabona* 16 (1974) 15.

[71] For the eastward extension of the *vicus*, cf. Gabler (1971a) 6–7; E. Szőnyi: Győr–Rákóczi út 59. *ArchÉrt* 105 (1978) 284.

The excavations conducted in 1977 in the plot of the house at 59 Rákóczi Street did not find the remains of a Roman settlement. The pottery found there probably originates from the western part of the Homokgödör cemetery that was destroyed by agicultural activites. The remains of a medieval (Árpádian Age) settlement found above the Roman layer proves unambiguously that most of the Turkish fortifications did not extend to this area. Stray Roman artefacts were also reported from the eastern part of the moat. Besides the stone *cippus* fragments found earlier in the plot of the house at 9 Kiss Street,[72] the 2nd century Roman jug brought to light from a depth of 1.5 m in 1980 is also worthy of note. Unfortunately, no detailed stratigraphic survey could be carried out on the site, but we could nevertheless observe a regular stratigraphic sequence in an approximately 15 m long section at the intersection of Rákóczi Street–Kiss Street, contrasting with the mixed debris fill of the moat noted elsewhere. This area may have been the site of one of the advanced gun emplacements of the Turkish fortification — the contemporary maps also support this suggestion —, and this may well account for the undisturbed earlier layers there. In all probability the Roman settlement did not extend to this area. A column and wall-plaster fragments found near the corner of Vas Gereben Street and the former Homok Street appear to have been the remains of a sepulchral structure, and thus they can be associated with the cemetery,[73] although they may also be considered finds originating from a detached *villa*-like building. In any case, the fact that the area of the *vicus* did not include this territory appears to be indisputable.

It was earlier thought that the civil settlement enclosed the camp in a semicircle: its area (implicitly, its built-in parts) was compared with that of the 18th century town.[74] The excavations conducted in 1977 in Gorkij Street yielded new evidence in this respect. The sections cut in the area of Gorkij Street–Varga Street–Saru Alley–Szük Alley helped us determine the southern edge of the *vicus*. Certain features observed in the northwestern edge of the excavated area suggested the proximity of a 2nd–3rd century settlement; the southern part remained open and unoccupied during the Roman period (it was dotted with pits for the extraction of clay) until the construction of the Turkish castle.[75] Accordingly, the most southerly possible end of the row of houses in the *vicus* can be placed at the line of the southern row of plots in present-day Liszt Ferenc Street. Towards the north the inhabited area presumably extended as far as the *limes* road or the adjoining cemetery. During the digging of a ditch in the section of Gorkij Street between Bástya Street and Rózsa Street we uncovered the remains of stone walls. Although their orientation — approximately northwest–southeast — de-

viated slightly from that typical for the structures of the fort, the walling technique (small ashlars), and the depth indisputably dated them to the Roman Period.

It may thus be considered highly probable that the houses of the *vicus*, built at various intervals, flanked a long section of the road leading to Brigetio. At least three rows of houses must have been built in the vicinity of Széchenyi Square — indicative of this were the two road sections running in an east–west direction that could be reconstructed after the 1954 and 1968–1969 campaigns. The 5 m wide and 15 m long section of the *limes* road was visible in the second half of the last century by the side of the then standing building of the gas-works. According to E. Méry, the road was bedded on a layer of stone and debris and was banked with large-sized flat slabs. In E. Szőnyi's opinion the road may have been subsequently widened and rebuilt, as suggested by one of the graves in the Homokgödör cemetery which was recovered from under the edge of the road.[76]

J. Czech presumed that the less explored southern part of the settlement lay by the side of the diagonal road leading to Savaria. Its boundaries have still not been fixed, owing to the extensive damage caused by the digging of the Turkish fortification. The Roman walls uncovered during the building of the office blocks of the department store were in all probability the remains of the *rivellino* kept as an enclave in the moat. The recent large-scale earthworks carried out east and west of this site (during the building of the foundations of the theatre, and around the site of the Arrabona department store) have brought to light only the fill of the moat. The remains of a settlement that J. Czech considered to have belonged to the consecutive row of houses of the *vicus* in the 3rd century should rather be regarded as being the remains of a detached group of houses. This suggestion is again based on J. Czech's description of 3rd century graves uncovered in this area. Although the distance between the fort and the *vicus* is unknown, it is most probable that in accordance with the military interests, an open area separated the *castellum* and the houses of the settlements to its east and south. Consequently, the southern part of the settlement must have covered a smaller area than the eastern part. This can probably be attributed to the growing importance of the *limes* road as against the other roads leading to the heart of the province during the 2nd–3rd centuries.

The low number of burials datable to the turn of the 2nd–3rd centuries, the brightest period of ancient Arrabona, was rather surprising. Graves dating from the 3rd century were conspicuously few in the vast Homokgödör cemetery. The latest inhumation burials were each dated by coins of Gallienus or Gordianus.[77] E. Szőnyi's investigations have proved that only a few Late Roman burials (dating from the 4th, or perhaps the 3rd century) may be reckoned with in the Kálvária cemetery on the evidence of the handful of Late Roman artefacts and coins, but these can by no means be taken to prove the uninterrupted use of the area as a burial ground. This was not the case with the so-called State Railway

[72] Lovas (1942) 14.

[73] E. Lovas: Győr város és vármegye feliratos és dombormíves római emlékei (Roman inscriptions and reliefs in the town and county of Győr). *Győri Szemle* 1 (1930) 200.

[74] Gabler (1971b) 27.

[75] P. Tomka: Győr–Gorkij u.–Varga u.–Saru köz–Szük köz. *ArchÉrt* 105 (1978) 278.

[76] Szőnyi (1976) 6.

[77] *Ibid.*, 31.

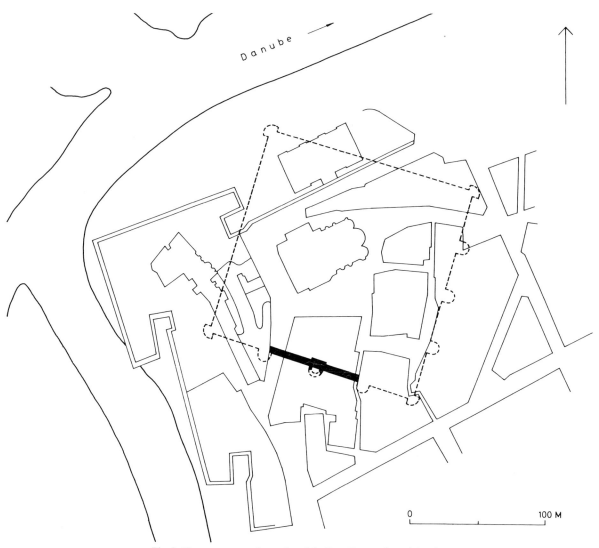

Fig. 2. The reconstructed remains of the Late Roman fort of Arrabona.

cemetery. The detailed analysis of the graves there has shown[78] that the farther the burial was from the settlement, the younger it may be considered. Accordingly, the burials of the late 4th century were located in the southernmost areas, those assigned to the mid-4th century were found in the northern part of Kálvária Street (6 Kálvária Street, Honvéd Street), and those datable to the turn of the 3rd–4th centuries, i.e. to the age of the tetrarchy, were discovered in the northern part of Honvéd Gardens and in the southern part of Tanácsköztársaság Street. Burials of the 3rd century have come to light in the area of the marketplace and also to its north. Thus it is the section farther north of the Savaria–Arrabona road, i.e. the area destroyed during the digging of the moat of the Turkish fortification, where the late 2nd–early 3rd century burials should be searched for.

---

[78] E. Szőnyi: A győri vasútállomás környéki későrómai temető (The Late Roman cemetery at Győr–Railway Station). *Arrabona* 21 (1979) 56–57.

## ARRABONA IN
## THE LATE ROMAN PERIOD

The Late Roman period brought about considerable changes in the general appearance of Arrabona. On the evidence of the 1978 campaign, this period saw large-scale reconstructions in the fort. After demolishing the still standing walls, the builders covered up the ruins with a thick levelling layer. This work was necessitated by plans to considerably reduce the area of the earlier fort (by approximately one-third) and to build new defensive structures and a new fort. During the excavations, part of the southern wing of the Late Roman fort was explored (Fig. 2), and another part was observed during bulldozing in the area. Along the approximately 40 m long section of a wall we could observe the facing stones and a cast core of rubble and mortar; the wall was 280 cm thick at the concrete-like raising sections. Together with the 20 cm socles on each side, the foundation was 320 cm thick. The buried ascending part was 180–300 cm high (Fig. 3). For certain static reasons the depth of the foundation could not be established. The

Fig. 3. Southern elevation of the outer side of the wall of the Late Roman fort of Arrabona (Győr, Martinovics Square 3, eastern side)

driver of the bulldozer claimed to have observed a 130 cm deep foundation during the excavation of the wall of the fort. Accordingly, the wall may have been as high as 430 cm at some points. During the excavation of this wall section the foundation of a tower and its walls also came to light. The presumably horseshoe-shaped tower (its southern part could not be excavated or even observed) projected considerably from the wall of the fort. It was 177–195 cm thick, the inner northern wall receded 93 cm from the wall, thus its wall was considerably thicker (420 cm). The northern face of the interior of the tower was the continuation of the outer southern face of the defensive wall. The tower was 300 cm wide. The builders of the Late Roman wall demolished some of the earlier structures and created an approximately 10 m wide (measured from the inner face of the wall), 1–1.5 m high, filled-in open space with the aim of reinforcing the walls and also to make the place more easily accessible. The new defensive wall was built on the line of one of the *scamni* of the earlier fort (presumably along the *via quintana*). The area of the fort was 150 m×150 m. The wall of the fort was first discovered in 1964 during A. Uzsoki's rescue excavations. In the lack of reliable stratigraphic observations, the wall was considered to be medieval.[79] The fort reconstructable from the recorded section of wall had preserved the northern and western—and presumably also the eastern—walls of the earlier fort. Minor reconstructions, walled up gates or rebuilt walls should of course be reckoned with within these areas as well. Regrettably enough, Káptalan hill is built in so densely that no further archaeological investigations can be carried out in the area. Consequently, the walls of Late Roman Arrabona can only be reconstructed on the evidence of the present-day building lines, the topography and earlier observations (Fig. 1). The exact dating of the large-scale construction is also rather problematic. The continuous stratification was disturbed next to the defensive wall as a result of the demolition of some of the houses there. We also had difficulties in examining the internal structures contemporaneous with the wall. Some of the internal buildings had demonstrably been occupied until the end of the 3rd century. Besides the early Roman pottery and coins, the level has also yielded sherds of Late Roman glazed pottery. In a Late Roman ditch dug into the layer, a coin of Maximinus Daia was found accompanied by another coin minted during the reign of the Constantinus dynasty. The ditches dug into the destroyed terrazzo of one of the buildings inside the 10 m rampart contained a number of coins of Valentinian or Valens. Accordingly, the laying of the terrazzo must be dated to a later period, most probably to the reign of Constantine. A coin of Constantine found in the destruction layer close to the wall of the fort appears to support this suggestion. In view of the general architecture of the fort, and the reconstructable position of the towers—all typical of the forts under

[79] K. Kozák: Adatok a győri vár középkori történetéhez (Beiträge zu der mittelalterlichen Geschichte der Burg Győr). *Arrabona* 9 (1967) 80, 82–84.

2*

19

Diocletian–Constantine[80]—we can date the building of the fort to the beginning of the 4th century. The fort must obviously have been occupied throughout the 4th century. The large number of coins dating from Valentinian's time suggests that new military tactical groups had taken up quarters in the fort, where new constructions had perhaps also been undertaken. The walls of the fort survived into the 5th century, giving shelter to the inhabitants, including the first population groups of the early Migration period. The debris layer beside the wall of the fort, containing finds diagnostic of the 5th century (pottery with latticed decoration, bone combs ornamented with dotted circles, etc.), can thus also be assigned to the 5th century. This period, however, marks the start of a new chapter in the settlement's history. According to the most significant 4th century source, the *Notitia Dignitatum*, cavalry had constantly been stationed in the fort until the 4th century. These troops included the *equites promoti*, the *cuneus equitum stablesianorum* and also the *milites liburnarii* (Liburnian combatant boats in the defense of the river), and the *XIV Gemina* fleet of the Carnuntum legion.[81] The fleet itself must definitely have been stationed in another fort, with a port and a fortress built not far off, at the confluence of the Danube and Rába rivers. Owing to the subsequent natural and artificial improvement of the waterways and the river bank, an attempt to locate them would be next to impossible. Following L. Várady D. Gabler earlier considered the *Notitia Dignitatum* to have been compiled from miscellaneous and non-contemporaneous data.[82] This suggestion was later refuted

by S. Soproni who, after his survey of the forts along the Pannonian section of the *limes*, argued that the various military troops could well have been stationed together in these forts, thus confirming the contemporary account.[83] It is quite possible that this suggestion is valid for Arrabona as well. If so, the diminished Late Roman fort lodged a cavalry 600–800 men strong (reckoning with an *equites* unit and a *cuneus equitum* that can be considered an élite troop), i.e. three-quarters or two-thirds of the earlier garrison troops. The diminution of the camp can obviously be associated with the reorganization of the troops during the Late Roman period, and also to the smaller number of the forces. (The later diminution of the forts and fortresses of Carnuntum, Almásfüzitő, Dunabogdány and Aquincum, however, can in no way be linked to these reconstructions.[84]) Only few of the internal structures of the Late Roman fort have survived. The walls of the above-mentioned building with *terrazzo* were in later times demolished, and its floor was repeatedly broken through. Extending into the northernmost part of the excavated area was the corner of a stone-walled house with *opus spicatum* foundations. Its good-quality *terrazzo* and thick walls were still in use during the 4th century. The stone walls found in 1904 south of the cathedral were presumably parts of this structure. The exact position and orientation of the walls, uncovered at a distance of 15.5 m from each other,[85] are unknown. Remains of Late Roman walls may also have been found during the excavation of the cathedral in 1969; unfortunately, these ruins could not be accurately dated.[86]

During the 4th century the area of the *vicus* gradually diminished and it was slowly abandoned. The excavations in Széchenyi Square have revealed that the large building there had probably been occupied in the first half of the 4th century, whereas to postholes dug into the earlier structures indicated small-scale constructions. The Late Roman period saw only one wattle-and-daub house erected in the area. The Quadic and Sarmatian incursions of 355–356 may have been of decisive importance in the depopulation of the area;[87]

[80] For the connections between fort type and defensive technique, cf. S. Johnson: *The Roman Forts of the Saxon Shore*. London (1979²) 60–62, 116. The semicircular projecting lateral towers were typical of the Late Roman forts, although they have not been precisely dated yet. Cf. Soproni (1978) 68–78 (Pilismarót), 55–57 (Visegrád), 68–71 (Szentendre); A. Mócsy: Pannonia-Forschung 1963–1968. *ActaArchHung* 21 (1969) 351; A. Mócsy: *Der römische Limes in Ungarn*. Ed. by J. Fitz. IKMK A. 22. Székesfehérvár (1976) 46–47 (Tokod); L. Nagy: Pest város eredete (Előzetes jelentés az eskütéri ásatásokról) (The Origins of Pest). *TBM* 3 (1934) 7–24 (Pest counter-forts). For the parallels of the U-shaped towers from Noricum, cf. H.-J. Ubl: Der österreichische Abschnitt des Donaulimes. Ein Forschungsbericht 1970–1979. *Roman Frontier Studies 1979. Papers presented to the 12th International Congress of Roman Frontier Studies*. Ed. by W. S. Hanson and L. J. F. Keppie. BAR International Series 71. Oxford (1980) 596; H. Thaller: Die Befestigungsanlage von Mautern a. d. Donau. *JÖAI* 40 (1953) 193ff. Since Favianae was one of the bases of the *liburnarii*, thus a port can also be assumed here, cf. Thaller, *ibid.*, 201. For the Pest counter-fort, cf. also T. Nagy: Budapest története az őskortól a honfoglalásig (History of Budapest from prehistoric times to the Magyar Conquest). *Budapest Története* I. Ed. by L. Gerevich. Budapest (1973) 122. For the development of the tower type, cf. T. Bechert: Römische Lagertore und ihre Bauinschriften. Ein Beitrag zur Entwicklung und Datierung kaiserzeitlicher Lagertorgrundrisse von Claudius bis Severus Alexander. *BJ* 171 (1971) 276–277.

[81] *Not.Dign.Occ* (Pann.I) 34,5; 34,16; 34,27.

[82] L. Várady: *Későrómai hadügyek és társadalmi alapjaik (Late Roman military affairs and their social background)*. Budapest (1961) 80, and later D. Gabler: Arrabona. *PWRE*, Suppl. XII. Stuttgart (1970) 94.

[83] Soproni (1978) 156–160.

[84] Cf. Carnuntum, H. Vetters: Zur Spätzeit des Lagers Carnuntum. *Österreichische Zeitschrift für Kunst- und Denkmalpflege* 17 (1963) 159ff; H. Vetters: Zum Problem der Kontinuität im niederösterreichischen Limesgebiet. *Jahrbuch des Vereins für Landeskunde von Niederösterreich* 38 (1968–1970) 48, 64; H. Stiglitz–M. Kandler–W. Jobst: Carnuntum. *ANRW* 88. 6 (1977) 656; Almásfüzitő, E. Biró: Azaum–Almásfüzitő. *Der römische Limes in Ungarn*. Ed. by J. Fitz. IKMK A. 22. Székesfehérvár (1976) 38–39; Dunabogdány, Á. Szalay: *A dunabogdányi római castellumról (Über das römische Castell von Dunabogdány)*. ArchHung 10. Budapest (1933) 36.

[85] A. Börzsönyi: Római régiségek Győr-Belváros területéről (Roman antiquities from the centre of Győr). *ArchÉrt* 27 (1907) 37ff; Lovas (1942) 7.

[86] K. Kozák–A. Uzsoki: A győri székesegyház feltárása (The excavation of Győr Cathedral). *Arrabona* 12 (1970) 115ff.

[87] D. Gabler: Későrómai éremlelet Ács–Vaspusztáról (Ein spätrömischer Münzfund aus Ács–Vaspuszta). *ArchÉrt* 99 (1972 [1973]) 236–237. For the abandonment of the settlements on the *limes*, cf. L. Barkóczi: *Brigetio*. Diss.Pann. II. 22.

this is suggested by the numerous coin hoards found at various sites of the province. The latest coins found at Széchenyi Square were minted between 351–354 under Constantius II.[88] The fact that no coin of Valentinian was found during the 1968–1969 campaigns is all the more significant since that was the very period when Pannonian currency was characterized by a marked expansion. The large number of coins dating from this period found in the area of the fort seems to imply that at the close of the 4th century the civilian population tended to gather near the defensible walls, in areas of the province lying farther in from the *limes*, or even in the fort itself.[89]

The reduced population in the second half of the 4th century began to use the area of the plots between the abandoned buildings in the former *vicus* as a burial ground. Moreover, Late Roman graves were also found in some of the rooms, and even over the walls. The latter burials suggest that parts of the walls were demolished as early as the turn of the 4th–5th centuries. In the area of the former *vicus*, the following sites have yielded groups of Late Roman graves:

(1) the plot of the house at 22 Rákóczi Street,
(2) in front of the house at 32–34 Rákóczi Street,
(3) the plots of the houses at 15 Liszt Ferenc Square (during construction) and 17 Liszt Ferenc Square,
(4) the plot of the house at 20 Liszt Ferenc Square (during construction).[90]

Slabs from earlier structures had often been used in erecting stone graves. Graves built of tiles have been reported from the plot of the Viczay-Mayer house at the corner of Széchenyi Square and Alkotmány Street in the western part of the *vicus*. A grave constructed of slabs was unearthed in the foreground of the fort, in the foundations of the house at 17 Kazinczy Street (Alexy house). Comparable graves have also come to light in the square in front of the Carmelites (today Köztársaság Square).[91] During the excavations conducted in 1977 on the plot of the house at 4 Saru Alley we also found graves dating from the Late Roman–early Migration period.

The large cemetery near the railway station, used throughout the 4th century,[92] has yielded inhumation burials, graves constructed of slabs, burial vaults and graves built of tiles. While the area of the *vicus* was in all probability the burial place of the population of the fort, this comparatively large cemetery in the south has yielded grave goods suggesting the burial of an agrarian Late Roman population who lived outside the walls, but enjoyed the protection of the fort. In his study P. Tomka reviews in detail the history of the town during the Migration period and also of the earlier periods that had led to the emergence of the medieval town.[93] His findings are summarized below.

In the early Migration period the area of the reconstructed and diminished Late Roman fort was inhabited by a civilian population. The 5th century layers have yielded pottery with latticed decoration, called 'foederati Keramik' for lack of a better term, sherds from glazed vessels of a later period and also several items of female jewellery, as well as various tools and implements. These finds and the rapid destruction of the walls suggest that by this period the fort no longer fulfilled an exclusively military function. The collapsed walls were never rebuilt, and the refuse gradually accumulated beside the high defensive wall (i.e. the ditch was no longer cleaned). The remains of the timber-framed store-building found beside the wall of the fort yielded seeds and fish-bones (3 Martinovics Square). The ruins of one of the towers of the Late Roman fort had also been used as a granary. Without assuming a complete change of population, we have every reason to believe that population groups from the Barbaricum had by this time also moved to the settlement (suggested by the hand-made pottery of Quadi and Suebians and the deformed skulls uncovered in the 5th century part of the cemetery at Széchenyi Square). The outlay of the town can be reconstructed on the evidence of the structures unearthed during the excavation in 1978. The excavated remains of timber-framed structures erected on stone foundation and the timber-framed houses were all built in line with the wall of the fort. The assumption based on observations made at the corner of a house extending into the excavated area— that some of the still extant Late Roman houses had been built into these structures—still remains to be proved.

The very same period saw the abandonment of the area of the former *vicus*. It is possible that the land outside the wall had been cultivated (horticulture?). Indicative of this were the grave groups (family burials?) dotting the area, the fence-posts found at the Gorkij Street site (the picket-fence was not accompanied by traces of a settlement!), the disturbedness of the Late Roman–early Migration period layer at Széchenyi Square and the topsoil that yielded small fragments of various artefacts. The find circumstances were reminis-

Budapest (1944–1951) 9; E. Swoboda: *Carnuntum* 3. Graz–Köln (1958) 159; K. Póczy: Aquincum a IV. században (Aquincum in the 4th century). *BudRég* 21 (1964) 55ff.

[88] For the increase in the coin circulation under Valentinian, cf. K. Biró–Sey: Coins from Identified Sites of Brigetio and the Question of Local Currency. *RégFüz.* II: 18 (1977) 27, Fig. 15. For the decrease in the money circulation in Arrabona, cf. E. Lovas: I risultati degli studi archeologici su Arrabona e dintorni. *Bolletino Assoziazione Internazionale Studi Mediterranei* 2 (1931) 6; E. Lovas: Győr város régészeti katasztere (An archaeological gazetteer of Győr). *Győri Szemle* 12 (1941) 178; Gabler (1971a) 6, 47.

[90] A. Börzsönyi: Római régiségek Győr–Belváros területéről (Roman antiquities from the centre of Győr) *ArchÉrt* 27 (1907) 40ff.

[91] A. Börzsönyi: Római emlékekről Győr-város területén (Roman antiquities from Győr.) *ArchÉrt* 24 (1904) 254; E. Lovas: Győr város régészeti katasztere (An archaeological gazetteer of Győr). *Győri Szemle* 12 (1941) 173.

[92] Szőnyi (1979) 56–57.

[93] P. Tomka: Ausgrabungen auf dem Káptalandomb in Győr (Jahresbericht 1978). *MittArchInst* 8–9 (1980) 139–141.

cent of sites uncovered on regularly ploughed farm-lands, where traces of pits, floor levels or levelled layers can no longer be observed. The accounts of life in comparable 5th century towns (e.g. *Vita Severini*) seem to confirm this assumption.

By the time of the Avar conquest this population too had disappeared. The stratification on Káptalan hill was not continuous, with a topsoil poor in finds or deposits containing traces of settlements dating from the dawn of the Magyar Conquest directly overlying the early Migra-tion period layer. Accordingly, no Avar centre can be assumed in the central part of Győr. The settlement patterns of the Avar Period, as reflected by cemeteries and the corresponding settlements are comparable with that of prehistoric periods: the territory occupied by the Avars included only the outer periphery of the present-day town (which in fact was rather congested: the Liqueur factory, Újszállás, the airport, Téglavető Balk, the New Cemetery, the Ritter estate on the road leading to Pápa, and Bokányi Dezső Street on the banks of the river Rábca).

The most probable date for the break in the continuity is 568, the year of the Langobard migration. Although no pottery of distinctly Langobardic origin has come to light in the town, the antler amulet (3 Martinovics Square) can most probably be assigned to the first half of the 6th century. Its closest parallels can be quoted from 6th century graves (Bezenye, Hegykő).

The preceding periods had a considerable influence on the development of the topography of early medieval Győr. The dilapidation of the walls of the Late Roman fort on Káptalan hill had considerably altered the shape of the hill, and its relative height was increased since this was the only site where the remains of the early Migration period settlement were stratigraphically super-imposed. Although the wall itself was by that time almost completely covered with the accumulated debris (as had been observed on the excavated southern section), the flat-topped high mound with relatively steep sides was well-suited for the creation of an economic military and political centre after the Magyar conquest.

The importance of this outstanding strategic point (with fords on the Danube and Rába rivers, at the intersection of the major land and water routes estab-lished in the Roman period) was only enhanced by the existence of the ditch of the Late Roman fort, no matter how desolate it was in the 10th century. The Danube outlet of the moat fed with water from the river Rába may have served as a port. The land at the foot of the hill was relatively even and was not endangered by inunda-tion: the flood-free area between the shore dunes of the Danube was gradually filled up in the course of the repeated demolition and rebuilding of the houses in the Roman *vicus*. This change in the topography contri-buted to the formation of the medieval settlement in the outlying grounds of the fortress, and it also accounts for the location of the settlement on an extended eastern axis along the Danube. The emergence of the settle-ments on the outskirts of the town was the result of the favourable geographic location, but the late Migration period settlements also influenced it.

## GYŐR IN THE MIDDLE AGES

In the lack of extensive excavations, studies on the early medieval history of the town of Győr had for a long time been based only on scanty written records, on reconstructions based on the late medieval conditions, on hypothetical and analogous reasoning. The past 20 years have brought about considerable changes in this respect. The archaeological excavations and observa-tions made during the large-scale building operations in the centre of the town have provided a firm basis for solving some of the main problems of the 10th–13th century architecture of the town.

We have already seen how the preceding periods had influenced the outlay of the town. The 'Roman heri-tage'[94] was fairly swiftly taken over by 10th century Hungarian society. A short while ago, 10th century finds were only known from the cemeteries in the above-mentioned outer periphery of the later town (Szeszgyár–1 km from the centre, Téglavető Balk–2 km, Lehel Street–1.5 km, Pós hill, on the opposite bank of the river Rába–3 km). Since these cemeteries are still under excavation, their dating, as well as the description of the community using them, cannot be considered fully accurate.[95] These burial grounds had been mostly used by commoners, although we have reason to believe that the graves at Téglavető Balk can be associated with a military middle-class community. Thus the 10th cen-tury settlement features found in 1978 on Káptalan hill, in the heart of the town, came as a surprise. The characteristic features and the relative chronology of these structures can be fitted into the chronological framework proposed by György Györffy in his study on the developement of the bailiff's (*comes*) castles.[96] A semi-subterranean hut, abandoned sometime in the mid-10th century, has yielded a remarkably large number of western import pottery. This fact, together with the stratigraphic position of the finds, was instru-mental in assigning them to a definite date. Moreover, this find suggests that this area became integrated into the long-distance trade network soon after the post-Conquest period consolidation. The small merchants' settlement built on the ruins of the ancient fort at the junction of the Danube and Rába rivers, at the intersec-tion of ancient routes and near the strategic river fords, soon developed into an important regional centre. The

[94] E. Fügedi: Die Entstehung des Städtewesens in Ungarn. *Alba Regia* 10 (1969) 102.

[95] N. Fettich–J. Nemeskéri: *Győr története a népvándorlás-korban (History of Győr in the Migration period)*. Győr (1943) 48–49; A. Börzsönyi: Pogány magyar sírokról Győr város határában (The burials of pagan Hungarians found in the environs of Győr). *ArchÉrt* 23 (1903) 67–70; A. Börzsönyi: Győri sírmező a régibb középkorból (A medieval burial ground in Győr). *ArchÉrt* 25 (1905) 31–33 and *ArchÉrt* 28 (1908) 220. G. Fehér–K. Éry–A. Kralovánszky: *A Közép-Duna-medence magyar honfoglalás- és kora Árpádkori sírleletei (The grave finds of the Conquest period and Árpádian Age burials from the Middle Danube Basin)*. Régészeti Tanulmányok II. Budapest (1962) 38–39. The excavations at Pós hill were led by Mária Albeker and Károly Mesterházy.

[96] Gy. Györffy: Die Entstehung der ungarischen Burgor-ganisation. *ActaArchHung* 28 (1976) 355.

immediate predecessor of the bailiff's castle was erected as early as the second half of the 10th century. Our excavations have brought to light a row of huge underground store-houses with the roofing supported by massive timber posts. The excavated part of this structure had a 2 m deep foundation on average, was 6.5 m wide and 40 m long. It was presumably built during the principality of Géza (972–997). Its mere existence implies a production system enabling the accumulation of large quantities of products, as well as expropriators able to see it executed. Consequently, it can be considered as definite proof of the presence of princely authority and indicates a level of social development considerably higher than previously assumed.

There is no data for the appearance of the hill, the oldest core of the later town. That there were defensive works in this area (rampart?, palisade?) is only a matter of conjecture based on a few excavation records, which are in fact rather difficult to interpret, and on the information recorded in our medieval chronicles that one part of the quartered corpse of the rebel leader Koppány was nailed onto the gate of the Győr fort in the first year of István's reign (997).[97]

The precincts proper outside the fort were at this time still uninhabited. The presence of a loose network of smaller settlements in the vicinity is suggested only by the above cemeteries. It may nonetheless be assumed that the core of the settlement already bore the name Győr (Gyeür, Jaurinum).[98]

The next landmark in the history of this princely economic and administrative centre (one of the most important ones in the country) occurred during the reign of King St. Stephen (997–1038). The building of the network of bailiff's castles on Káptalan hill and in its immediate vicinity had brought about considerable changes in the outlay of the settlement. First the timber-framed bailiff's castle with a defensive rampart was erected on the mound.[99] A new row of aboveground timber-framed (Blockwerk) store-houses was built south of the rampart, on the very same spot where the underground store-houses had stood. The bailiff's castle became the ecclesiastic centre, and the episcopal cathedral was built in the middle of the castle. Unfortunately, nothing else is known of other constructions in the period. In all likelihood, there were also the residences of the bailiff and the bishop (the bishopric at Győr was one of the first set up by King Stephen[100]), the

lodgings of the officers (agricultural and military), and servants and the buildings of the bailiff's castle. Unfortunately, the few contemporaneous fireplaces uncovered during the excavations offered little information about the structures containing them. Nevertheless, we have to reckon with a relatively densely built-in settlement in the barely 150 m × 150 m area.

Following the completion of the bailiff's castle, the first groups of people settled in the precincts outside the wall. This settlement, called Váralja (i.e. *suburbium*), was built according to country customs (the excavations at Széchenyi Square have brought to light underground furnaces, refuse pits and postholes). The small, detached settlements lying at a distance of 1–2 km from the centre of the town were thus replaced by chains of adjacent, though still loosely connected, settlements flanking the main roads and extending as far as the castle, or to be more precise, as far as the marketplace at the intersection of the roads. Most of the archaeological data at our disposal comes from the settlements lying on the road leading eastward along the Danube: the 'nameless village'[101] at Szeszgyár–Újszállások can apparently be linked with the finds made in Rákóczi Ferenc Street and the features uncovered in the centre of the town. The parish church named after St. Stephen the Martyr, that has been dated to the reign of King St. Stephen by some scholars had probably stood somewhere near this road (presumably near the corner of present-day Liszt Ferenc Street–Nefelejcs Alley). The settlements built on the roads leading to Fehérvár and to the south along the river Rába are known only from written sources (Benedekfalva, Királyfölde–Kertesszer–Adalbertfalva).

The next remarkable change in the topography of the area occurred in the 13th century. The reign of King Béla IV saw the building of a new donjon for the bishop within the castle wall (on Káptalan hill). This major construction presumably took place in the 1250s or 60s.[102] To all appearances, this building lay outside the original boundaries of the bailiff's castle, but close to its northwestern wing, with a moat separating the two constructions. In other words, the tower was built at the strategically most important point of the fortress, thus strengthening its defences (Fig. 5). This construction indirectly reflects the changes in the relations between the ecclesiastic and secular (royal) powers, and also the

[97] *Képes Krónika (Chronicon Pictum).* Ed. by D. Dercsényi–K. Cs. Gárdonyi–L. Mezey. Budapest (1964) 98.

[98] The name originates from a proper name and has a root in common with the name Géza (Gyeücsa). D. Pais: Bő. *Magyar Nyelv* 23 (1927) 507; Gy. Németh: Géza. *Magyar Nyelv* 24 (1928) 149. Gy. Györffy: *Tanulmányok a magyar állam eredetéről (Studies on the origins of the Hungarian state).* Budapest (1959) 23, also derives it from a proper name, but in a different way.

[99] P. Tomka: Erforschung der Gespannschaftsburgen in Komitat Győr-Sopron. *ActaArchHung* 28 (1976) 402–408.

[100] Gy. Balanyi: Szent István, mint a magyar keresztény egyház megalapítója és szervezője (St. Stephen, the founder and organizer of the Christian Church in Hungary). *SZIE I,* 346–347.

[101] Quite a number of archaeological finds coming from the area of Vagongyár–Szeszgyár–Viztorony–Újszállások are housed in the local museum. The most recent rescue excavation in the area was conducted by András Uzsoki in 1967. Most of the finds are still unpublished. For a detailed summary, cf. E. Lovas (1942) 16–18. Lovas calls attention to the fact that the name of the settlement is still unknown. Borbiró–Valló (1956) 77–78 refers to it as a nameless village. B. Szőke: Fejezetek Győr koraközépkori történetéből (The early medieval history of Győr). *Arrabona* 1 (1959) 93, identifies it with Szt. Benedekfalva. In our opinion there is no need to search for a toponym— the name of the settlement was simply Győr, similarly to the annexed inner regions.

[102] K. Kozák: Adatok a győri Püspökvár történetéhez. (The history of the bishop's castle in Győr). *Arrabona* 3 (1961) 33–55.

Fig. 4. The castle of Győr in Domenico Zeno's engraving

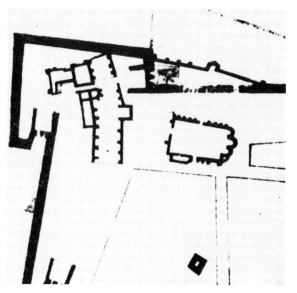

Fig. 5. The castle of Győr in Nicolò Aginelli's engraving

growing importance of the bishopric in the topographic record. The cathedral, which was rebuilt in the meantime, still lay within the castle walls. Little is known of the architectural sequence of the other structures inside the walls owing to the lack of excavations. These buildings include another tower (donjon) in front of the southern side of the castle (depicted in 16th century engravings), or the palace of the comes Hectore mentioned in a charter. The castle was defended by the river Rába in the west, by the Danube in the north and by a moat starting from the bank of the Rába in the south and east. The Danube outlet of the moat perhaps served as an inner port. The engravings only depict a single gate of the castle (in the east), but it is hardly imaginable that there was no direct access from the castle to the marketplace in the south.

As a result of these large-scale constructions, the settlement of Váralja also grew in importance. Indicative of this are the contemporary commercial regulations. Idrīsi, the 12th century Arabian geographer, describes it as a busy commercial centre. The customs regulations of Győr, issued in 1260,[103] offer a glimpse into the contemporary life of the town (mention is made of German and Italian merchants, and of trade in grain crops and fodder, cheese, fruit, wine, honey, fish, livestock, leather, furs and textiles, pottery, salt, gold, silver and glassware). The income from the duty of the thirtieth amounted to 500 *gira*s even during the reign of King László IV.[104] This trade was conducted on the above described west–east and north–south trade routes and on the Danube waterway. In addition, we can also reckon with local production, evidence of which has been furnished by the finds discovered in the pottery kilns of the 'nameless village', the eastern suburb destroyed in the 1270s. The inhabitants of this settlement probably specialized in a kind of industrial production as early as this period.

The arrival of the mendicant orders and the construction of various churches similarly reflect Váralja's rapid development. The first church of the Franciscan order was erected between 1235–1250, and that of the Dominicans was completed by 1221. Churches built in some of the nearby villages are also mentioned in the sources (the existence of the provostship of St. Adalbert is confirmed in an 1138 document, the Benedictine church is referred to in 1116). The church and monastery of the Johannine Order, which settled down in the area in 1209, could not be located. Studies on the history of the settlement tend to locate it to a site farther south from the town.

The period also brought about considerable changes in the social breakdown of the population living in the environs of the emerging town (besides peasants and servants, the new elements included tradesmen, merchants, mendicant friars and *hospites*). Culminating these transformations, the settlement was granted the privileges of a town in 1271. Since Erik Fügedi's recent study gives a detailed account of the charter,[105] we shall here only descibe the topographic consequences.

The skirmishes in the 70s brought desolation to the settlement, especially to its outlying areas. The potters' settlement on the eastern road was rebuilt only in the 14th–15th centuries, but as the blacksmiths' quarter. The reconstructions in the inner town also involved large-scale building operations. After removing a remarkably large amount of earth, the townsmen rebuilt the central marketplace (its late 13th century gravelled level was found during the 1968–1969 excavations in Széchenyi Square). The bazaar, extending as far as the

[103] *AUO* VII, 523.

[104] *CD*, 327; Borbiró–Valló (1956) 40.

[105] E. Fügedi: Győr városának 1271. évi kiváltságlevele (The 1271 franchises of Győr). *Győr. Várostörténeti tanulmányok*. Ed. by L. Dávid–A. Lengyel–L. Z. Szabó. Győr (1971) 111–117.

Danube, flanked the wide open space of the marketplace (this quarter with winding roads and narrow passage-ways was called Kalmár [Merchant] Street). The port and the fish-market on the Danube bank also belonged to this complex. The building of the palisade (rampart) encircling the town was another large-scale project (its traces were discovered near Szük Alley, in the southern end of the plots in Liszt Ferenc Street, during the excavations preceding the building of the Gorkij Street housing estate). This palisade bordered and defended the town until the mid-16th century, when the large-scale military constructions shifted the boundaries towards the south and reduced the enclosed area in the east.

Most of the studies on the medieval history of Győr draw a sharp distinction between the 'royal town' *(civitas regalis)*, which had the bailiff and the town as its authority, and the 'capitular town' *(civitas capitularis)*, headed by the bishop of the chapter. This essentially legal distinction is not reflected in the topographic record. It appears to be logical to presume—especially for the early period—that the royal and church manorial lands (which included also private lands, e.g. the land and the peasantry of the Hédervári family) would be easily discernible. Consequently, the settlement lying to the east on the riverside hills may have fallen under the bailiff's power, while the villages extending southward paid their taxes to the bishopric. The granting of urban privileges abolished these topographically assessible differences, since from this period on royal and episcopal subjects both settled within the walls of the town.

The 13th century developments brought an end to the first stage in the history of the town. The ensuing periods require a separate study.

## REFERENCES

Borbiró, V.–Valló, I. (1956): *Győr városépítésének története (The architectural history of Győr)*. Budapest.

Gabler, D. (1971a): Kutatások Arrabona canabaejában (Investigations in the canabae of Győr). *Arrabona* 13, 5–54.

Gabler, D. (1971b): Győr a rómaiak korában (Győr in Roman times). *Győr. Várostörténeti Tanulmányok*. Edited by L. Dávid–A. Lengyel–L. Z. Szabó. Győr, 21–47.

Gabler, D.–Lőrincz, B. (1977): A dunai limes I–II. századi történetének néhány kérdése (Remarks on the history of the Danubian limes in the 1st–2nd centuries). *Arch Ért* 104, 145–175.

Lovas, E. (1942): *Győr város régészeti katasztere (Archaeological gazetteer of Győr)*. Győri Szemle Könyvtára 19. Győr.

Mócsy, A. (1974): *Pannonia and Upper Moesia. A History of the Middle Danubian Provinces of the Roman Empire*. London–Boston.

Soproni, S. (1978): *Der spätrömische Limes zwischen Esztergom und Szentendre*. Budapest.

Szőke, B. M.–Szőnyi, E. T.–Tomka, P. (1976): Sondierungsgrabung in Győr–Káptalandomb. *MittArchInst* 6, 107–113.

Szőnyi, E. (1976): A győri "homokgödri" római temető (The Roman cemetery of Győr-Homokgödrök). *Arrabona* 18, 5–47.

Szőnyi, E. (1979): Arrabona késő római temetői I. Vasútállomás környéki temetők (Die spätrömische Gräberfelder von Győr (Raab) I. Das Gräberfeld um die Eisenbahnstation). *Arrabona* 21, 5–57.

# THE RISE OF HUNGARIAN TOWNS ALONG
# THE DANUBE

## L. Gerevich

In Roman times the Danube formed an important central part of the *limes*. This network of forts and towns could hardly have evolved without the strategic and commercial role of the waterway.[1] At first the trade of Pannonia had been directed towards the Italian, and later, to western markets; from the late 3rd century the region gradually merged with the Balkanic–Dalmatian trade area.

We are hardly mistaken if we assume that the immediate 'geomorphological' factors stimulating the emergence of the settlements and the system of European roads and waterways played a similar role after the Magyar conquest.

A glance at a map showing the towns of Hungary in the 11th and 12th centuries reveals an astonishing variety; the position and proximity of these towns to each other also allows a number of far-reaching conclusions, extending beyond the obvious geographical data and the historical factors characteristic of the area. The early settlements which eventually grew into the most significant towns all lie along, or in close proximity to, the Danube; in this respect one must also bear in mind the west–east valleys of the Felvidék (Slovakia) as well as the flat, southerly area of the Hungarian section of the Danube and the region of Lake Balaton as most important in the Pannonian area, with the Danube Bend occupying a central place.

The importance of the settlements that grew into medieval towns was enhanced by the fact that Stephen I (St. Stephen, 997–1001–1038) founded important church institutions in them: bishoprics and abbeys. Of the ten bishoprics and arch-bishoprics only four (Eger, Bihar, Gyulafehérvár and Csanád) lie outside this area, two of which lie beside the river Maros (Gyulafehérvár and Csanád). The significance of the Danube and the Transdanubian area had been recognized already by the first Magyar settlers:[2] the region was occupied by the

chief tribe, and it is in this area that we find the family estates of the princes and the kings of the House of Árpád. This is the territory that later became the scene of early missionary activities. It would appear that while the Hungarian tribes needed the proximity of the river for their semi-nomadic way of life based on stockbreeding (their previous homelands all lay along major rivers), they also appreciated the architectural heritage of the former Roman civilization, preserved by the Slavic and other peoples they found here. Furthermore, we also have to assume that traffic on the Danube, that had temporarily halted in the beginning, offered great strategic, political and commercial possibilities, reminiscent of the time when Pannonia had been a Roman province.

The 200-years long debate over the existence of eastern trade on the Danube was finally closed with its rejection; the arguments in favour of this possibility were based on late medieval conditions when eastern trade had indeed become almost impossible, and had for the most part been taken over by Venice. Archaeological data, such as the hoard of Byzantine coins from Óbuda, the distribution of various wares and a wide array of building techniques originating from the south, the fleets accompanying various western military expeditions (791; and the campaings of Henry III: 1043, 1051), and, most important, the morphology of the ports and ferries of the bigger towns on the Danube, as well as the data indicating an increase in water traffic during the 11th and 12th centuries have all contributed to a better understanding of the role played by the Danube in the emergence of towns.[3]

---

[1] A. Mócsy: *Pannonia a késő császárkorban (Pannonia in the late Imperial Period)*. Budapest (1975) 21, 72; I. Tóth: *A rómaiak Magyarországon (The Romans in Hungary)*. Budapest (1979) 18–19.

[2] *Cum ergo Kusid venieset in medium Vngarie et circa partes Danubii descendisset, vidit locum amenum ... fluvium bonum et pratosum, placuit ei. SRH* I, 288.

[3] The Bavarian statutes on duties and tolls dated between 903 and 907 also proved that trade with Moravia, and perhaps also with a country as far away as Poland, was overwhelmingly realized by Danube shipping. Cf. S. Kohn: *A zsidók története Magyarországon (The History of the Jews in Hungary)*. Budapest (1884) 7–9. It is probable that little had changed a hundred years later. The remains from this period—though few and far between—also testify to the early existence and role of settlements along the Danube. As regards Győr, this has been proved by Péter Váczi. Around 1028–30: *Arnoldus monachus Ratisponensis ... Cumque periclitarer sepius in profundis Danubii decursibus ... CD* VII/4, 43; *MES* I, 42; 1089:

We can add that a part of the population of 11th century Hungarian settlements had arrived from the French-speaking area on the northeastern border of the German Empire,[4] an area that was quoted by Pirenne as an example for the role played by ferries and ports *(portus)* in urbanisation.[5] To illustrate this point we have chosen the two most significant towns of the Hungarian section of the Danube, two former capitals, Esztergom and Buda-Pest (even though the latter in fact comprises a series of ferries and ports, towns and settlements).

Eastern trade was mostly concentrated in the hands of Jews and Ismaelites. We know of a somewhat telling incident about the year 1050: On their way from Russia to Regensburg two Jewish merchants crossed the river near Esztergom and, instead of going to the synagogue, they stopped to repair their cart.[6]

One of the earliest references to Pest is an allusion to its *portus* from 1046: *Deinde perrexerunt pariter versus portum Danubii … Cum que ad predictum portum Pest venisset, …*; St. Gellért was killed in front of its ferry in 1046.[7] It cannot be mere coincidence that in contemporary chronicles and documents these towns are usually mentioned in connection with their *portus*. Géza II's deed of settlement gives the Chapter of Buda (Óbuda) *(capitulum Budensis ecclesie)* the toll of the Óbuda and Pest *portus* and ferries, and, even more significant, the duties on ships carrying salt and wine upstream or any goods downstream (1148: *… ad usum fratrum Budensis ecclesie tributum fori Geysa et tributum portus Pest et Kerepes, navium etiam cum vino sive cum salibus ascendentium sive cum aliis venalibus descendentium eidem ecclesie regie maestatis auctoritate condonare curavi…*).[8]

There is also the lively description by Odo de Deogilo of the town of Esztergom at the time of the 1147 crusade: on her ships the Danube carried the wealth of many a country to the noble town of Estrigun.[9] Mention was made as late as 1295 of duties paid on various goods, brought by way of the Danube, and on being sold below the Castle of Buda (1295: *… quod, licet ipsi de antiqua et approbata et hectenus pacifice observata consuetudine de omnibus mercimoniis et rebus venalibus, que per fluvium Danubii iuxta Castrum Bude navigio deferuntur,*[10] and *navium etiam tributum cum vino sive cum salibus ascendentium sive cum aliis venalibus descendentium…*).[11]

The significance of the Danube traffic is reflected not only by early, 11th–12th century travels, or the (merchant) fleets of towns and monasteries,[12] but also by the

*Gebhardus, Pragensis episcopus … Strigonii moritur … et quia prope urbem erat Strigoniam, illuc mittit cum rex navigio, …* MGH IX, 95; MES I, 61–62; "Walter Sans-Avoir … set out on the road to Hungary. Marching up the Rhine and the Neckar and down the Danube, … From Cologne Peter took the usual road up the Rhine and the Neckar to the Danube. When they reached the Danube, some of his company decided to travel by boat down the river: .." St. Runciman: *A History of the Crusades.* I. Cambridge (1951) 122–123; "… als König Stephan der Heilige (995–1038) die Bekehrung der Ungarn angebahnt hatte, konnte der Weltverkehr wieder seinen Weg durch die Länder an der Mittleren Donau nehmen. … Das Hauptverkehrsmittel bleiben auch jetzt noch die Wasserstrassen, trotz der Gefahren. … Bei dieser Sachlage erschien die Einrichtung eines allgemeinen Umschlagplatzes zu Wien als das beste Mittel, um den Landeskindern mindestens den Gewinn des Zwischenhandels nach Ungarn und den südlichen Donauländern vorzubehalten, eine Massregel, … Die Fahrzeuge, mit welchen die Flüsse befahren wurden, hat man schon im XIII. Jahrhundert als zweiwändiges Schiff, Einbaum, Zille und Floss unterschieden; die zweiwändigen Schiffe waren vorne und rückwärts etwas verjüngt und hatten einen breiten Boden. Sie massen im mittleren Sechstel 6–12 Werkschuh und darüber, was auf eine Länge von 36–72 Schuh oder von etwa 12–24 Metern schliessen lässt. … Die starke Verwendung der Flüsse als Verkehrsmittel erklärt sich aus der Beschaffenheit der Wege und durch die Seltenheit von Brücken in dieser Zeit." A. Luschin v. Ebengreuth: *Handel, Verkehr und Münzwesen. Geschichte der Stadt Wien* I. Ed. by H. Zimmermann. Wien (1897) 407, 408, 413, 422–423.

[4] G. Bárczi: A középkori vallon–magyar érintkezésekhez (The Walloon–Hungarian contacts in the Middle Ages). *Századok* (1937) 399–416; H. Ammann: Die französische Südostwanderung im Rahmen der mittelalterlichen französischen Wanderungen. *Festgabe Steinacker.* München (1955) 259–281; Gy. Székely: Wallons et italiens en Europe Centrale aux XIᵉ et XVIᵉ siècles. *AnnUnivBud Sectio Historica* 6 (1964) 3–71; Gy. Györffy: A székesfehérvári latinok betelepülésének kérdése (The settlement of the Latini in Székesfehérvár). *Székesfehérvár Évszázadai* 2. Ed. by A. Kralovánszky. Székesfehérvár (1972) 37–44; E. Fügedi: Das mittelalterliche Ungarn als Gastland. *Die deutsche Ostsiedlung des Mittelalters als Problem der europäischen Geschichte.* Ed. by W. Schlesinger. Sigmaringen (1975) 471–50.

[5] H. Pirenne: *Les villes et les institutions urbaines* I. Paris–Bruxelles (1939) 151–156, 382–391. In that territory (Maas) there were names suggesting a Hungarian origin also later, e.g. in 1371. *Ibid.,* II, 75; H. Pirenne: *Economic and Social History of Medieval Europe.* London (1947) 43, 56.

[6] S. Kohn: *A zsidók története Magyarországon (The history of Jews in Hungary).* Budapest (1884) 57–61, 359–367, 405–508.

[7] *Inter hac autem Endre et Levente cum eadem multitudine procedentes per medium Hungariae appropinquaverunt ad portum, qui vulgo dicitur Pesth.* SRH I, 339, 340; A. Chédeville: De la cité à la ville 1000–1150. *Histoire de la France urbaine.* Ed. by G. Duby and J. Le Goff. Paris (1980²) 62: "En Flandre, en particulier, où l'essor urbain fut aussi vigoureux que précoce, on continua d'employer, comme à l'époque carolingienne, le mot *portus*: à Gand, il est attesté régulièrement de 941 au XIIIᵉ siècle mais on le rencontre aussi dans diverses sources des Xᵉ et XIᵉ siècles relatives à Bruges, Valenciennes et Tournai"; 72: "Tous les châteaux, à l'exception des nids d'aigle encore peu nombreux, étaient doublés d'une agglomération. C'est le cas de ceux qui avaient été établis auprès d'une *villa*, d'un ancien *vicus* ou d'un *portus* plus récent qui leur donna son nom …"

[8] *MonBp,* 3.

[9] Odo de Deogilo. MGH XXV, 62; SRH I, 458–459; H. Marczali: Árpádkori emlékek külföldi könyvtárakban (Heritage of the Árpádian Age in Foreign Libraries). *Történeti Tár* (1878) 167–170, 168.

[10] *MonBp,* 291.

[11] *MonBp,* 297. Ladomér, Archbishop of Esztergom, refers to the privileges of Géza, concerning the payment of tolls.

[12] E. g. the Knights Hospitallers of Esztergom–Szentkirály had a fleet of 12 ships. 1187: *… monasterium sancti Stephani regis … hospitalem domum, positam in loco, qui Obon nuncupatur, et insuper duodecim naves …* MES I, 133; *… currus … cum Bombardis nostris … ad naves disponare et usque Budam*

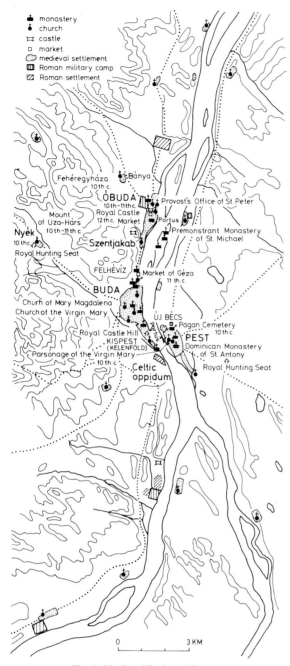

Fehéregyháza
10th c.

ÓBUDA
10th–11th c.    Provost's Office of St. Peter
Royal Castle
12th c. Market    Portus
Mount
of Uza–Hárs
10th–11th c.    Premonstrant Monastery
of St. Michael

Nyék
10th c.
Royal Hunting Seat

Szentjakab

FELHÉVÍZ    Market of Géza
11th c.

BUDA

Churh of Mary Magdalena
Church of the Virgin Mary

ÚJ BÉCS
Pagan Cemetery
10th c.
Royal Castle Hill    PEST
KISPEST
(KELENFÖLD)    Dominican Monastery
of St. Antony
Parsonage of the Virgin Mary
10th c.    Royal Hunting Seat

Celtic
oppidum

0    3 KM

Fig. 1. Medieval Buda and Pest

bricks, as well as timber were transported to Hungary and, particularly, to Buda.[14]

These random references leave no doubt about the urbanizing function of the Danube. The river linked the waterways and roads of Western and Central Europe and was, at that time, the main artery of its trade, somewhat reminiscent of the situation in the late Roman Empire.

In the following we shall attempt to outline some of the common features of the emergence, history and morphology of these towns.

The Castle Hill of Esztergom occupies an area beside the Danube roughly corresponding to the width of a road. It widens into a valley further south; the valley is divided by a marsh[15] (Tapolca). All these settlement areas were densely populated since the Neolithic, Copper and Bronze Ages. The Celts and, afterwards, the Romans had built a fort on the hill. Below the hill, along one of the tributaries of the Danube, a harbour was built in Roman times.[16]

The fact that Esztergom grew into the capital[17] of the country can be traced to the new political and economic situation following the Battle of Augsburg (955), which brought an end to Hungarian raids, and particularly after the accession of Prince Géza to the throne (971). This explanation is in fact the assumption of a westward-oriented long-distance trade on the Danube. This suggestion is supported by the disappearance of the dirhems and also the decline of Arabic commercial relations to which hundreds of these coins bore witness. On the other hand, a lively north–south trade is suggested by the large number of denars minted by Stephen I found along the rivers flowing into the North Sea.[18] The river Garam which flows into the Danube almost opposite the town of Esztergom, and its valley linked this northern

fact of major merchant shipping. Later trade with the Levant or its alleged importance have not yet been sufficiently proven.[13] It was from Germany and, primarily, from Vienna that bulky and heavy goods, pottery,

... destinare velitis ..., quia ad Castrum Nandoralbam multa victualium genera in navibus mittere habemus, ... 1454: ... Puchsen und zewge schiff ... gen Offen awffen Wasser zu schiken. T. Ortvay: Pozsony város története II (History of Pozsony II). Pozsony (1898) 412–413.

[13] For a comprehensive survey and a review of the relevant international literature on the basic questions of medieval Hungarian trade, see Zs. P. Pach: Egy évszázados történész-vitáról: áthaladt-e levantei kereskedelem útja a középkori

Magyarországon (A century-long historical debate: did the Levantine trade route pass through medieval Hungary). Századok (1972) 849–891; Zs. P. Pach: A Levante-kereskedelem erdélyi útvonala I. Lajos és Zsigmond korában (The Levantine trade route through Transylvania under Louis I and Sigismund). Századok (1975) 3–32; Zs. P. Pach: A nemzetközi kereskedelmi útvonalak XV–XVII. századi áthelyeződésének kérdéséhez (On the shifting of international trade routes in the 15th–17th centuries). Századok (1968) 863–888; Zs. P. Pach: Levantine Trade and Hungary in the Middle Ages. Theses, controversies, arguments. Études historiques hongorises 1975. Ed. by D. Nemes–E. Andics–E. Arató. Budapest(1975) 283–307.

[14] Even in the 15th century the transportation of building materials was carried out on the Danube. 1425; CD X/6, 730; 1497; Hofkammer Österreichische Gedenkbücher. Vol. 3/a. 607.

[15] MES II, 520: ... balneum in aquis calidis de Tapulcha; its drain operated mills. MES II, 350 (1294), 371 (1295), 520 (1303); Schünemann (1929) 55.

[16] I. Horváth: Esztergom. MRT 5, 78–84, with abundant bibliography. Schünemann (1929) 45–46.

[17] Schünemann (1929) 47 (1131); A. F. Gombos: Catalogus fontium historiae Hungaricae. Vol. III. Budapest (1938) 2326; Vita Conradi archiepiscop. Salisburgensis (1106–1147). MGH XI, 63–77; MES I, 84.

[18] L. Huszár: Szent István pénzei (St. Stephen's Coins). SzIE II, 335–364.

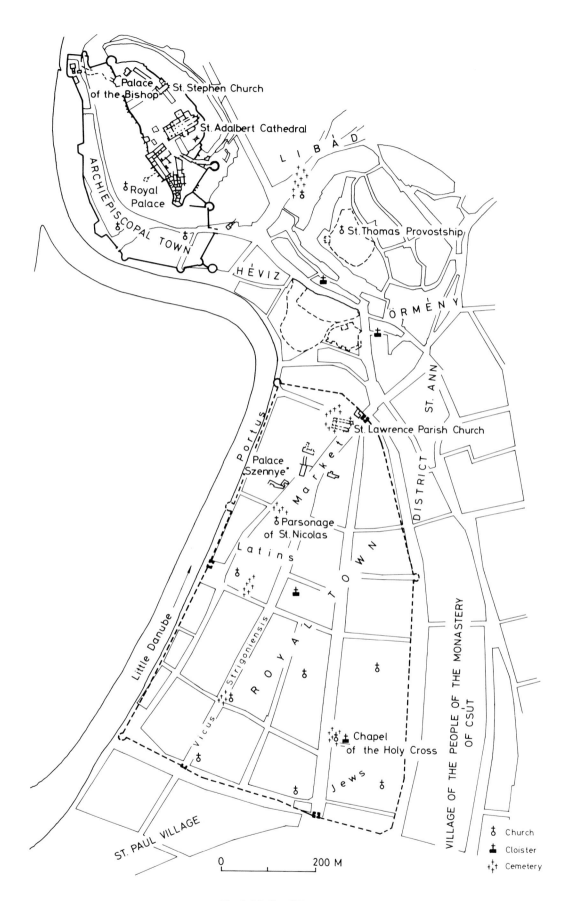

Palace
of the Bishop — St. Stephen Church

St. Adalbert Cathedral

LIBÁD

ARCHIEPISCOPAL TOWN

Royal Palace

St. Thomas Provostship

HÉVIZ

ÖRMÉNY

St. ANN

St. Lawrence Parish Church

Portus

Palace
"Szennye"

Market

ROYAL TOWN DISTRICT

Parsonage
of St. Nicolas

Latins

Little Danube

Vicus Strigoniensis

Chapel
of the Holy Cross

VILLAGE OF THE PEOPLE OF THE MONASTERY OF CSÚT

Jews

ST. PAUL VILLAGE

0        200 M

Church

Cloister

Cemetery

Fig. 2. Medieval Esztergom

29

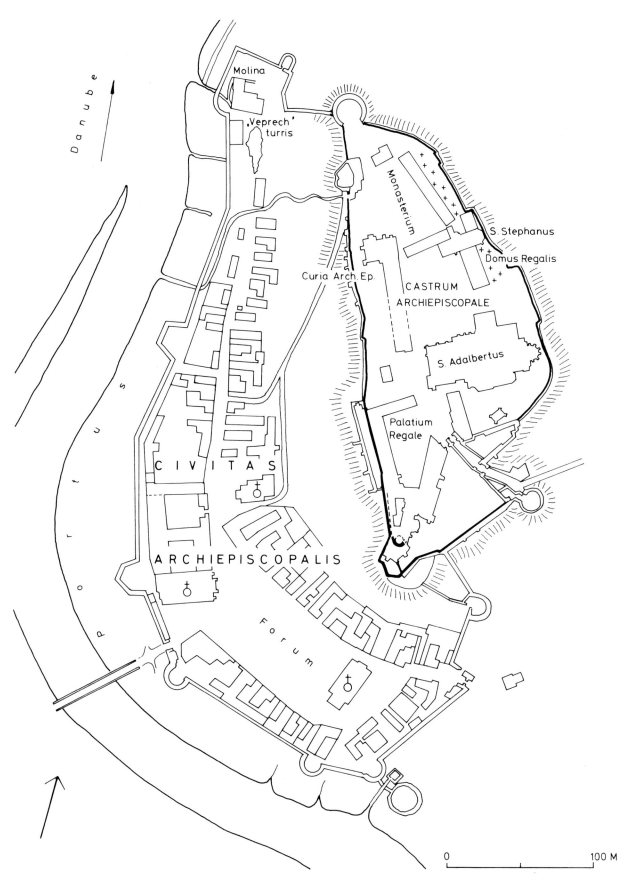

Fig. 3. Esztergom. The Royal Castle and the *civitas archiepiscopalis*

Danube

Molina

„Veprech'
turris

Monasterium

S. Stephanus

Domus Regalis

Curia Arch. Ep.

CASTRUM
ARCHIEPISCOPALE

S. Adalbertus

Palatium
Regale

C I V I T A S

A R C H I E P I S C O P A L I S

P o r t u s

f o r u m

0                    100 M

trade to the Danube waterway—hence the German name of the town, Gran. Its medieval Latin name, Strigonium, is usually derived from Slavic, and suggests the presence of a Slavic earthwork on the hill rising above the river, which in pre-Hungarian times perhaps controlled the crossing between Moravia and Pannonia, then dependent on the Carolingian empire. There is little in favour of the theory that it had been a bishop's seat in these early times, but is must at any rate have been church property and an ecclesiastical centre before actually becoming a royal seat; otherwise the area at the foot of the fortified hill, protected from the south by the marshes, and the important harbour would not have remained in the possession of the church. The people and retinue of the king were settled further down, beyond the marshland, in what later became the 'royal city' (1184: *Quidam udvornicorum regis de suburbio Strigoniensi. ...*).[19]

It was on the hill that Prince Géza held his court from the very beginning of his reign; later, he erected stone walls around the castle.[20] After embracing Christianity together with his entire family he built a small 20 meters long church dedicated to the protomartyr Stephen near his palace; his son, the future Stephen I (St. Stephen, born in the palace of Esztergom in 969) was baptized in this church by the *clerici* of Bishop Pilgrim.[21] This event is recorded in the Legends of St. Stephen,[22] as well as in later deeds and documents. Until the 18th and early 19th centuries the ruins of the small church and scattered remains of the palace were visible on the hill, together with the foundation walls and cellars of the archiepiscopal palace.[23] Their traces were erased by the large-scale building activity (that in some points penetrated to a depth of 11 metres) in connection with the construction of the present-day Basilica. However, their memory is preserved by a collection of early carved stones, some of which were recarved at the close of the 12th century. This is another piece of evidence for the rebuilding of St. Stephen's church at that time.

Stephen I established Esztergom as his royal residence and had it developed accordingly. He had already founded an archbishopric there in 1001 and had the imposing cathedral of St. Adalbert built at the turn of the century, in memory of the missionary who had been active in the region. He ordered his new palace to be constructed on the southern crest of Castle Hill; its foundation walls were first uncovered in 1933–1938[24] and later in the 1960s during the excavations conducted by Mrs. Emese Nagy.[25] The southern 'new' palace of Stephen I encompassed a separate courtyard of its own. The castle, divided in this way, controlled two separate settlements at the foot of the hill.

The distance of the royal city from the castle suggests that an earlier settlement in ecclesiastical possession lay at the foot of the hill.

The first area to be settled lay in the north, very near to the castle, while the royal town, occupied by the court personnel and the retinue (the *udvornici*)[26] emerged south of the marshland along the Little Danube, in the neighbourhood of the Danube port (the branch where the river never freezes, owing to hot springs). The *udvornici* built their houses on the northern side of the large marketplace. Further to the south, around the Church of St. Nicholas, we find the Latini, who settled here from the mid-11th century on,[27] and the Jews, who were attracted by the long-distance trade, as well as by the prosperity and protection offered by the royal residence.

As mentioned before, the development and the status of a city, both of the *Regalis Civitas Strigoniensis* and of the *Civitas Archiepiscopalis (Aquatica Civitas)*, were ensured by their right to stop the traffic of the markets beside and belonging to the harbours, and to levy a toll on the goods. This latter right was of particular importance since tolls were not only levied on commodities from foreign countries shipped on the river or transported on roads along the Danube, but also on wares that

[19] *CD* II, 219; *MES* I, 129.

[20] *..., dictam ecclesiam esse fundatam ante tempora beati regis Stephani, scilicet per dominum Geyzam regem, patrem eiusdem, qui construxit etiam castrum Strigoniense.* A. Pór: *Az esztergomi Szent István első Vértanuról nevezett prépostság története (A history of the Esztergom provostry named after St. Stephen, the First Martyr)*. Budapest (1909) 105. From the *Canonica visitatio*, held in 1397, which makes its authenticity incontestable.

[21] J. L. Csóka: A magyarok és a kereszténység Géza fejedelem korában (The Magyars and Christianity at the time of Prince Géza). *SZIE* I, 280–281; B. Hóman–Gy. Szekfű: *Magyar történet (Hungarian History)*. Vol. I. Budapest (1935) 167; According to the tradition he was baptized by Adalbertus. *SRH* II, 380, 406.

[22] *SRH* II, 394, 407.

[23] Gy. Széless: *Rudera Ecclesiarum ... S. Adalberti ...* Manuscript in the Primate Archive of Esztergom. Archivum Vetus, No. 1344. A part of it was published in 1765. Adalbert Cathedral. *SRH* II, 412; J. N. Máthes: *Veteris arcis Strigoniensis, monumentorum ibidem erutorum, aliorumque antiquitatum lythographicis tabulis ornata descriptio.* Strigonii (1827).

[24] T. Gerevich: *Magyarország románkori emlékei (Romanesque monuments in Hungary)*. Budapest (1938) 76–98; A. Leopold: Az esztergomi várhegyen folyó régészeti kutatások történeti vonatkozásai (Historic implications of the archaeological research conducted on Castle Hill in Esztergom). *Annales Strigonieses* 7 (1934) 34; A. Leopold: Az Esztergomban feltárt műemlékek ikonográfiája (Iconography of the momuments uncovered in Esztergom). *Katholikus Szemle* (1935) 623; K. Lux: *Die königliche Burg Stephans des Heiligen in Esztergom.* Burgenwart (1935).

[25] E. Nagy: Előzetes jelentés a 1964–1967. évi esztergomi várfeltárásokról (Preliminary report on the 1964–1967 excavations of Esztergom Castle). *ArchÉrt* 95 (1968) 102–107; E. Nagy: Rapport préliminaire des fouilles d'Esztergom 1964–1969. *ActaArchHung* 23 (1971) 181–198; E. Nagy: Le premier palais royal de la Hongrie. *Actès du XXIIᵉ Congrès International d'Histoire de l'Art. Budapest 1969.* Ed. by Gy. Rózsa. Budapest (1972) II, 863–865, III, 631–632; Z. Nagy: *Esztergom.* Budapest (1973).

[26] Schünemann (1929) 62; *Quidam Udvornicorum regis de suborbio Strigoniensi.* CD II, 219.

[27] *..., nostris Ciuibus de Strigonio, qui remanserant de inuasione Tartarorum, et qui de terra latina ex post facto superuenerant, ...* MES I, 440 (1256); *RegArp*, 348.

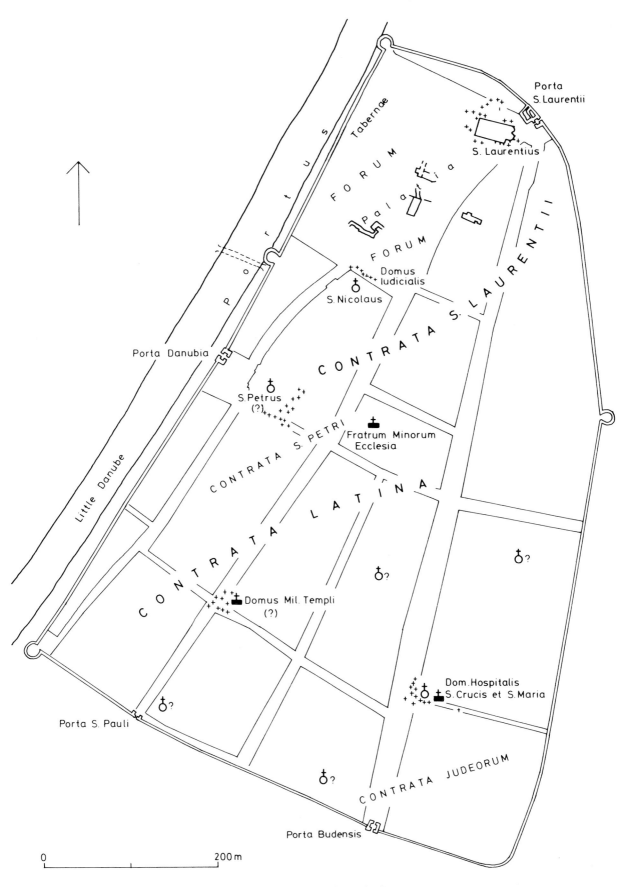

Fig. 4. *Regalis civitas Strigoniensis*

32

Fig. 5. View of Esztergom from the Danube. 17th century engraving (British Museum, Sloane 5233f13)

were transported from other Hungarian towns. The toll was gradually transferred into the hands of the Church.[28]

In 1198 King Imre (1196–1204) presented the archbishop with an unfinished royal house—the *domum regalem*. This can probably be identified with the old palace[29] of Prince Géza, then under reconstruction,

which was wedged in among the buildings of the archiepiscopal palace, around the closed courtyard in the north. From that time the two castles, or courts, came to be partly separated. The partition also necessitated the construction of a new Royal Chapel.

The heyday of the town began in the middle, and continued in the second half of the 12th century. This is reflected and recorded not only by deeds and by various chroniclers of the Holy Crusades that passed through Hungary (the second crusade in 1147, the third in 1189), but also by the remains of monuments reflecting a peak of Hungarian art and architecture. The royal and archiepiscopal palaces were rebuilt at that time, as was the Cathedral of St. Adalbert.

The emergence and joint wielding of secular and ecclesiastical power, as well as their influence on the culture and the groundplan of towns has since long been recognised as one of the basic stimuli to urban development in Europe.[30] An identical source of power and law—secular and ecclesiastical power being domiciled in the same castle—was therefore established. Esztergom Castle is one of the most typical examples of this

---

[28] A. Pór: Háborúság Esztergom város és az esztergomi káptalan közt a vám miatt (Conflict between the city of Esztergom and the chapter of Esztergom over the tolls). *Magyar Gazdaságtörténeti Szemle* (1904) 167–168; S. Domanovszky: *A harmincadvám eredete (Origin of the thirtieth toll)*. Budapest (1916) 29–30; Schünemann (1929) 49–50; *MES* II, 253: ... *cum ex praerogativa civitatis Strigoniensis et ex consuetudine, cuius temporis non extat memoria, sit locus apud Strigonium omnibus mercatoribus descendendi et explicatis suis mercibus tricesimam reginalem et tributum Strigoniensis capituli persolvendi.*

[29] 1198: ... *rex Hungarie quicumque fuerit a deo coronatus per sedem Strigoniensem, in signum catolice fidei, decimam soluere deberet archiepiscopo Strigon., a quo fidem baptizmatis et coronam receperunt; nos eadem fide, qua ipsi salvari volentes, in perpetuum satuimus, quod de omnibus proventibus regalibus archiepiscopus Strigon. decimam ad plenum recipere debeat, prout semper receperunt. Item decimam tributorum in terra Scipiensi et in Posonio, ipsi domino archiepiscopo Strigon. in perpetuum pro mensa sua, sicut per sanctos reges erant donate. Item pro salute nostra et pro discordia vitanda, exemplo sanctorum regum, donavimus in perpetuum domum regalem in Castro Strigon., que nondum fuit opere consumata, eidem Strigon. archiepiscopatui; tamen tempore necessitatis nostre ipse dominus Archiepiscopus nos in eadem recipere teneatur. Datum per manus domini Kaptapani [sic] episcopi agriensis, aule nostre cancellarii. Anno ab incarnacione Domini Mᵒ. Cᵒ. nonagesimo octauo. MES* I, 156; *RegArp* I, 54; L. Gerevich: Esztergom. *Enzyklopädie zur Frühgeschichte Europas* (Arbeitsmaterial). Berlin (1980) 102.

[30] A. Chédeville: De la cité à la ville 1000–1150. *Histoire de la France urbaine* II. Ed. by G. Duby–J. Le Goff. Paris (1980) states the following: "Tout château important avait ainsi deux bourgs au moins, l'un laïque, l'autre ecclésiastique. Ils ne se pressaient pas au pied de la muraille à la manière de faubourgs: les nécessités de la défense exigeaient un glacis, il fallait également que les bourgs puissent grandir sans se gêner mutuellement. Il semble aussi que l'on ait tenu à imiter la structure polynucléaire des anciennes cités qui servaient encore de modèle urbain: ..." (p. 77). "Les bourgs ecclésiastiques reparaissent dès la première moitié du Xᵉ siècle, abrités par une muraille, d'abord au nord de la Seine, puis un peu plus tard au sud" (p. 84).

model with the Prince's palace and chapel (Géza, after 972), and also with the king and his archbishop living in the same castle. The various texts surveyed in the above leave little doubt about the 'L' or 'T' form, in which the first royal palace and its chapel were connected with each other.

In the 13th century the castle became the archbishop's property, but the explanations provided by the deeds of gift do not solve the various contradictions. It has already been mentioned that King Imre had endowed the archbishop with a royal house in 1198.

Most of the earlier scholars and some of the contemporary ones interpreted this deed of 1198 as being the transfer of the castle, in spite of the fact that all of these quoted the deeds of 1249 and 1256, which they considered to have been two additional, later donations.[31] Regarding the topography of the castle the deeds were fully utilized, but most scholars virtually never tried to solve the contradiction of the threefold donation.[32] As a matter of fact, the unfinished state of the construction mentioned in the first deed—from 1198 – seemed to justify the correctness of superficial explanations, even though it only mentioned the donation of Prince Géza's palace that had been contiguous with St. Stephen's church. The palace was a simple house containing the room where St. Stephen was born, which later became a chapel.[33] The deed contained the donation of the tithes,

and the transfer of the royal house is mentioned but briefly in the last sentences: no mention is made of the castle or its accessories. Géza's palace, the *domus regalis*, wedged into the northern archiepiscopal castle—which was separated from the rest of the royal palaces—was given to the archbishop in 1198 *pro discordia vitanda*.[34] The transfer of the entire royal castle and the palaces would have made the continuation of the reconstruction of the royal palace up to beyond the turn of the century pointless. The error was brought to light by archaeological investigations which proved that the palace had been rebuilt at the end of the 12th and the beginning of the 13th centuries. It also escaped the notice of former research that St. Stephen's chapel and, evidently, also the old royal house, could have been reconstructed at the same time as the palace and the cathedral.

According to the next deed (1249), the king, fearing another Mongolian invasion, had the remaining citizens moved to the castle and endowed them with the part owned by the archbishop within the castle, with the exception of the canon's houses and St. Adalbert's church. In exchange the archbishop received the royal palace and its accessories.[35] Since it was rather old, the palace was in a poor state, and its renovation proved to be rather costly.

After the Mongolian invasion (1241–1242) the royal palace was rarely inhabited, nor was it repaired. It would appear from the text of the deed (1249) that the archbishop did not receive the royal palace with too great enthusiasm: ... *si ipsi titulo donacionis illa acceptassent et possidere voluissent*.[36]

The 1256 deed offers the final solution, together with the legal formulae for the donation of the whole castle and its appropriate value, expressed by the repetitions characteristic of the texts of deeds, as well as with a presentation of antecedents and a topographical description: *et totum residuum infra muros Castri ... et tota antiqui Castri circuicione*.[37]

In their very forms these deeds differ significantly from the one dated to 1198, which—we must repeatedly emphasize—cannot be interpreted as a donation of the entire castle. The historic evidence also contradicts this: the royal family often sojourned at Esztergom palace, even if the king himself was a rare guest. Important

[31] *MES* I, 375–376, 439–411; *RegArp* I, 271, 348.

[32] A. Lepold: Szent István király születéshelye (The birthplace of King St. Stephen). *Annales Strigonienses* 9 (1938) 4; I. Sinka: Magyarország Árpád-kori fő- és székvárosa Esztergom (Esztergom, the capital and royal residence of Hungary in the Árpádian Age). *Annales Strigonienses* 8 (1936) 26–27. Even though the author accepted the fact of the donation, generally acknowledged, he remarked that the king seldom resided in Esztergom, while his family lived there permanently.

[33] *Utrum omnia et singula altaria dicte ecclesie, que cum uni existente in sacristia, et alio existente in capella, in qua natus fuit beatus rex Stephanus, ...* A. Pór: *Az esztergomi Szent István első vértanúról nevezett prépostság története (History of St Stephen protomartyr's chapter on the hill of Esztergom).* Budapest (1909); A. Lepold: Szent István király születéshelye (The birth-place of King St. Stephen). *Annales Strigonienses* 9 (1938) 5. This assumption is confirmed by the text of several documents, thus, for example, ... *eorundem Canonicorum hospicia iuxta eandem ecclesiam s. Stephani prothomartiris, ubi beatissimus Rext Staphanus sanctum nomen suum proprium et nativitatis sue pronunciacionem per os sancti Stephani prothomartiris omnipotentis Dei veri nuncii, recepit. MES* I, 608; *RegArp* II, 27; The situation might have been similar in France in the 9th century since ... *episcopus in domo ante altare Sanctae Mariae ... et regina in oratorio Sancti Petri iuxta domum regiam. ... Sed et rex alacriter ei obviam prosilivit ... cum ipso et venerabili coniuge in oratorium beatissimi apostolorum principis Petri, quod ut diximus, cubiculo regis contiguum erat, processit ...* (Hinkmar: *Vita S. Remigii*, around 878). "Diese Erzählung lässt m. E. deutlich erkennen, dass Königspfalz, Kathedrale, Petersoratorium und Baptisterium auf engem Raum beieinander lagen: ... der Erzbischof habe sich an dieser Stelle festgesetzt, wo einst der römische Statthalter residierte trifft dies zu, so wäre damit auch die Lage der Königspfalz geklärt: Sie hätte sich auf der Südseite der Kathedrale, an der Stelle der erzbischöflichen Pfalz befunden, die im 12. Jahrhundert als das Palatium Tau bekannt war." (*Vita S. Gildardi–*

*basilica S. Petri, quae ad palatium dicitur.*) C. Brühl: *Palatium und Civitas*. Köln (1975) 63, 64, 65. Numerous stones, clustered columns, plinths, consoles and, probably, even the tympanum originate from the reconstruction of St. Stephen's chapel which coincided with the rebuilding of the palace.

[34] *MES* I, 156; *RegArp* I, 53–54. The 1256 deed alludes only to King András's donation.

[35] *MES* I, 375–376. ... *residuum populi de Civitate Strigon., ... una cum Venerabili Patre nostro, ... quod edificia et Curiae, ad archiepiscopum pertinencia, locum spaciosum obtinebant; Palacium /nostrum regium cum om/nibus Domibus et utilitatibus, ac pertinencijs suis, que vetustate diruta fuerant et reparacione sumptuose indi/gerent, cum venerab/ili Patre nostro Stephano Strigon. Archiepiscopo commutauimus, ... tradidimus; RegArp* I, 271.

[36] *MES* I, 376.

[37] *MES* I, 439, 441; *RegArp* I (2), 348.

historical events also took place there and it was there that the king exercised direct judgement.[38]

In Esztergom the dignitaries of the church played a prominent role in the life of the town;[39] the right of trade free from duty, valid for the whole territory of the country, was granted to them, as well as the right to establish a town in the *suburbium* and to hold fairs there that was given to the archbishopric in 1239.[40] Nevertheless, the slow decline that gradually overtook ecclesiastical towns became apparent in Esztergom—and later also in Óbuda.[41] However, this did not affect the castle, which had been transferred into the archbishop's ownership, where works of extension and decoration were carried out, particularly from the mid-14th century on. The entire fortifications system was completed after several reconstructions in the 14th century under the archbishop's supervision.[42]

In the first half of the 13th century the royal court was shifted to the square, palace-like Óbuda (Buda) Castle, in order to be nearer the cluster of towns and settlements headed by Buda and Pest, whose commercial and strategic importance increased considerably at that time.

The Budapest of our days can be traced back to three medieval settlement nuclei. Their relationship and the change in their names have not yet been fully clarified. The walls of a 3rd–4th century Roman camp *(Contra Aquincum)* defending the bridge-head leading to the *barbaricum* stood on the site of the present City of Pest. The later Pest evolved on the site and the surroundings of this camp; its fortress was donated to the Volga-Bul-

garian nobles Billa and Bocsu and their people by the Magyar prince Taksony (947–972). The fortress has been identified with the former Roman *castrum*,[43] which, however, is inconsistent with the fact that as early as the 11th–12th century this area was principally used as a burial ground.

A trilobe chapel, a *trichora* of an earlier date stood in its southeastern corner, sheltered by the walls of the fortress.[44] The remains of its curved foundation walls suggest that it was rebuilt into the sanctuary of a basilical church, of which nothing has survived except the fragment of a door frame with a carved interlacing pattern, a decorative motif extremely popular in Italy and Dalmatia in the 9th–11th centuries. By the time the site was reorganised it had been functioning as the parish church of Pest.

The walls of the Roman *castrum* were demolished at least 1 metre below the surface level of around 1200. This would suggest that the defensive role of the Roman walls had diminished long before the town emerged. There is no evidence for repairs in the fortress walls from the early Middle Ages. The narrowing of the sallyport, on which the 'Pest Castle' theory was based, actually turned out to be the remains of a later reconstruction into a cellar. While planning and organising the site its function was also clarified: it had been used as a door in the cellar of a late medieval house with its stone jambs having been chamfered.[45]

By the 13th century the rapidly developing commercial settlement had grown into an extensive and rich—*magna et ditissima*—German merchant town.[46]

Across the river the boat-shaped ridge of Castle Hill of Buda runs parallel to the Danube, its steep slope allowing only one road along the river, which was of Roman origin and extremely busy in medieval times too. On the hill above the crossing point of two main roads we excavated between 1946–1961 the remains of ancient Hungarian royal palaces, which surrounded three courts of the castle. Some parts of the south and east front, the chapel, the great hall, cellars, towers and walls dating from the 14th–15th centuries were reconstructed. In fact the vestiges of the earlier castle were also uncovered: basements, walls and foundations as well as fragments of vaulting, supported by seven metres high columns, which were subsequently built into the eastern outer wall of the later castle.[47]

Another road running on the other side of the Castle Hill linked the Pest harbour with Esztergom. Buda Castle was in a position to control both roads, as well as the port, which was the crossing place, the port of transshipment.[48] (Some goods had arrived by ship on the Danube to be transported further on roads and *vice*

[38] The most important events took place there; thus, for example, the wedding of Emerich and the daughter of Alphonse II, King of Aragon (Dubravius: *Hist. Boh.* I, 378), having captured his rebel brother, had him probably imprisoned in the palace of Esztergom. *MES* I, 168. On administering justice; *MES* I, 287–288; *RegArp* I, 156; Stephen's son was born in Esztergom in 1239. *MES* I, 331; L. Sinka: Magyarország Árpádkori fő- és székvárosa Esztergom (Esztergom, the capital and royal residence of Hungary in the Árpádian Age). *Annales Strigonienses* 8 (1936) 27, 29, 33. *Ipse enim (Rex) de Strigoniensi et Albensi civitatibus, quae ad unam tantum diaetam distabant, exercitu congregato.* (Rogerius: *Carmen Miserabile*, Cap. 16). *SRH* II, 562.

[39] *RegArp* I, 59–60. L. Erdélyi: Árpádkori társadalomtörténetünk legkritikusabb kérdései (Critical problems of social history in the Árpádian Age). *Történeti Szemle* 3 (1915) 338. The forged deed of 1201, tried to legalize and to explain the strengthening of ecclesiastical power.

[40] *RegArp* I, 201.

[41] The houses and churches of religious orders are key points. The Monastery of the Holy Cross of Jerusalem founded by St. Stephen appears later to have become connected with the Order of the Knights of St. John.

[42] For several centuries Esztergom was the centre of constructions and of architectural arts to which others were strongly linked. Several masterpieces of this period have been preserved in the Cathedral Treasury. In the *suburbium* the remains of a goldsmith's workshop were unearthed. The most significant among foreign masterpieces is the Matthias Calvary. The upper part was made in the same Burgundy workshop as the reliquary of Christ's thorn preserved in the British Museum, and it is possible that it had in part been wrought by the same goldsmith.

[43] L. Nagy: *Az Eskü-téri római erőd, Pest város őse (The Roman fort of Eskü Place, the ancestor of the city of Pest).* Budapest (1946) 101–103.

[44] Gerevich (1976) 45–47.

[45] Gerevich (1971) 90.

[46] *SRH* II, 562 (Rogerius).

[47] L. Gerevich: *A budai vár feltárása (Excavations of Buda Castle).* Budapest (1966) 48–53; Gerevich (1976) 49, 50, 55, 56.

[48] Gerevich (1971) 15.

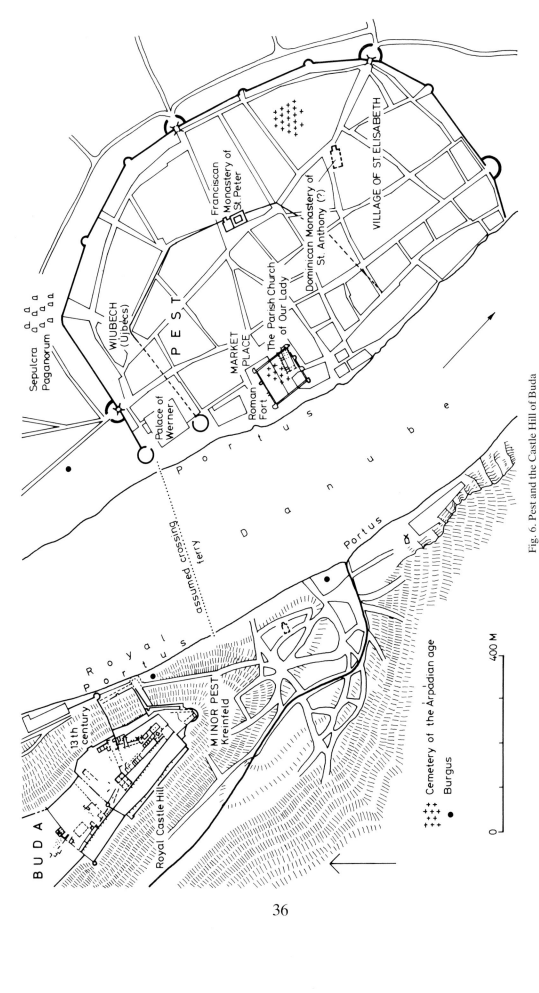

Fig. 6. Pest and the Castle Hill of Buda

Sepulcra Paganorum

WIUBECH (Újbécs)

Palace of Werner

PEST

MARKET PLACE

Roman Fort

Franciscan Monastery of St. Peter

The Parish Church of Our Lady

Dominican Monastery of St. Anthony (?)

VILLAGE OF ST ELISABETH

Portus

Portus

assumed crossing ferry

D a n u b e

BUDA

13th century

Royal Castle Hill

MINOR PEST Kreinfeld

Royal Portus

Portus

Cemetery of the Árpadian age

Burgus

0                    400 M

36

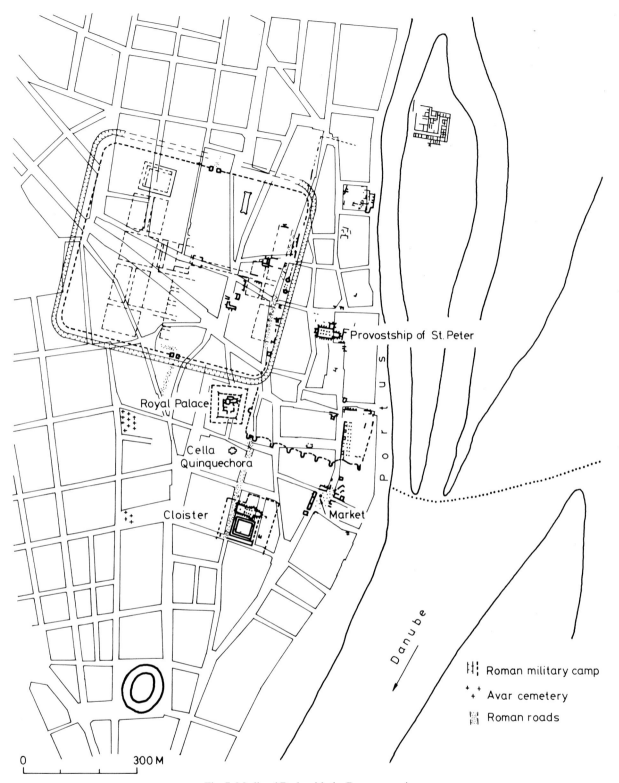

Fig. 7. Medieval Buda with the Roman remains

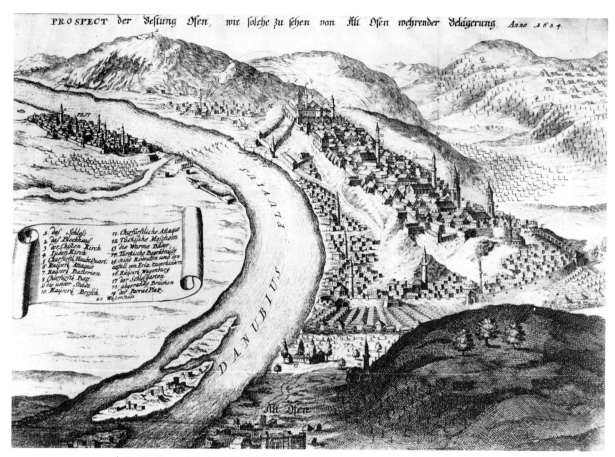

Fig. 8. Siege of Buda, 1684. View from the north (Hallart del., Wening engraving)

*versa*.) At the foot of the hill, where the two roads met — with Pest on the opposite bank, connected by the ferry — , there was the settlement Kis-Pest (Little Pest) that had earlier belonged to an older castle.

The identical name of Pest[49] for the two settlements clearly underlines their close relation that can, besides the extremely busy water traffic, be partly ascribed to the fact that the probably most important crossing point of the Hungarian section of the Danube was here. This ferry-town, sprawled over the river, has retained this characteristic feature until the present. The two sides of the ferry should in fact be considered as parts of one and the same town; yet a number of studies have been devoted to the problem of which of the two should be regarded as the earlier formation. The toponym 'Pest' which can be derived from Bulgarian suggests the right bank as the original bearer of the name that means 'oven' which may have referred to the troughs and caves with hot springs which abound at the foot of the two

hills. Perhaps the probable German variant of the Slavic name — 'Ofen' — had, beside the twin settlements, referred to the area north of the right bank of the river, Buda (the later Óbuda) that overlay the former Roman town, and extended to the wide, open plain of the Danube. Apparently the German inhabitants used the same denomination for all three settlements.[50]

Even in this case 'Ofen' can be considered an equivalent to the name 'Pest', which may have been transmitted by the German population. It is possible that the Hungarian variant is the toponym 'Héviz', meaning 'hot water'. This linguistic argument would suggest that the denominating locality should be considered as the first medieval settlement. Strangely enough, one is tempted to conclude from this that the local Celtic population may have survived (Tabán, Gellérthegy, Óbuda).

The Hungarian name can in all probability be traced back to the personal name 'Buda'. In the Buda hills several Magyar cemeteries were found with their characteristically small number of graves, which obviously points to the importance of the Magyar settlement at Óbuda. Árpád, the leader of the tribal confederation, was buried here, and the church erected over his tomb at

[49] J. Melich: *A honfoglaláskori Magyarország (Hungary at the time of the Hungarian Conquest)*. Budapest (1925); Gy. Györffy: Budapest története az Árpád-korban (History of Budapest in the Árpádian Age). *Budapest története* I. Ed. by L. Gerevich. Budapest (1973) 259–261. Following several authors, L. Nagy locates the name 'Ptolemaius' to this area and derives the name of Pest from 'Pestium'.

[50] L. Gerevich: Hungary. *European Towns. Their Archaeology and Early History*. Ed. by M. W. Barley. London (1977) 431–455.

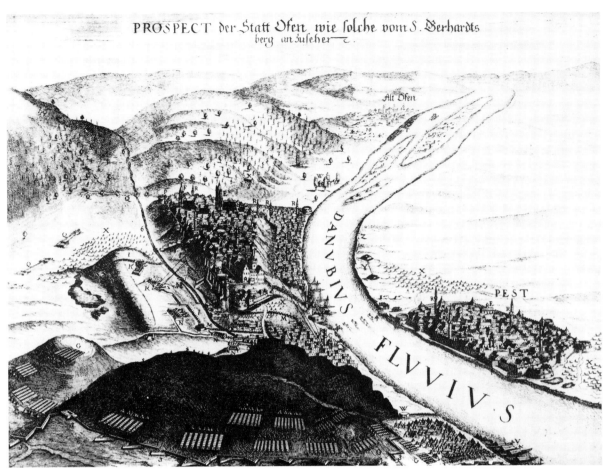

PROSPECT der Statt Ofen wie solche vom S. Berhardts berg anzusehen.

Fig. 9. Siege of Buda, 1684. View from the south (Hallart del., Wening engraving)

Fehéregyháza (White Church), probably dates to the same period—the 10th century.[51]

After the Magyar conquest the settlement of Buda fell behind Fehérvár and Esztergom, even though the collegiate church of the chapter of St. Peter, founded by Stephen I or by Peter, was ornamented with palmettes in a style inspired by Balkanic stone carving and by the traditional, tribal Hungarian style of silverwork. The substantial donations of St. Ladislaus (1077–1095) and Géza II (1141–1162) to the Buda chapter prove the importance of the place in economic geography.[52] The settlement lying in the centre of the road network that was also equipped with a harbour, whose winter use was ensured by a river-branch (fed by hot springs) and whose importance was enhanced by the growing traffic on the northeastern and southwestern roads, soon rivalled Esztergom. The privilage of 1212 established the jurisdiction of the *prepositus;* in 1212 the king ceded the town to the chapter and, in accordance with the existing situation, it was divided into two parts in 1355: the royal district and the ecclesiastical precinct,[53] reflecting the characteristic arrangement of major royal and episcopal towns.

The large-scale excavations carried out in recent years have unearthed a wealth of remains and yielded exciting new data on the history of the settlement. Its

[51] Fl. Rómer: Magyar régészeti krónika (Chronicle of Hungarian archaeology). *ArchKözl* (1868) 192; I. Henszlmann: *Ásatások a Victoria téglagyár telkén Ó-Budán (Excavations on the site of the Victoria Brick Factory at Óbuda).* Budapest (1886); L. Wekerle: *Árpád sírja kimutatva az ó-budai Viktória-téglagyár telkén megtalált Fehéregyház szentélyében (Árpád's grave unearthed in the sanctuary of Fehéregyháza found on the site of the Viktória Brick Factory in Óbuda).* Budapest (1886); T. Tholt: *Fehéregyháza és Árpád sírja holfekvése és kutatásaim (The whereabouts of Fehéregyháza and Árpád's grave, and my explorations).* Budapest (1886); S. Gömöri–Havas: Az óbudai Fehéregyház (Fehéregyház of Óbuda). *BudRég* 2 (1890) 33–41; E. Foerk: Újabb leletek a Victoria telkén (Further finds in the Victoria area). *BudRég* (1923) 74–80; see also *Budapest Műemlékei* II. Ed. by F. Pogány. Budapest (1962) 499–502. The chapel was integrated into a church of the Paulites which King Matthias had built in 1483. In spite of this no pre-Romanesque or Romanesque stones were found in the area of the Victoria Brick Yard; only graves with lockrings were discovered.

[52] E. Fügedi: Topográfia és városi fejlődés a középkori Óbudán (Topograhy and urban development in medieval Óbuda). *TBM* 13 (1959) 16–20.
[53] L. B. Kumorivitz: Óbuda 1355. évi felosztása (The division of Óbuda in 1355). *Bud Rég* 14:1 (1976) 279–302.

location sheds light on its relation to the Roman *castrum* and *canabae*. Its nuclei were the collegiate church and the royal castle. The former lies on the site of the *castrum* defended by the Roman walls, the latter outside the walls. The medieval settlement spread over the extended *castrum* of the 4th century and the area of the *canabae* as well as the vast Roman cemetery.[54] The two centres were linked by a former Roman road which traversed the 4th century camp and became the main street of the first settlement, the so-called Kovács (Smiths') Street, indicating by its name one of the principal crafts practised by its inhabitants. The marketplace, the 'forum' of later times probably lay northeast of the doubly fortified royal castle[55] and the road; it probably extended until a small branch of the Danube where, similarly to the other port towns on the Danube, it was bordered by the harbour. This was controlled by the royal castle, and protected on the north side by the collegiate church and its walls.[56] The site of the Roman harbour is indicated by the remains of warehouses; the medieval port probably occupied the same site or its immediate neighbourhood.

None of the excavations conducted so far has yielded irrefutable proof for the medieval use of Roman buildings. However, the frequent proximity or merging of settlement levels, as well as the use of some Roman buildings, the remains of medieval walls found along the main road and in the vicinity of the earlier walls of the Roman camp nonetheless seem to support this possibility. But, similarly to other early Hungarian towns in Pannonia, the basic outlay of the settlement at Óbuda was determined by the position of the Roman centres; the Roman suburb that survived longest, the *canabae*, as well as the early Christian cemetery and church along the main road, the *cella trichora* and *cella quinquechora* (*septichora* in Pécs) suggest that—as the example of Western European towns shows—it was the settlement of the poor eking out a miserable existence in the vicinity of the first Christian graves and churches that later developed into the first centres of early medieval towns.

Beside manufactured goods, shipping also supplied the town with raw materials. We know of ships that transported ores in the early 14th century. Several smaller streams, partly fed by warm springs, flowed into the Danube; the watermills worked by them can from the 12th century on be considered as the power plants of that period which supplied energy to the various industries in the Óbuda and Héviz area. For example one of the mills operated glass-works in the mid-15th century. Their high value is amply reflected by the numerous lawsuits between the church proprietors of the mills and their tenants.

Héviz, lying to the south of Óbuda (and later separated from it by Jakabfalva), and extending until Viziváros (Water-town) at the foot of Castle Hill also belonged to the House of Árpád.[57] Just as the royal castles of Óbuda, Pestújhegy *(novus mons Pestiensis)* and Buda controlled the harbours of Pest and Óbuda, in Héviz, too, a royal *curia* supervised the ferry, the market and the harbour of Jenő. Géza I (1074–1077) established here the renowned 'Géza Fair' *(Géza vására)*, attracting not only the tradesmen of the east-bound road leading to the Great Hungarian Plain and Transylvania, but administering, due to its harbour fed by warm springs and accessible all the year round, a long-distance water trade as well. In 1148 Géza II gave some sort of toll of the Géza Fair, and the harbour of Pest and Kerepes, to the Chapter of Buda.[58]

By the end of the century the control over the fords had been more or less taken over by the order of the Hospitallers who had already received large donations from the royal estates. The order's characteristic square castle with four corner towers provided powerful protection for the harbour and the ford.[59] Thus it was also "... on two hills facing each other that the secular and ecclesiastical centres of the settlement arose",[60] at the early settlement of Héviz which included the 'Géza Fair', the ferry and the harbour.

Besides the above-mentioned representative models of towns along the Danube, the towns of Győr and Pozsony (Bratislava), which played a key part also in the Middle Ages can be considered equally characteristic.

[54] H. Bertalan: Adalékok Óbuda középkori helyrajzához (Data on the topography of medieval Óbuda). *BudRég* 23 (1973) 23, 99–110; K. Póczy: Az aquincumi legios tábor és katonaváros romjainak feltárása és a műemléki bemutatása (Investigation of the Aquincum Legionary Camp and the restoration of its ruins). *BudRég* 24:1 (1976) 11–30. H. Bertalan: A középkori ásatások-kutatások története Óbudán (1850–1975) (A review of the investigations and excavations on the territory of medieval Óbuda, 1850–1975). *BudRég* 29:1 (1981) 31–42.

[55] J. Csemegi: Hol állott egykor az óbudai királyi vár? (Where did the royal palace of Óbuda stand?) *A Magyar Mérnök- és Építészegylet Közlönye* 5 (1943) 34–35; K. Lux: Árpádkori építészeti maradványok Óbudán (Architectural remains from the Árpádian period in Óbuda). *A Magyar Mérnök- és Építészegylet Közlönye* (1916) 193–205; L. Gerevich: Az óbudai királynéi vár maradványai a Kálvin-közben (Remains of the Queen's Castle in Kálvin köz in Óbuda). *Budapest Műemlékei* II. Ed. by F. Pogány. Budapest (1962) 372–382.

[56] H. Bertalan: Az óbudai prépostság középkori templomának maradványai a Korvin Ottó tér alatt (Remains of the Medieval Church of the Óbuda Provostry below Korvin Ottó tér). *Budapest Műemlékei* II. Ed. by F. Pogány. Budapest (1962) 399–401.

[57] Kubinyi (1964) 12, 21, 26.

[58] *MonBp*, 3, 1148: ... *tributum fori Geysa et tributum portus Pest et Kerepes, navium etiam cum vino sive cum salibus ascendentium sive cum aliis venalibus descendentium eidem ecclesie regis maiestatis auctoritate condonare curavi.* Salt and wine were the principal commodities transported on the Austrian section of the Danube and its tributaries. W. Rausch: *Handel an der Donau.* I. Linz (1969) 17, 26, 27. ... *in deducendis ... suis victualibus, vino et rebus aliis ...* (1269). Kubinyi (1964) 88.

[59] E. Reiszig: *A jeruzsálemi Szent János-lovagrend Magyarországon (The Jerusalem Order of the Knights of St. John in Hungary).* Vol. II. Budapest (1928) 28; I. Radványi: *Margitsziget története (The History of Margaret Island).* Pest (1858) 136–137; Gy. Osváth: *Szent Margit-sziget hajdan és most (The Isle of St. Margeret in the Past and Today).* Budafok (1901) 67; Kubinyi (1964) 115.

[60] Kubinyi (1964) 98–99.

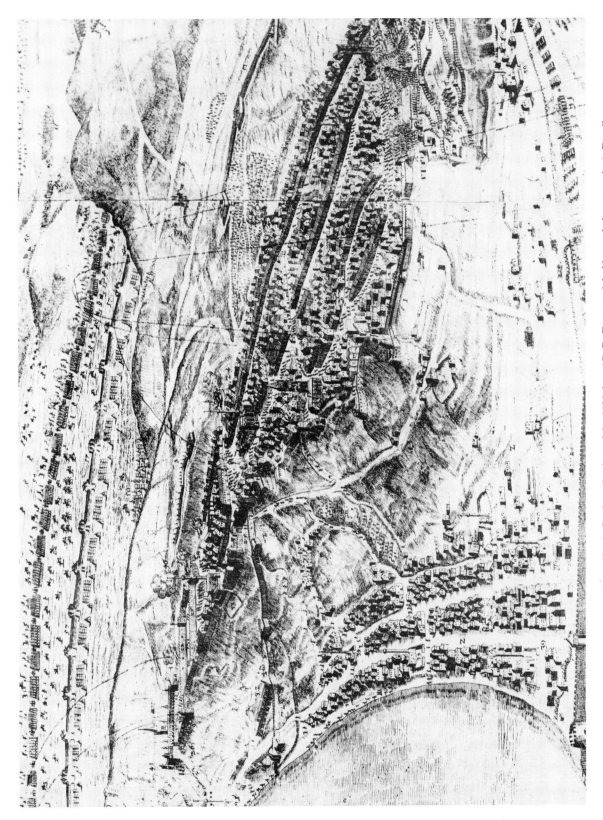

Fig. 10. View of Buda Castle at the time of the 1686 siege (G. D. Fontana del., Nessenthaler engraving). Detail

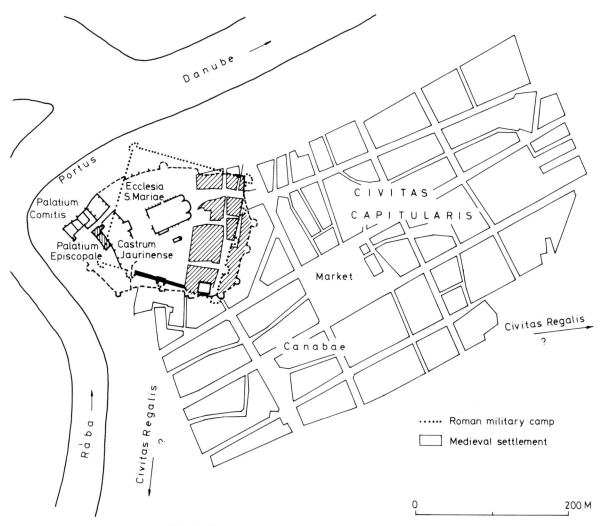

Fig. 11. Sketch of Győr, showing the position of the castle

The latter supervised the Danube where it leaves the Alpine–Carpathian gate, overlooked by a Slavic 'Burg-wall' and later by Dévény (Devin) castle,[61] some 15 km to the west, which stood where the navigable river Morava, a busy waterway to the north, flows into the Danube. Following the Hallstatt, La Tène and Roman period settlements, the 9th century saw a large-size earthwork protecting the Brezalauspure (907) *(Reslava civitae),*[62] one of the centres of the defence system of the Moravian–Slav territory. After 907 the castle came to

defend the Hungarian border. The fortress housed two authorities: the seat of the comes and the *prepositus* of the chapter,[63] and controlled also the harbour at the foot of the hill which—just as in Esztergom, Visegrád or Buda—enjoyed the immediate protection of a recon-structed Roman tower, a justified precaution since the town was one of the most important toll-collecting stations of the country. It was in the area of Vedricz (Verpruch) where, due to the donations of Béla III or Endre II, the abbot of Pilis took one-third of the Pozsony toll *(tricesima)* in his own tower and houses *(domus aquae).*[64]

[61] L. Kraskovská: Slovenské hradisko pri Devinskej Novej Vsi (Ein Slawischer Burgwall bei Devinska Nová Ves). *Slov Arch* 10 (1962) 241–250; L. Kraskovská: Slovenské hradisko v Devinskej Novej Vsi Nad lomom (Der slawische Burgwall in Devinska Nova Ves "Nad lomom"). *SlovArch* 14 (1966) 147–161.

[62] J. Stanislav: Bratislava–Presporok–Pressburg–Pozsony. *Slovanská Bratislava* 1 (1948) 22–35; S. Rospond: Bratislava–Braslav-j. *Sbornik Univ. Komenského, Philologica* 16 (1964) 67–70; V. Hatz: (B)BRESLAVA CIV(ITAS) zum Beginn der ungarischen Münzprägung. *Dona Numismatica.* Hamburg (1965) 75–85.

[63] *Bratislava.* Ed. by S. Pison. Bratislava (1961) 11.

[64] R. Békefi: *A pilisi apátság története (History of the Abbey of Pilis).* Pécs (1891) 206–216; 316–319, 345–349. *Preterea medietas tributi regalis de Posonio; cum due partes tocius tributi Posoniensis ad nos pertinet, de quibus unam partem habet ecclesia Sancti Martini de Sacro Monte Pannonie, aliam partem possidet ecclesia de Plys antedicta; ...* 28 June, 1254, *RegArp* I, 313. Beside the Danube the tower of the Archbishop of Esztergom played a similar role and was also called Veprech: *... a parte Danubii incipiendo a quodam fonte calido scaturienti,*

Fig. 12. View of Győr (Jaurinum) in 1566, based on a drawing by N. Aginelli (communicat N. Houfnagel, 1597)

The top of Castle Hill was surrounded by earthworks that can be dated to the 9th century. On the top there stood an oblong building of two joined parts reinforced by ashlars and surrounded by small huts, that were not built of stone. At right angles to the building, though a bit farther away, the remains of another oblong edifice were detected. Their dating was based on comparing their construction technique with that of Moravian basilicas. The larger edifices had apparently been built later in the 12th century.[65]

In spite of their rather modest dimensions and building technique they are reminiscent of the servant people's dwellings at Dömös (11th–13th ceturies). A basilica with a nave and two aisles, that incorporated also Roman building material and columns, rose on the gently sloping eastern terrace of Castle Hill in Pozsony (Bratislava). The position of the edifice is surprisingly similar to that of the Cathedral in the outer castle court of the Bishop's Castle of Győr, which is further from the palace. By the 13th century the defence of the castles appears to have called for the building of a keep[66] on Castle Hill in Pozsony, too.

In the second half of the 13th century one keep was built in the northwestern corner of the internal court of the Bishop's Castle of Győr.[67] Whether the corridor with stairs in the thick northwestern wall can be architecturally termed as a keep is debatable: this type of dwelling was already obsolete in the west. The direction of the former chapel of the palace is connected at right angles to the thick wall. The form of the mouldings and ribs of the lower church suggests a date around the close

---

qui est sub castro [Esztergom] et fluit ad ripam fluminis Kysduna vocati, usque ad turrem archiepiscopalem, Veprech vocatam. Magyar Sion (1863) 396.

[65] T. Stefanovicová: Bratislavsky Hrad. 9–12. storici (Die Burg Bratislava im 9–12. Jahrhundert). Bratislava (1975) 65–73, 114–119, 148–153.

[66] In the light of previous evidence Borbiró–Valló (1956) 53, proved the existence of the 'ancient keep'. While unearthing cellars Károly Kozák found its northern wall. For the excavation reports, see K. Kozák: Adatok a győri Püspökvár középkori történetéhez (The medieval history of the bishop's castle in Győr). Arrabona 3 (1961) 33–35; K. Kozák–A. Uzsoki: Régészeti és műemléki kutatás a győri Püspökvárban (Archaeological investigations in the bishop's castle of Győr). Arrabona 4 (1962) 53–65; K. Kozák: Adatok a győri vár középkori történetéhez (The medieval history of the Győr castle). Arrabona 9 (1967) 67–84; K. Kozák–A. Uzsoki: A győri székesegyház feltárása (The excavation of the cathedral in Győr). Arrabona 12 (1970) 111–159.

[67] The best guidelines to the area of the internal castle (castellum) was provided by Nicolò Aginelli's general plan of 1566 (now kept in the Nationalbibliothek of Vienna, Cod.

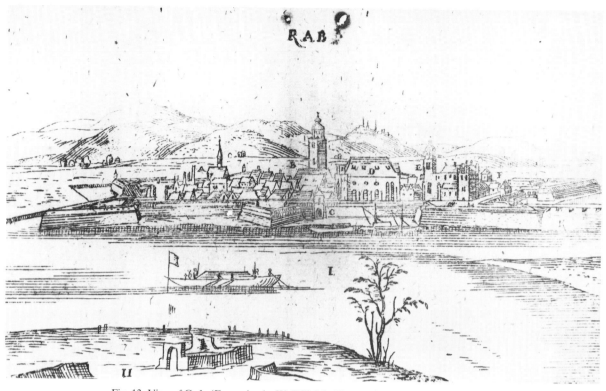

Fig. 13. View of Győr (Engraving by W. Dilich in *Ungarische Chronica*. Cassel 1600)

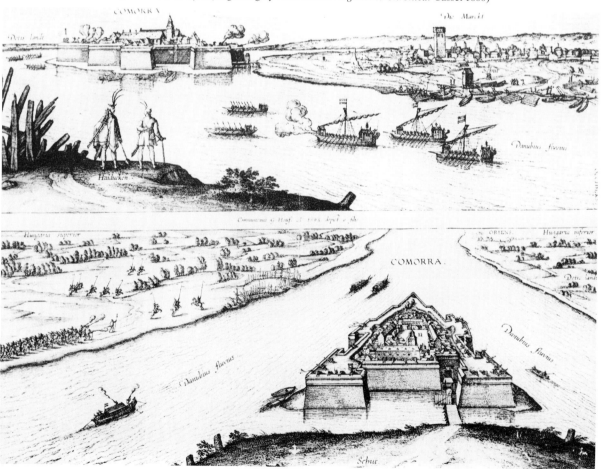

Fig. 14. View of Komárom. The castle and the town (engraving by G. Hoefnagel, depict. a filio)

44

Fig. 15. Thomas of Kolozsvár: St. Nicholas' Miracle of the Grain. Panel from the former Calvary altarpiece of the Garamszentbenedek monastery (1427). Probably showing the buildings of Esztergom and the boat traffic on the Danube

45

Fig. 16. View of Visegrád. The Castle Hill and the *suburbium* in the 17th century (British Museum, Sloane 5233f19)

of the 13th century. There is little doubt that, even if it was completely reconstructed, it had been the southeastern continuation of the former *palacium;* otherwise there would have been no sense in building the double chapel — that would, in this way, have been inaccessible. The inner castle was separated from the outer one by a wide moat, that has since filled up. Its arrangement has been revealed by the gardens lying below the Bishop's Palace. The moat, among other things, suggests that the palace of the inner castle that lay outside the walls of the Roman *castrum* had formerly been in the possession of the *comes*. The Bishop resided near the cathedral, in the Roman *castrum;* he came into the possession of the palace only later. This double castle, however, not only suggests a strengthening of the defence works but also a slow separation of ecclesiastical and secular power. The separation of the settlements can be observed also in the settlements of the servant people and in the growth of their settlements into towns *(Civitas regalis, civitas capitularis, castrum Jaurinense)*. The *Castrum Jaurinense* practically coincided with the site of the Roman *castrum,* in whose centre the bishop's cathedral was later erected. The stone fragments ornamented

with carved interlaced patterns brought to light by Péter Tomka also seem to suggest that by the time the bishopric was established, a church had stood there. Christianity possibly looked back on nearly 200 years' tradition in that late Avar centre, and it could well be that the Cathedral was built as early as the end of the 10th century, perhaps on the site of an earlier church.

The *civitas capitularis* was the *suburbium* of the medieval castle built on the site of the Roman *castrum*. The *suburbium* also extended to the Roman tombs (settlements) and the remains of an early medieval settlement. The groundplan of the *civitas capitularis* that lay below the castle and was fortified by walls, with a large central square and a network of streets crossing at right angles, undoubtedly displays the characteristic features of a pre-planned city. As in the case of Esztergom's Viziváros ('water-front town'), presumably here, too, a royal patent contributed to its foundation in an area formerly inhabited by the servant people of the church. Neither in Esztergom, nor in Győr did the royal city cover the area of the former Roman settlement, but extended beyond it.

The survey of the two capital towns on the Danube and the major medieval towns offers the following conclusions: the river Danube, which traverses Europe, played a decisive role in the development of strategic relations, as well as in the emergence of long-distance trade. Along the river and, in particular, where it changed its course we witness the crystallization of the centre of the country, the evolution of its first capitals, Esztergom, Fehérvár, Óbuda and Buda.

The major influence on the emergence of towns was the locations of the ferries to the roads which cross the

8609, fol 37); Borbiró–Valló (1956) 55. This groundplan also proves the medieval origin of the oblong Episcopal Palace; however, in view of the late, 13th century date of the palace chapel, this internal nucleus had belonged to the comes, and the Episcopal Palace had stood in the cathedral part. It was also there that the houses of the canons and provosts were to be found. Meanwhile, this may have changed, since it was in that area that a house of Comes Hector was sold in 1265. Borbiró–Valló (1956) 59, 299. From the research of F. Jenei.

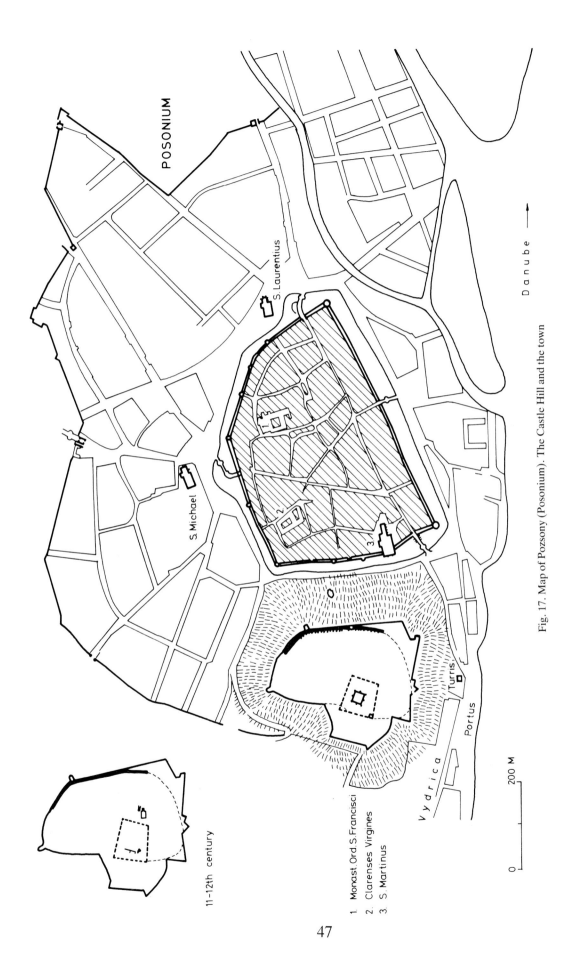

POSONIUM

S. Laurentius

S. Michael

Danube →

V y d r i c a

Turris

Portus

0    200 M

11–12th century

1. Monast. Ord. S. Francisci
2. Clarenses Virgines
3. S. Martinus

Fig. 17. Map of Pozsony (Posonium). The Castle Hill and the town

47

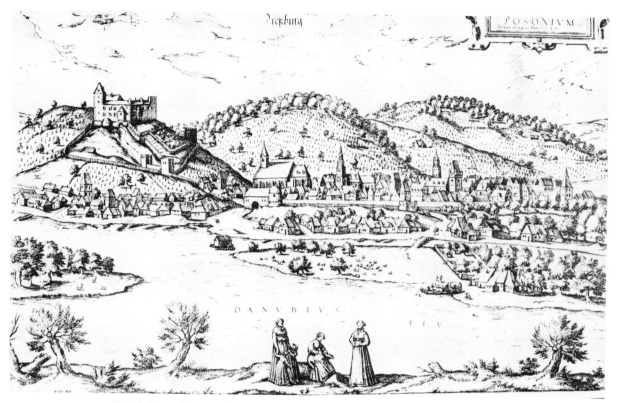

Fig. 18. View of Pozsony from the south (after G. Braun–F. Hogenberg: Köln 1572. I.)

Fig. 19. View of Pozsony from the north (after M. Merian: *Neuwe Archontologia cosmica.* Frankfurt 1638)

Fig. 20. Detail of Fig. 9. The harbour below the Royal Castle in 1684

WAITZEN

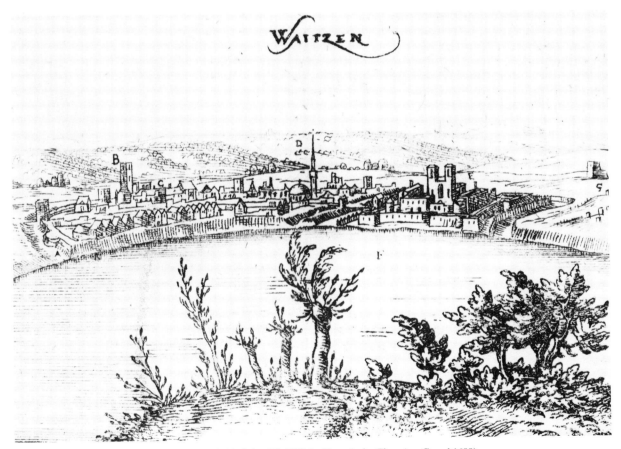

Fig. 21. View of Vác (after W. Dillich: *Ungarische Chronica.* Cassel 1600)

4

49

Danube to link far-away highly-civilized countries; the fords were without exception controlled by royal episcopal or county fortresses (the Buda and Pest castles, Óbuda, Felhéviz, Vác, Esztergom, Győr, Komárom, Pozsony), and were mostly built on a hill or elevation rising above the river (Buda, Esztergom, Pozsony).

This system can be traced as far back as the Neolithic and the Bronze Age. The fords often also acted as ports for the river traffic and stopping points for the Danube road traffic, fortified by huge towers and walls, extending from the castles to keep them under strict control (Buda, Visegrád, Esztergom, Pozsony). In most cases the harbours were located in a narrow branch of the Danube or in the cove of a tributary—streams partly fed by the waters of hot springs (Óbuda, Buda, Esztergom, Győr).

The castles were seats of a dual power: they included the churches and palaces of the king and sometimes of the *comes* of the county and the church dignitaries, the bishop or dean. The division of power is reflected in the dual castle, and in the settlements, too: the royal and ecclesiastical towns lay side by side with their separate nuclei, parishes, harbours and marketplaces (Győr, Esztergom, Óbuda).

The beginnings and antecedents of this separation are still unclear, but we may assume that it was not independent of the settlements of the surviving local Pannonian population and the areas occupied by the conquering Magyar tribes.[68] In Italy, too, the Germanic conquerors settled down beside the cities in the beginning. The various toponyms can also be traced to the settlements and populations of different periods of time. The population groups of various periods who survived and abandoned the Roman customs they had previously adopted are to be sought in the old place names: In the Roman *castra* and in the *canabae*. The existence of local Christian communities within the Roman walls or in the cemeteries can also be assumed. In addition to these localities the conquerors, in all probability, settled near, but nonetheless outside these earlier settlements, in what later became the royal cities and the seats of the *comes*—though perhaps only temporarily.

This may explain why the archiepiscopal city of Esztergom was only founded in 1239, even though the settlement at the foot of the hill had existed long before.

The internal arrangement of districts according to their various functions is a rare phenomenon in cities of other countries, too—let alone in Hungary, where it is almost unknown. It is rather the construction and the groundplan of the interior of the castle that can serve as a guideline. The oblong groundplan of palaces and their location beside the church occurs in numerous variations in 9th and 10th century German and French models, as well as in Eastern Europe and the Balkans, or else their later forms can be traced back to them. Along the Danube several residences of kings and bishops, internal castles of *comites* and barons can be traced back to this form. It is the ancient royal mansion of Dömös, the later royal chapter, that has survived in its purest, 11th century, hardly changed form. This simple outlay of oblong secular buildings can also be found in *curiae*, surviving in their original form in villages and in the simplest urban dwelling houses.

In the groundplan of the castles lying in the earliest centres the link between church and state is expressed in this way. This, however, is true not only of the castle, but even more of the settlements *(suburbia)* of the peoples serving the ecclesiastical and royal power: the settlements which later grew into towns, as has been shown by the quoted royal and ecclesiastical charters, gradually became more and more separate as in Esztergom, Buda and Győr.

It cannot be mere coincidence that under these topographical circumstances the centre of the medieval settlements—the church—lies inside the late Roman *castra* and cemeteries (Óbuda, Pécs, Győr), while the palaces of the secular officials and their people usually lie outside the walls (Győr, Buda).

We are perhaps also justified in assuming that the Magyar settlers occupied the vicinity of the areas that still had some remnants of Roman buildings that could be put to use, and also that they favoured the neighbourhood of early Christian sites, defended by the massive walls of Roman *castra* and towns; these areas had already attracted the local population, too, who had somehow weathered the storms of the Migration period and preserved the occasionally interrupted continuity of a modest Roman civilization as in Óbuda, Pest, Buda, Esztergom, Győr, Szombathely, Pécs, or Sopron. These traits are clearly discernible in the emergence of both Western and, later, the Eastern and Central European towns. Consequently their role in the emergence of a homogeneous Europen civilization is incontestable.

### REFERENCES

Borbiró, V.–Valló, I. (1956): *Győr városépítésének története (The architectural history of Győr)*. Budapest.

Gerevich, L. (1971): *The Art of Buda and Pest in the Middle Ages*. Budapest.

Gerevich, L. (1976): A pesti és budai vár (The Pest and Buda castles). *BudRég* 24, 43–54.

Kubinyi, A. (1964): Budafelhévíz topográfiája és gazdasági fejlődése (The topography and economic development of Budafelhévíz). *TBM* 16, 85–148.

Schünemann, K. (1929): *Die Entstehung des Städtewesens in Südösteuropa*. Breslau.

---

[68] P. Váczy: A város az ókor és a középkor fordulóján (The town at the turn of Antiquity and the Middle Ages). *Győr. Várostörténeti Tanulmányok*. Ed. by L. Dávid–A. Lengyel–L. Z. Szabó. Győr (1971) 53.

# THE SETTLEMENT HISTORY OF VESZPRÉM
# AND SZÉKESFEHÉRVÁR IN THE MIDDLE AGES

## A. Kralovánszky

The aim of the present paper is to shed light on the divergent development of Veszprém and Székesfehérvár during the 13th–14th centuries, in spite of the almost identical conditions and circumstances that shaped the history of these two towns in the 10th–12th centuries. Veszprém had remained a settlement resembling a market town in ecclesiastical property, where only the landowner-bishop acted as a high dignitary of the country. Székesfehérvár, on the other hand, acquired a high national rank through the privileges granted to the town on account of its ecclesiastic and civil institutions.

We also wish to underline the increasing significance—compared with the written sources—of the historical evidence uncovered in the course of archaeological investigations in clarifying the medieval settlement history of the towns. We made use of both types of sources proportionately, since they conversely support or contradict each other, and thus often enlarge our knowledge. The usefulness of this 'Janus-faced' method has already been proved by a series of pioneering studies.[1]

Several scholars consider the history of Hungarian towns to have followed the eastern course of development. In their opinion the only exceptions to this general trend were Esztergom, Székesfehérvár, Buda, the North Hungarian mining towns and the Saxon settlements in Transylvania, where the settling Western European (Latin, Walloon, German, etc.) merchants and craftsmen introduced a western type of development.[2]

Obviously enough, the conquering Magyar tribes who reached the Carpathian Basin at the turn of the 9th–10th centuries and made their livelihood primarily from animal husbandry and agriculture, lacked the inner economic and social drive that could have led to the evolution of eastern-type urban settlements, including the building of stone structures. It is well-known that the emergence of towns in or near their earlier homelands can be attributed either to some ancient precursors (Pontus region), or to the proximity to continental waterways linking Asia and Europe, or to certain economic and strategic considerations of emergent states. This course of development was stimulated by the regular exchange of goods produced as a consequence of an ever-increasing division of labour, and also by the formation of state organizations that had, in turn, brought about a concentration of the population.[3]

On reaching their ultimate homeland in an alliance of seven + one + (x?) tribes, the conquering Magyars did not find a single urban settlement whose occupation and perpetuation could have led to a subsequent urban development. The Magyar tribes could not establish day-to-day contacts with the settlements lying outside the southern and western confines of their newly-conquered territory (Sirmium and Poetovio, Emona, Vindobona) basically on account of their geographic location (all lay beyond the march-land).[4] The goods required by them (fine textiles, rare metals) were primarily acquired through the taxes paid by the highly industrialized foreign countries (Byzantium, Lombardy, etc.) and also from the booty of the raids organized against foreign countries through diplomatic channels.[5] Non-luxury goods—such as textiles, leather, bone implements, wood, etc.—which were obviously more in demand, were provided by their own craftsmen.

---

[1] See the studies by Györffy (1973) and L. Gerevich: Budapest művészete az Árpád-korban (The art of Budapest in the Árpádian Age). *Budapest története I.* Ed. by L. Gerevich. Budapest (1973) 351–401; and *European Towns. Their Archaeology and Early History.* Ed. by M. W. Barley. London–New York–San Francisco (1977).

[2] This apparently over-simplified distinction serves primarily investigational purposes. Obviously this process was much more complex and varied according to the countries. For an outline of this tendency, cf. E. Fügedi: Die Entstehung des Städtewesens in Ungarn. *Alba Regia* 9 (1969) 101–118.

[3] B. A. Rybakov: Trade and trade routes (in Russian). *The cultural history of the ancient Rus.* Vol. I. Moscow (1948) 315–369; M. I. Artamonov: *The history of the Khazars* (in Russian). Leningrad (1962) 385–399. For the latter cf. also S. A. Pletneva: *Die Chasaren.* Leipzig (1978) 96–126; Gy. Györffy (1973) 219–235.

[4] Gy. Komoróczy: *A kereskedelem és ipar Szent István korában (Trade and commerce under King St. Stephen).* Budapest (1938).

[5] Sz. Vajay: *Der Eintritt des ungarischen Stämmebundes in die europäische Geschichte.* Mainz (1968) 862–933; Györffy (1977) 40–53.

The crushing military defeats in 955 at Augsburg and in 970 at Arkadiapolis, and the inseparable development in the organization of the state and the church brought about radical changes in the development of the country. While around 950 the emperor of Byzantium relates[6] that the Hungarians were ruled by a number of kings instead of a superior prince, the archaeological, linguistic and historical evidence from the close of the 10th century unambiguously indicates an accelerated social development which was coupled with a large-scale reorganization of the military—all promoting the interests of a central power (these developments included the military occupation of the main intersection points on the roads and waterways in the country, the occurrence of toponyms derived from the names of the tribes in various parts of the country, the visit of Emperor Otto's envoy in 972, a suffragan bishop in Prince Géza's court and the participation of 12 Hungarian leaders in the imperial assembly of Quedlinburg in the following year).[7] The partial displacement of the tribal clans who had probably occupied separate areas in the preceding periods could only be executed by means of a strong military power. The newly organized central power must have established new centres to replace the earlier ones (for example, at Buda), and those on the territory of the princely tribe.[8] These centres were located on the right bank of the Danube or in the area to its west: Esztergom, Fehérvár, Veszprém. The late 10th century existence of these three main centres is supported by the following facts. Esztergom was the birth-place of King St. Stephen (970s).[9] According to the historical sources, Veszprém, Prince Géza's settlement, was a place *"ubi regalis (ducalis) accessus et conversatio habebatur"*.[10] And finally Géza was buried in Fehérvár in 997.[11] The written sources relating the life of Géza often refer to settlements without specifying them by name.[12] On the

strength of this 'negative evidence' we may feel justified in assigning the rise of these three settlements, which had played an important role during the ensuing centuries, to the last quarter of the 10th century. All three settlements had a demonstrably sporadic population in the first half of the 10th century. However, the burials dated to this period also suggest that the cemeteries and their associated settlements were located at sites differing from those that became the nuclei of later settlements. In all three cases the distance between the site of the early 10th century burials and that of the late 10th century settlements ranged between a few hundred metres and one or two kilometres.[13]

Characteristic of all the three settlements was their location on the territory of the princely tribe related to the tribe of Megyer, after which the Hungarian people were named (Magyar), and also on, or nearby, the main Roman roads.[14] From a strategic point of view, Esztergom and Veszprém had had outstanding geographical potential, while in Fehérvár artificial structures had to be erected. The historical evidence and the reconstructions both support the assumption that the three settlements were established artificially, based on a conscious choice of the sites, in the last decades of the 10th century. Esztergom could become a central settlement through its proximity to the Danubian waterway, which had been constantly used since prehistoric times, especially by the Romans. The geographical potential of the site permitted the supervision of international trade on the Danube, which also protected the settlement from possible attacks. Veszprém was characterized by similar features, although it lay 12 km from Lake Balaton (also a potential defence), but in the thick forests of the Bakony Mts. The lofty rock pinnacles at both sites proved to be ideal for erecting the princely-royal and church structures around the turn of the 10th–11th centuries. In Fehérvár the core of the new settlement was built on the narrow elevations rising above the surrounding marshland, which at the same time defend-

[6] Gy. Moravcsik: *Bíborban született Konstantin: A birodalom kormányzása (Constantine Porphyrogenitus: De administrando imperio)*. Budapest (1950) 179.

[7] Pauler (1893) 22; Gy. László: Budapest a népvándorlás korában (Budapest in the Migration Period). *Budapest története*. Vol. I. 2. Ed. by K. Szendy. Budapest (1942) 805–809; Gy. Kristó–F. Makk–L. Szegfű: Adatok korai helyneveink ismeretéhez (Data on early Hungarian toponyms). *Acta Universitatis Szegediensis de Attila József nominatae. Acta Historica* 44 (1973) 1–94; I. Rákos: IV. Béla birtokrestaurációs politikája (Béla IV's policy of restoring estates). *Acta Universitatis Szegediensis de Attila József nominatae. Acta Historica* 47 (1974) 1–29.

[8] Györffy (1973) 251–258.

[9] *Hic Strigoniensi oppido nativitatis exordium habuit.* Leg. Minor S. Stephani regis. *SRH* II, 394.

[10] *Ibid.*, 395. Hartvik's legend of 1112–1116 has *ducalis* instead of *regalis. Ibid.*, 408.

[11] *... ad ecclesiam SS Petri et Pauli in foro sitam, in qua sepultus fuisse Gieza pater B. Stephani...*, says Ionnanis Dlugos in his account of the crowning of Ulászló I in 1440 in Székesfehérvár: *Hist. Polonicae Libri XII.* Lipsiae (1711) Vol I, 742–743.

[12] Györffy (1970) 191–192, deals with the following toponyms formed of personal names. Décséd in Baranya County, the two Décses in Békés County, Décséd in Inner Szolnok County, Devicse in Hont County, Divics in Krassó County,

Décsi in Nyitra County and Décséd puszta in Torda County. These toponyms were assigned to the reign of Géza by Györffy. Since these toponyms are considered marks of proprietorship (Géza=Décse, cf. K. Czeglédy: Géza nevünk eredete (The origins of the name Géza). *Magyar Nyelv* 52 (1956) 325–333) we left them out of consideration here. We likewise disregarded the reference in the charter of Pannonhalma of 1002 that the construction of this monastery was begun under Géza (972–997) since Pannonhalma was founded as a special churched settlement. Erdélyi (1902) 589–590.

[13] *MRT* 2, 224–256; *MRT* 5, 78–231; Bakay (1966) 43–88, and Bakay (1968) 57–84. A. Kralovánszky: Székesfehérvár kialakulása a régészeti adatok alapján (Formation of Székesfehérvár on the evidence of the archaeological data). *Székesfehérvár évszázadai* 1. Ed. by A. Kralovánszky. Székesfehérvár (1967) 7–18.

[14] The geographical location of the ancient settlement of Solva coincided with that of Esztergom; Gorsium lay 8 km from Székesfehérvár, and Caesariana 7 km from Veszprém: L. Glaser: Dunántúl középkori úthálózata (The medieval road network of Transdanubia). *Századok* 63 (1929) 139–167; Györffy (1970) 191–242; A. Mócsy: *Pannonia a korai császárság idején (Pannonia in the Early Imperial Period)*. Budapest (1974) 176–177.

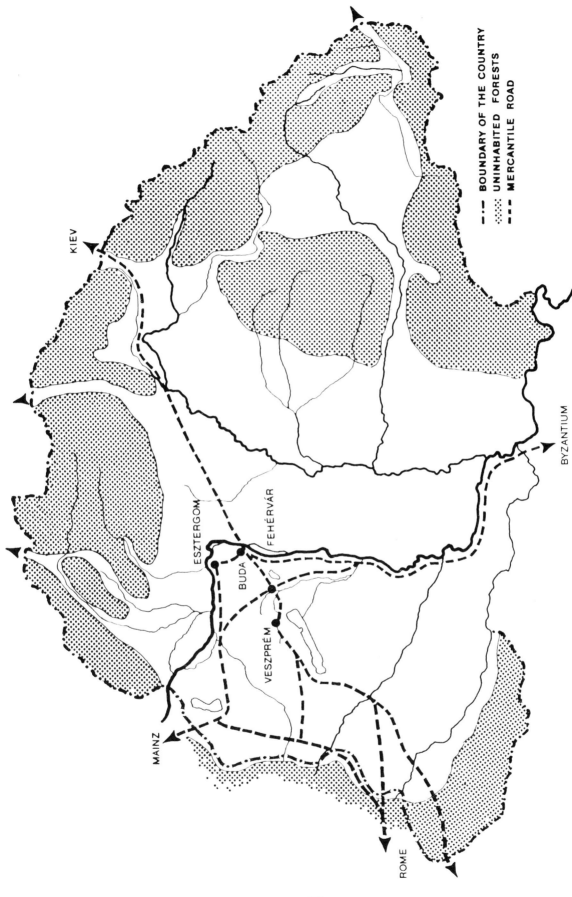

Fig. 1. A reconstruction of the international roads through Hungary in the 10th–13th centuries

BOUNDARY OF THE COUNTRY
UNINHABITED FORESTS
MERCANTILE ROAD

KIEV

ESZTERGOM

FEHÉRVÁR

BUDA

VESZPRÉM

BYZANTIUM

MAINZ

ROME

ed the settlement at an angle of about 270 degrees. Owing to its geographical location, Esztergom could keep a check on the waterway, and Veszprém and Fehérvár on the main roads. In each settlement a *capella regia* was built in connection with the conversion of the reigning dynasty to Christianity. The conversion of Géza's dynasty took place in 973 (Princess Sarolt had been baptized in Transylvania in her early youth), but still we cannot assign a specific date to such buildings that also functioned as an *ecclesia baptismalis*. We nevertheless have grounds for presuming that these structures had existed, since all three settlements were county seats and, moreover, Veszprém also functioned as an episcopal see and Esztergom as an archsee, where the baptism of the people of the neighbourhood was supervised.[15]

The first part of the present paper is devoted to the discussion of the questions we consider to be cardinal to the history of these settlements. This is followed by suggestions on the possible approaches to tracing the birth of, and the reconstruction of, surviving structures in the two towns. The occasional disproportions in the text are the regrettable results of our efforts to review both the earlier and the more recent findings of settlement historical studies.

## VESZPRÉM

Most linguists and historians derive the name of the settlement from the proper name of Besprim (which first occurs in 1002/1009) borne by the child of the daughter of Prince Géza (972–997)—her name has not come down to us—and Boleslav the Bold, a Polish prince. Boleslav's wife, who was sent packing around 987 when the prince remarried, returned to Hungary with her new-born child and presumably took refuge in one of the courts of the prince (princess?). Since the first heads or bailiffs of the counties, which were established around the turn of the 10th–11th centuries, also gave their names to the new administrative centres (e.g. Sopron, Szolnok, Doboka, etc.), we share the view that Prince Veszprém, who later became a Polish prince, was one of the first overlords *(comes)* of one of these new administrative units.[16]

The emergence and the early history of Veszprém is first related by the chroniclers Anonymus and Simon de Kézai. According to Anonymus, the conquering Magyars met with 'Romans' in the area of Veszprém around 900.[17] On the other hand, Simon Kézai notes that Veszprém had been inhabited by Marót, the aging father of the Moravian prince Svatopluk, and his people at the time of the Magyar conquest.[18] Most historians would agree that these data are both unauthentic, but the significant role assigned to the settlement of Veszprém by these 13th century sources can nevertheless be accepted without reservations. These chronicles were conceived in the courts of the kings of the Árpád dynasty, where the practice of recording past events gained in importance only in the 13th century, although it appeared as early as the early 11th century, simultaneously with the adoption of Christianity and the founding of the state. Consequently, the 13th century chroniclers could only fall back on the unwritten, oral tradition when compiling the history of the preceding 200–400 years. However, it has been pointed out earlier that oral tradition can only be considered trustworthy if it spans a period not longer than 100 years, i.e. three generations.

Nevertheless, there are 10th–12th century written sources which, amplified by other historical sources, allow the reconstruction of the early history of Veszprém.

While it is fairly difficult to assign a date to the course of events that transformed certain settlements into county seats, it is all the more easier to date the episcopal sees. As outlined in the plan for organizing the church in Hungary passed by the Council of Ravenna in 1001, the formation of the archbishopric at Esztergom and the bishoprics at Eger, Kalocsa and Veszprém was soon commenced.[19] On the testimony of the deed of Pannonhalma's foundation (1002) and also that of the Veszprém bishopric (1009) we can safely state that the bishopric, dedicated to St. Michael, had already functioned as an ecclesiastic and county seat in this period.[20]

The latter document clearly implies that the Veszprém bishopric (that included the areas of Somogy, Zala, Veszprém, Fejér and Pilis Counties lying on the right bank of the Danube, but not the territory of Esztergom) had, on account of its dimensions and location, been granted more privileges compared with the higher-ranking Esztergom archbishopric.[21] This apparently fits in with the fact that the 11th century territory of Pilis, Fejér and Veszprém Counties had

---

[15] L. Mezey: Csutmonostor alapítástörténete és első oklevelei (The founding of Csutmonostor and its first charters). *TBM* 15 (1963) 9–12; Györffy (1969a) 214–219.

[16] J.: Melich; *A honfoglaláskori Magyarország (Hungary in the Conquest Period)*. Budapest (1931) 398–401; Györffy (1958) 589; for more details cf. Vajay (1967) 85, note 78. In our opinion the assumption that the settlement of Veszprém was called Ortahu in the 9th century cannot be conclusively proven, cf. T. Bogyay: Die Kirchenorte der Conversio Bagoariorum et Carantanorum. *Südostforschungen* 19 (1960) 69. This theory is based on the fact that in 865 Adalwin, the archbishop of Salzburg, consecrated a church to St. Michael on the estate of Kocel. The name of the church was thus identical with that of the cathedral in Veszprém. Cf. Gutheil (1977) 24. However, no Frankish finds have yet been reported from either the minutely investigated Balaton highland (cf. the volumes of *MRT*), or from the castle hill in Veszprém. Accordingly the identity of

the *patrocinii* cannot be considered sufficient proof for this theory.

[17] Anonymus: Gesta Hungarorum: ... *contra Romanos milites, qui castrum Bezprem custodiebant*. SRH I, 97.

[18] Simonis de Keza: Gesta Hungarorum: ... *Morot ... confectus senio repausabat in castro, quod Bezprem nominatur*. SRH I, 164.

[19] Györffy (1969) 214; Györffy (1977) 117–118.

[20] 1002: I. Szentpétery: Szent István oklevelei (Charters of St. Stephen). *SZIE* II, 183–194; 1009: Karácsonyi (1891) 57–58. Györffy (1967) 22–23.

[21] In his review of the present study András Kubinyi remarked that "in my opinion the unusual extension of the Veszprém diocese should rather be attributed to the efforts of

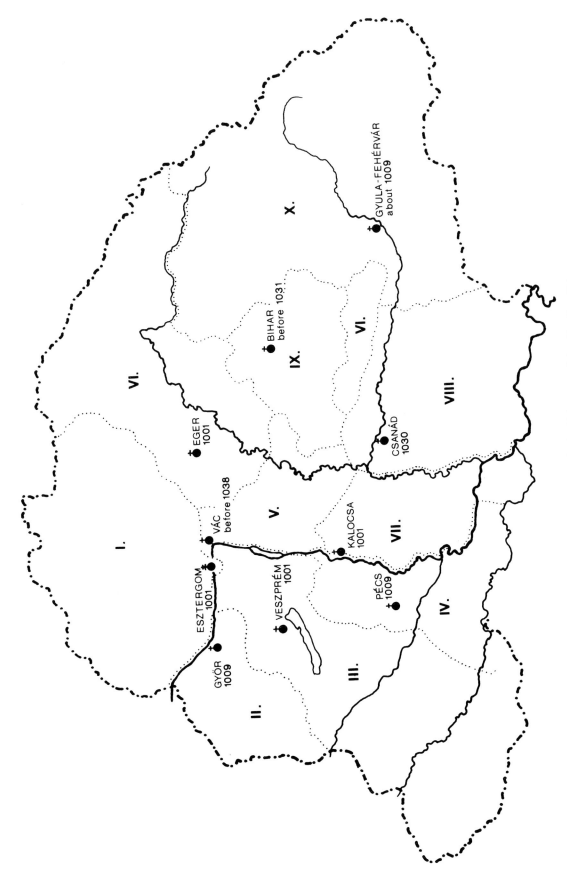

Fig. 2. The bishoprics of Hungary in the 11th century (after Gy. Györffy)

GYULA-FEHÉRVÁR
about 1009

X.

BIHAR
before 1031

IX.

VI.

EGER
1001

VÁC
before 1038

V.

CSANÁD
1030

VIII.

I.

ESZTERGOM
1001

KALOCSA
1001

VII.

VESZPRÉM
1001

PÉCS
1009

GYŐR
1009

II.

III.

IV.

already been the princely property of the Árpáds one century earlier, and also with the local church tradition that claimed the Veszprém bishopric to be the oldest in the country.[22]

In our opinion, the answer to this question is related to an earlier event, more precisely to the sending of a bishop to Hungary in 972. In the autumn of 972 Brunus of the St. Gallen monastery was ordained the converting bishop of Hungary by the Holy Roman Emperor Otto I in the chapel of the palace at Ingelheim near Mainz. According to Gy. Györffy, Brunus, who soon afterwards visited Hungary, must obviously have been the man who brought the relics of St. Gall, St. Martin and St. Brictius (Bereck in Hungarian) to Hungary.[23] Five of the seven churches known to have been consecrated to St. Gall in Hungary are to be found in the Veszprém bishopric (of the remaining two, one is situated on the river Ipoly, the other near the town of Kalocsa). The churches of Martin (Pannonhalma) and Bereck both lie in Győr and Zala Counties, i.e. on the territory of the earliest Veszprém bishoprics (it was only after the founding of further bishoprics in 1009 that the two churches were taken over by other dioceses). These data apparently support the assumption that the activity of Brunus was restricted to Transdanubia, or more precisely, to the possession of the Árpáds. Supporting him in his mission were Prince Géza, who had been baptized by him, and Princess Sarolt, the daughter of the Transylvanian Gyula who was baptized in her early youth. Consequently, Brunus often visited the seasonal quarters of Géza and Sarolt, which included also the settlement named Veszprém in later times.[24]

The church tradition at Veszprém that claimed the local bishopric to be the oldest in the country, may perhaps be accounted for by Brunus' frequent visits to this central settlement (which can by no means be considered a canonically and politically approved episcopal see!). These visits soon became politically undesirable, and thus could only be perpetuated in tradition. We have every reason for assuming that King Stephen and his advisers did not desire these visits, which had been associated with the Holy Roman Emperor and which therefore were feared to have bad effects on the new-born Hungarian state, by becoming legally valid, i.e. they acted against the survival of the remembrances in a form Emperor Otto I was presumed to have liked. The Christian Hungarian state sought to establish a self-governing church independent of outside secular powers. With this aim in mind, the preceding events which were considered detrimental to further develop-

ment were meticulously weeded out. In a related development, King Stephen and his advisers may have been aware of the fact that in the years 973–977 Piligrim, the bishop of Passau, and his superior, Frederick, the archbishop of Salzburg, made repeated attempts to substantiate their claims to the canonical control over Pannonia by presenting forged charters to the Pope. In other words, their schemings meant a real threat to the ecclesiastical sovereignty of the Hungarian church. Consequently, they decided on turning to the Pope as an ecclesiastical authority, with the obvious intent of facing the lesser evil.

Similar motives must have forced Stephen to found a new bishopric in Transylvania following his military victory there in 1003–1004. This bishopric also ignored the legal claims of the converting bishops sent to the region in the mid-10th century by Byzantium. Also confirming the parallelism between the two cases is the fact that both the Veszprém and the Transylvanian bishopric had Archangel St. Michael as their patron saint, who at the same time was also venerated as the most outstanding patron saint of both the Byzantine and the Holy Roman Empire. It cannot be mere chance that two of the bishoprics had the same patron saint.

These developments raise yet another question concerning the peculiar and unique way the cathedral of the bishopric at Veszprém had been founded. Curiously enough, the only episcopal cathedral in the country whose founder was not the king or his bishop was that of Veszprém—it was established by Queen Gizella, the wife of King Stephen.

This may presumably be explained by King Stephen's god-sent realisation that Queen Gizella's ancestors were Bavarians, and that she was kin of the Holy Roman Emperors (Otto II, 983–1002, was her second cousin and Henrik, the Bavarian prince, 995–1002, and later Holy Roman Emperor, 1002–1024, was her brother). Consequently, the decision to entitle (?) or compel (?) the queen to become the donor of the Veszprém bishopric, founded by King Stephen, but conceived by the Holy Roman Emperor following the missions sponsored by the Bavarian high priest, was designed to stir the least possible unrest and tension.

This decision may well be connected with the exclusive right granted to the bishop of Veszprém in power (perhaps stipulated at the very outset) to crown the queen in power.[25] (It should be borne in mind that the royal insignia were kept in the king's own church in Székesfehérvár, and thus the crowning archbishop of Esztergom or the bishop of Veszprém were compelled to visit Székesfehérvár before each coronation. In other words, by this decision the king managed to avoid throwing himself, and the insignia of the royal succession, at the mercy of the high priests.[26])

---

the organizers of the first church institutions to make the dioceses continuous with at least one main waterway. ... I have already noted this elsewhere: Diskussionsbeitrag. *Die Stadt am Fluss*. Ed. by E. Maschke and J. Sydow. Sigmaringen (1978) 199." We wholly accept his opinion.

[22] 1276/1469: ... *sancta Vesprimiensis ecclesia prima omnium kathedralium regni sedium*. The private archives of the Veszprém chapter, Insula magna 5. Quoted by Gutheil (1977) 52; 1277: ... *valde priorem et antiquiorem interpontificales sedes Hungarie regni Vesprimiensem basilicam*. CD IX/7, 692–696.

[23] Györffy (1977) 68–74.

[24] *Ibid.*

[25] For the papal decree and charter of 1216 cf. G. Fraknói: *Monumenta Romana Episcopatus Vesprimiensis*. Tom I. Budapestini (1896) 35–36.

[26] A. Kralovánszky: A székesfehérvári királyi bazilika alapításának és István királlyá koronázásának kérdéséhez (On the questions of the foundation of the royal basilica in Székesfehérvár and the crowning of King Stephen). *Fejér megyei Szemle* (1967) 52.

This fortunate realization, in fact a master stroke of diplomacy, also accounts for the fact that while Veszprém managed to avoid the fate of Gniezno or Prague, it could, at the same time, retain its special legal status.

And yet another question: was Veszprém really the residence of the medieval queens of Hungary, the place where they were crowned and buried?[27]

Numerous scholars consider it a proof that the Greek cloister in Veszprém valley was reportedly founded by Prince Géza under the influence of Princess Sarolt, who was baptized according to the Greek rite.[28] The sources also record that Koppány, the pretender pagan chieftain, wanted to seize Veszprém in 997 with the alleged aim of taking the dowager princess in marriage and thus climbing to power, and that Veszprém, after whom the settlement was named, was given shelter by Sarolt in her assumed lodging in Veszprém after he was expelled from Poland. Moreover, the sources also mention that the queen's crown, kept in Veszprém until 1217, was donated by Gizella to the Veszprém cathedral as a memorial of her crowning there. The cathedral is also reported to have served as the burial place of the widowed Queen Gizella and Adelhaid, the wife of King St. Ladislaus. The account of the life of the queen's servants in Veszprém can also be considered indicative of the town's status as the queen's seat. The questions concerning the education of Princess Margaret in Veszprém are also regarded as relevant to this problem.[29] The following quotations from the contemporary charters apparently support the assumptions listed above: according to them, Veszprém housed "... the queen's throne, and it is the esteemed right and privilege of the [town's] bishops to anoint and crown the queen of Hungary...";[30] "... our Veszprém church, of which we are special patrons, where the queen's throne is kept...";[31] "[your Veszprém] ... church where the queens' chapels are and where they are crowned...";[32] "... we have been told of the custom that the Hungarian queens are crowned in the cathedral of Veszprém, and they also receive the queen's regalia there...".[33]

The above listed views and data can apparently be set beside with each other. However, we have to emphasize that for the most part these should only be considered assumptions and inferences rather than historical facts!

According to the deed of the foundation of the Greek cloister in Veszprém valley, this institution was subordinated to the archbishopric of Esztergom. Consequently, it cannot be dated to the reign of Géza (972–997), since the archbishopric was founded by King Stephen only after 1001.[34] We have found no data in support of Grand Duchess Sarolt's assumed stay in Veszprém in 997. It is likewise mere guesswork to conclude that the keeping of Queen Gizella's crown in the town is a proof of her being crowned there. There is also nothing to substantiate the reports on the burial of Queen Gizella in Veszprém. According to Bonfinius, the late 15th century chronicler, the cathedral of Veszprém housed a crumbling tombstone with the following inscription: "... *Ladislai sanctissimorum Pannoniae regum consortum hic ossa quiescunt*" (... the Ladislauses, the saintliest kings of Hungary, had their wives' bones buried here).[35] Since Bonfinius knew that Ladislaus and Stephen were the only kings sainted in Hungary, he presumed Stephen's name before that of Ladislaus. This is why he considered the tomb to be the burial place of Queen Gizella and Adelhaid. His conclusion may well have been influenced by the fact that he knew of the above-cited papal charter of 1377, which the Pope wrote to Elizabeth, the wife of King Louis the Great. The charter, an answer to the queen's earlier application for the right to hold patronal festivals in Veszprém cathedral (obviously a paying concern), declares that the right can be granted "since ... we have been told that ... [Veszprém] is the queens' burial place".[36] The strange thing about this is that only two queens, the wives of the two sainted kings, are referred to as having been buried in the cathedral. Had these burials been more than mere rumours, they would definitely have survived in other, earlier references as well, since the repeated and emphatic assertion of such a 'privilege' would undeniably have concerned the financial and moral interests of the bishop of Veszprém in power. However, we know of no such references. According to contemporary sources, Bavarian Gizella returned to her homeland a few years after the death of King Stephen, and she died there as a nun.[37] Adelhaid died in 1090, five years before her husband's death,[38] so in principle she may have been buried in Veszprém. However, this is not mentioned in the charters issued by King Ladislaus following Adelhaid's death, or by King Imre (1203) and King Béla IV (1254). These charters confirm Queen Adelhaid's donation of the village of Merenye to the bishop of

---

[27] Most recently Gutheil (1977).

[28] A. Balogh: A veszprémvölgyi görög monostor alapítása (The foundation of the Greek monastery in Veszprém Valley). *Regnum* (1944–46) 21–30; Komjáthy (1973) 33–49; Gutheil (1977) 138–165.

[29] For Koppány, cf. Gy. Györffy: Koppány lázadása (Koppány's rebellion). *Somogy megye múltjából. Levéltári Évkönyv* 1 (1970) 18; cf. also Gutheil (1977).

[30] ... *in qua quidem ecclesia est sedes reginalis, in reginam Hungarie inuncte fuissemus et Deo propitio suscepissemus pariter reginale dyadema*. The private archives of the Veszprém chapter, 1280. Nagy- and Kisberény 6. Cited by J. Gutheil (1977) 264.

[31] 1300: ... *nos ecclesie Wesprimiensi cuius specialis sumus patrona, in qua est sedes reginalis*. Gutheil (1977) 264.

[32] 1341: ... *illius ecclesie vestre, que specialis capella et locus coronationis reginalis existit*. Gutheil (1977) 264.

[33] 1377: ... *cum itaque, sicut accepimus, regina Ungarie pro tempora existens in ecclesia Wesprimiensi coronari et alia insignia reginalia recipere*. Fraknói–Lukcsics (1896–1907) vol. II, 246.

[34] Gy. Moravcsik: Görögnyelvű monostorok Szent István korában (Greek-speaking monasteries under St. Stephen). *SZIE* I, 416; Györffy (1977) 321–323; for the improbability of the donation under Géza, cf. Komjáthy (1973) 33.

[35] I. Fogel–B. Iványi–L. Juhász: *Antonius de Bonfinis, Rerum Ungaricarum decades*. Dec. II. Lib. IV. Lipsiae (1936) II. 91.

[36] 1377: ... *regine Ungarie ... sepeliri consueverint* ... Cf. note 33.

[37] For a recent summary cf. Vajay (1967) 89.

[38] Wertner (1892) 193–205.

Veszprém.[39] However, the bishop's application for this confirmation does not make any reference to the burial of Adelhaid in the cathedral, and to his related obligations, to support the plea. Furthermore, we know of no authentic reference to the above-mentioned papal authorization to hold patronal festivals, and neither do we know of pilgrims to the queen's assumed tomb; and neither is there evidence for the burial of other queens in the cathedral of Veszprém after 1377. The presence of the queen's servants and the other princely people cannot be considered as conclusive evidence since this type of court was quite common at that time. The education of St. Margaret in Veszprém cannot be explained by the assumption that in this way she could stay near her mother. In the year 1246, when Margaret moved to the Dominican cloister in Veszprém, the only nuns representing this order in Hungary were those whom the fugitive royal couple had met on the Dalmatian sea-coast. It was there that King Béla IV and his wife took a vow to give the life of their next daughter to God. Consequently, the only cloister where they could send Margaret was that of the Dominicans. But since Veszprém lay far from Buda, the royal seat, the king founded another Dominican cloister on Rabbit Island (today Margaret Island) near the queen's palace there. Margaret and eighteen other nuns were brought to the new cloister in 1252.[40] Had our queens lived in Veszprém, they would obviously have given birth to their children there. However, there are only scant references to the royal birthplaces: Esztergom around 970 (St. Stephen), Fehérvár (?) in 1007 (St. Imre), Pozsony (Bratislava) or Sárospatak around 1207 (St. Elizabeth).[41] Moreover, there are queenly charters that had been issued in Veszprém, a town which was otherwise entitled to make up charters independently. The same applies to the royal charters, of which only one was issued in Veszprém during the Árpádian Age (1000–1301). (Cp. Székesfehérvár: 18 charters on 10 occasions, Esztergom: 13 charters on 11 occasions, Buda: 128 charters on 37 occasions.[42]) The situation is the same if we consider the royal dwellings, mentioned in various types of written sources. In the period before 1313, i.e. when the king granted the bishop of Veszprém the right to succeed the status of county bailiff, thus centralizing the church and secular power in Veszprém castle, only 3 confirmed and 1 unconfirmed royal visits are known to have been completed (for the same period: Esztergom:

22, Székesfehérvár: 52, Buda: 67).[43] Mention must be made here of the fact that the royal charter does not contain provisions concerning the possessory right of his assumed palace in Veszprém castle. Had the king had such problems to solve, he would probably have mentioned it in the charter.[44]

Let us finally turn to the questions concerning the coronation of the queens in Veszprém. None of our sources offer sound proof in this respect. The verifiable coronations of Hungarian queens all took place in the royal basilica in Székesfehérvár: N. N., 1038 (wife of Peter); N. N., 1041 (wife of Aba Samuel); Anastasia, 1046 (wife of Endre I); Rixa, 1061 (wife of Béla I); Judit, 1063 (wife of Salamon); Synadéné, 1074 (wife of Géza I); Adelheid, 1078 (wife of László I); N. N., 1097, Eufemia, 1112 (wife I, II of Kálmán); N. N., after 1120 (wife of Stephen II); Helen, 1131 (wife of Béla II); Eufrozsina, 1146 (wife of Géza II); Maria, 1163 (wife I, II of Béla III); Konstancia, 1198 (wife of Stephen III); Anna, 1173, Margaret, 1186 (wife I, II of Béla III); Konstancia, 1198 (wife of Imre); Gertrud, 1205, Jolantha, 1215, Beatrix, 1234 (wife I, II, III of Endre); Elizabeth, 1270 (wife of Stephen V); Isabella, 1272 (wife of László IV); Fennena, 1290, Ágnes, 1297 (wife I, II of Endre III); Maria, 1310, Beatrix, 1318, Elizabeth, 1320 (wife I, II, III of Charles); Margaret, 1345, Elizabeth, 1353 (wife I, II of Louis I); Maria, 1382, Borbala, 1405 (wife I, II of Sigismund); Elizabeth, 1438 (wife of Albert); Beatrix, 1476 (wife of Matthias); Anna, 1502 (wife of Ulászló II); Maria, 1522 (wife of Louis II); Anna, 1527 (wife of Ferdinand I); and Izabel, 1539 (wife of János Zápolyai).[45] On the evidence of the medieval legal custom the assumption that the queens not listed in the above were also crowned in Székesfehérvár is susceptible without proof. Moreover, in view of the great importance attached to these events, it is more than intriguing that none of the local or foreign dignitaries attending the marriage or the coronation mention the event and the related programmes of the high priests conducting the ceremonies, or of the presence of the king, etc.

What, then, are the historical facts that can be gleaned from the authentic data concerning the emergence, the early history and the significance of Veszprém?

In my opinion, the answer is to be sought in Queen Gizella's donorship. We know that she was the one who ensured the building and the ornamentation of the cathedral of the Veszprém bishopric, and thus she can be considered its real founder, the *fundatrix*.[46] The

---

[39] *Ibid.*, 194.

[40] M. Pfeiffer: *A Domonkos rend magyar zárdáinak vázlatos története (Brief history of the Dominican cloisters in Hungary).* Kassa (1917) 83–85; L. Gerevich: Budapest művészete az Árpád-korban (The Art of Budapest in the Árpádian Age). *Budapest története.* Ed. by L. Gerevich. Budapest (1973) 376; I. Király: *Árpádházi Szent Margit és a sziget (St. Margaret of the Árpád Dynasty and the Island).* Budapest (1979) 43–60.

[41] Cf. note 9; Wertner (1892) 438.

[42] I. Szentpétery: *Árpádházi királyaink okleveleinek kritikai jegyzéke (Critical edition of the charters of the kings of the Árpád Dynasty).* Vols I–II. Budapest (1927–1943); The charter in question: 1171: *Actum est in civitate W.* The initial 'W' does not necessarily stand for Veszprém, all the more so, since in this period the name normally began with 'B'. *Ibid.*, 118.

[43] B. Sebestyén: *A magyar királyok tartózkodási helyei (Residences of the Hungarian kings).* Budapest (1938).

[44] *CD* VIII/2, 155.

[45] P. Engel: Temetkezések a középkori székesfehérvári bazilikában. Függelék: A székesfehérvári koronázások (Burials in the medieval basilica of Székesfehérvár. Appendix: The coronations at Székesfehérvár). *Századok* 122 (1988) 632–637.

[46] Around 1083: ... *Pre cunctis tamen episcopatus Besprimiensis, quam ipsa a fundamenta ceptam omnibus sufficientiis ad servitium in auro vel argumento vestimentisque multiplicibus adornavit. SRH* II, 384–385; 1277: ... *Kesule regina*

bishops and the chapter of Veszprém obviously tried to assure the continuity of this early queenly foundation and donorship, and they never missed an occasion to bring this fact to the attention of the ruling sovereign and his consort, if she was non-Hungarian. This appears to have been considered natural by the ecclesiastic and wordly nobility, as well as by the king. This is why one of the charters from the age of Charles Robert describes the Veszprém cathedral as a "special queenly chapel" *(specialis reginalis capella)*.[47] This donorship in turn offer a plausible explanation for the coronation of the queens. We know of a medieval custom which involved the coronation of the ruling sovereign by the priest of the cathedral or private chapel founded by the king at Christmas and at Easter, partly to honour the founder, and partly to enhance the ceremony itself. The practice of this custom in Hungary during the Árpádian Age is attested for Kings Sámuel Aba and Solomon. The former was crowned at Csanád, the latter at Pécs at Easter.[48] There is no evidence that this right befitted also the queen in each cathedral founded by the king. However, the charters that contain references to Veszprém definitely suggest that the queen had in fact enjoyed this honour by right of her donorship. In this case, then, her coronation was not state, but ecclesiastic law which in turn suggests entirely different historical conclusions!

The other question relevant to the coronation is the existence and location of the queen's 'throne'. It is often mentioned in medieval charters that the founding patron or his successor had to attend the holy mass in the sanctuary, to which only the clergy had access. This seating implied both rights and liabilities. The patron's seat was situated at the northern wall of the sanctuary, while the clergy sat in its southern end.[49] The contemporary sources draw a distinction between the *sedes reginalis* (the queen's seat) and the *solium* or *tronus regis* (the king's throne), thus underlining that only the king was entitled to sit on a throne![50]

It is not mere chance that after the 1280s the sources lay special emphasis on the fact that the queen's seat in Veszprém stood in the church attributed to the queen herself. Rogerius, the contemporary chronicler relates that after ascending the throne in 1235 King Béla IV "came to the town of Székesfehérvár ... was given the royal crown and ... thereupon he ruled that ... whoever of the barons, except for the archbishops and bishops, takes the liberty to sit down on a chair in his presence, will receive an appropriate punishment. Then he had

the seats of these dignitaries burnt."[51] Following the death of King Béla IV, the secular aristocrats and barons made every effort to regain their centuries-old privilege. Queen Elizabeth and her prelate, the bishop of Veszprém (the originator of the 1280 charter which first mentions the queen's seat in the cathedral), may have acted in concert when they decided on leaving the king's ruling unchanged. This decision was only facilitated by the fact that in the preceding year (1279) the papal legate excommunicated both the king and the country on account of their pagan conduct. Following this ruling, the king was compelled to rescind many of his orders, to dismiss several of this dignitaries and to change his own, and also the court's way of life.[52]

In short, the assumption that Veszprém was a queen's seat and that they were crowned and buried there is supported by the following facts: the founding of the cathedral of Veszprém by Queen Gizella, the privilege of the bishop of Veszprém to crown the queens (in the Coronation Basilica of Székesfehérvár!), and the seat identified as that of the queen in the cathedral of Veszprém. The written sources containing references to these events all date from the period following the destruction by fire and the subsequent plundering of the cathedral in 1276 (this coincided with the rapidly spreading use of written records in the second half of the 13th century). These events are mentioned again in the charters issued during the reign of the Angevin dynasty in the 14th century, and are repeated and elaborated by Bonfinius in the late 15th century. In the 18th–20th centuries the historians (primarily the church historians) treated this medley of facts, gracious misconceptions and deliberate overestimations as tradition and based their so-called scholarly findings on them. It would nonetheless appear that the coexistence of the settlement (princely dwelling, and later county seat) and the bishopric (the events preceding its foundation, the rights granted to it at the actual founding and those obtained in later times) in Veszprém must have raised the prestige of the town, which in turn must have had its effect on the population.

However, the settlement history of Veszprém was also determined by its economic standing.

In the 13th–14th centuries the number of persons owning an estate or a house in Veszprém included the king, the queen, the bishop, the chapel and some of his canons, the nuns in Veszprém valley and those in the Dominican order, certain noblemen and a handful of craftsmen. The population of the town also included the royal heralds, the servants of the queen and the prince, and the bishop's serfs. The latter people lived on communal land.[53]

*beate memorie fundatricis ecclesie Vesprimiensis.* The private archives of the Veszprém chapter. Kál. 13. Quoted by Gutheil (1977) 59–60.

[47] 1341: Gutheil (1977) 264, note 17.

[48] Pauler (1893) 110, 146.

[49] 1347: ... *nobiles de superiori Dörögd praefatae ecclesiae patroni stabunt et orabunt coram majori Altari Beati Andreae...* I. Ádám: A felsődörögdi templom (The church at Felsődörögd). *Egyházművészeti Lap* (1882) 213–215. The archaeological excavations have revealed that the patron family sat at the norhern wall.

[50] Cf. note 30.

[51] Rogerius, Carmen Miserabile. *SRH* II, 555. For the eastern antecedents, cf. J. Horváth: Középkori irodalmunk székesfehérvári vonatkozásai (Medieval literary references to Székesfehérvár). *Székesfehérvár évszázadai* 2. Ed. by A. Kralovánszky. Székesfehérvár (1972) 123–127.

[52] Pauler (1893) 447–484.

[53] Mályusz (1953) 162–166; Gy. Székely: A földközösség és szerepe az osztályharcban (The community of land and its role in class struggle). *Tanulmányok a parasztság történetéhez*

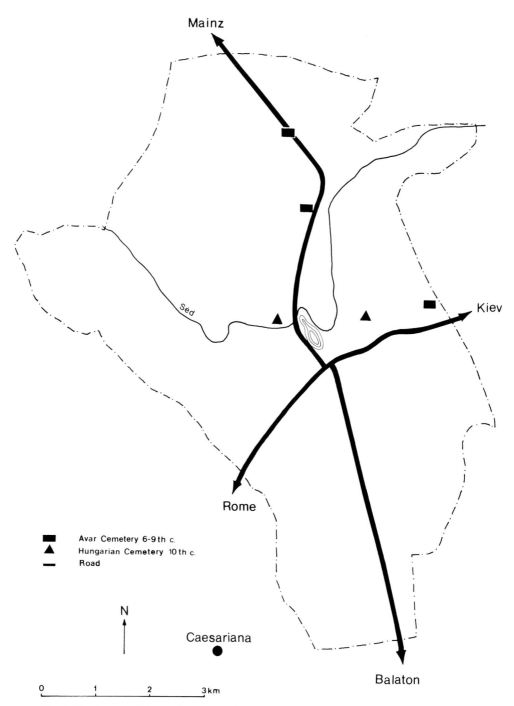

Mainz

Séd

Kiev

Rome

Balaton

■ Avar Cemetery 6-9th c.
▲ Hungarian Cemetery 10th c.
— Road

N

Caesariana ●

0    1    2    3km

Fig. 3. The Avar and Magyar Conquest period cemeteries around Veszprém. 6th–10th centuries

The economically most significant people in the town were the bishop and the chaplain who, after gradually buying or inheriting further plots, finally became the only landowners in the area. However, their enrichment did not stimulate the strengthening of the craftsmen and merchants, who in fact were the backbone of urbanisa-

tion.[54] The low number of these people can also be accounted for by the town's disadvantageous geographical location. The customs revenues that could be collect-

[54] The bishopric controlled—fully or partly—some 70 villages and market towns in the 14th century. Meanwhile, the chapter owned about 140 villages and estates: J. Holub: *Egy dunántúli egyházi nagybirtok története a középkor végén (History of a Transdanubian church estate in the Late Middle Ages)*. Pécs (1943); Kumorowitz (1953) 7–9; Gutheil (1977) 301–341.

*Magyarországon a XIV. században.* Ed. by Gy. Székely. Budapest (1953), 86-87, 89, 99-100.

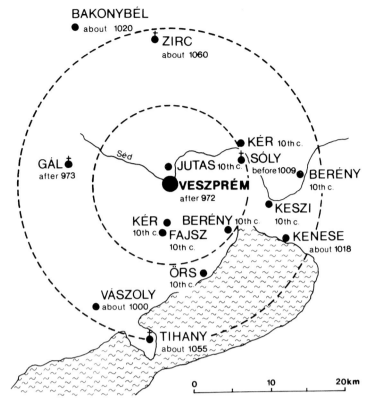

Fig. 4. The 10th–11th century settlements around Veszprém

ed on the main roads and waterways in the country were considerably tapped by the staple right of Esztergom (11th century), Buda (1224) and Győr (1271), the right of Vasvár, Pécs and Zagreb to exact toll and the privilege of Székesfehérvár and Buda to hold annual fairs.[55] In a related development, the population of Esztergom and Székesfehérvár (after 1147) and of Buda and Pest (around 1250) was increased by the arrival and settlement of Latin and German immigrants. This again was not the case in Veszprém. These Latin and German merchants soon proved their worth in turning these settlements into towns proper.[56]

As is known, Veszprém was not independent legally in the Middle Ages. The burghers of the town, who lived under the seigniory of the mainly clerical landowners, did not have the right to take justice into their own hands, to elect a parson or to enjoy free trade. In return for a profit-yielding tenth in Csepel Island, in 1313 the king donated the bishop of Veszprém the right to

succeed the status of the county bailiff.[57] This meant the centralization of church and secular power, although in 1278 Endre III, then the prince of Slavonia, and again in 1294 as king, granted the people of the bishop of Veszprém immunity from the bailiff's jurisdiction and subjected them to the bishop himself.[58]

The economic status of Veszprém was further strengthened by the granting of the right to mint money to bishop Mátyás Gathalóczy (1440–1457).[59] Nonetheless, Veszprém ranked only 7th among the 14 bishoprics in Hungary in terms of finances.[60] The so-called 'bigger palace' of the bishop lay on the castle hill in Veszprém.[61]

[55] For a recent summary, see Györffy (1973) 217–247.

[56] Francus lived in Veszprém in the late 11th century: Gy. Székely: A székesfehérvári latinok és vallonok a középkori Magyarországon (The Latins and Walloons of Székesfehérvár in Medieval Hungary). *Székesfehérvár évszázadai* 2. Ed. by A. Kralovánszky. Székesfehérvár (1972) 56–58. Bishop Robertus (1209–1226) was Walloon by origin. Cf. A. Kubinyi: Székesfehérvár középkori oklevéladása és pecsétei (Medieval charters and seals of Székesfehérvár). *Székesfehérvár évszázadai* 2. Ed. by A. Kralovánszky. Székesfehérvár (1972) 151–168; E. Fügedi: A középkori magyar városprivilégiumok (Privileges of the medieval Hungarian towns). *TBM* 14 (1961) 17–107.

[57] *comes perpetuus: CD* VII/2, 155.

[58] 1278: *CD* V/2, 471–472; 1294: *CD* VI/1, 303–304. Jenő Major kindly pointed out this data for me. I wish to express my gratitude.

[59] L. Huszár: Pénzverés Veszprémben a XV. században (Minting in Veszprém in the 15th century). *VMMK* 2 (1964) 199–204. This may have been preceded by the following event, noted by J. Major: "According to a 1338 source (*AO* III, 514) the monetary unit in the area was the Veszprém mark, which implies that the town had been a regional economic centre."

[60] L. Fejérpataky: Pápai adószedők Magyarországon a XIII–XIV. században (Papal tax-collectors in Hungary in the 13th–14th centuries). *Századok* (1887) 606. Revised by E. Mályusz: *Egyházi társadalom a középkori Magyarországon (Clerical society in medieval Hungary)*. Budapest (1971) 180–181; E. Fügedi: A XV. századi magyar püspökök (Bishops in 15th century Hungary). *Történeti Szemle* 8 (1965) 496.

[61] 1448: ... *in maiore palatio castri Wesprimiensis.* The private archives of the Veszprém chapter. Veszprém eccl. et capit. 38. Cited by Gutheil (1977) 274.

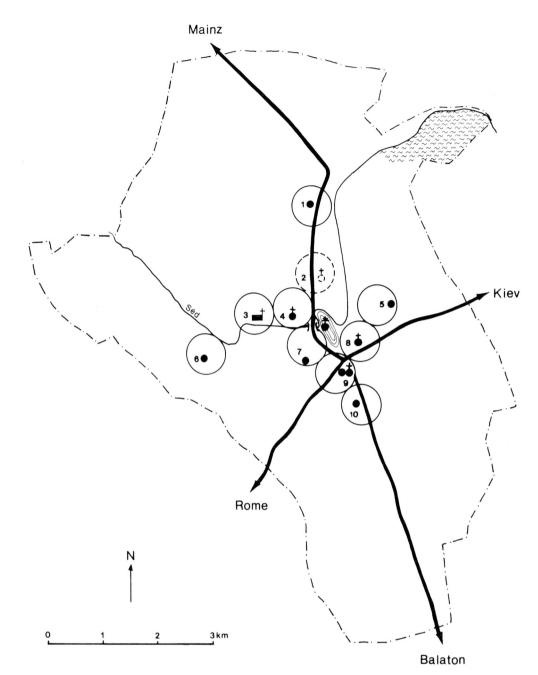

Fig. 5. The churches and cemeteries of Veszprém in the 11th–13th centuries, 1 Jutas; 2. St. Thomas' church; 3. Veszprémvölgy, Greek cloister; 4. St. Catherine's Dominican nunnery; 5. Madách Imre street; 6. Sashegy; 7. Mt. Jerusalem; 8. Cserhát, church of St. John the Baptist; 9. St. Nicholas' church; 10. Komarov street

The town's chapel had not more than 36 members, 32 of whom are identified by name in a 1469 document. Most of them lived in their own house in the capitular quarter under the castle hill.[62]

In the Middle Ages, Veszprém functioned as the centre of three different estates: of the princely and later royal estate (from which the queen's and the prince's estates had seceded), of the bishop's estate (which also included the chapel's possession), and finally of the royal county estate.

According to the archaeological data at our disposal,[63] 9th–10th century original settlers are known to have lived only in the territory 1.5 km from the castle hill

[62] The charters cited by Gutheil (1977) 107–109, 182–212.

[63] The archaeological observations and research into the medieval history of Veszprém are linked to the activities of I. Ádám and Gy. Rhé and, more recently, K. Gyürky and S. Tóth (we look forward to the publication of the latter's

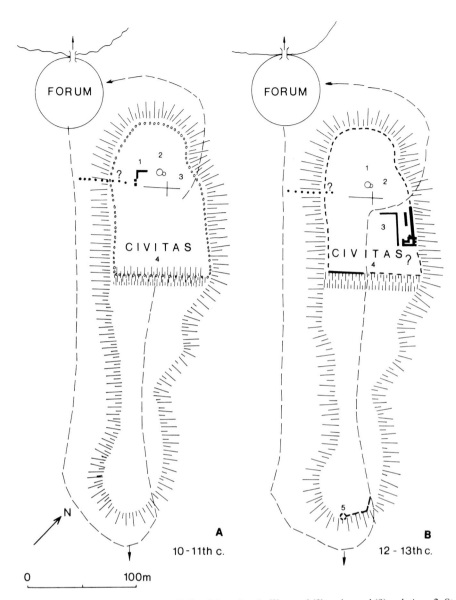

Fig. 6. Veszprém Castle. A. 10th–11th centuries. 1. Walls of the princely (?)–royal (?)–episcopal (?) *palatium;* 2. St. George's chapel; 3. St. Michael's cathedral; 4. earthwork ditch. B. 12th–13th centuries. 1. St. George's chapel; 2. St. Michael's cathedral; 3. episcopal residence; 4. castle walls; 5. watchtower

named, perhaps not accidentally, Árpádfia (Jutas).[64] Early Magyar burials datable to the first half of the 10th century—one authentic and one that can no longer be located—have come to light on the hill-side by the

stream Séd which crosses the town.[65] A concentration of settlements can be noted around Veszprém from the mid-10th century. The approximately 40 metres high castle hill had been the seat of the bishopric, founded around the turn of the 10th–11th centuries and, on the strength of later data, the bailiff's court can also be located there. Of these early structures only the episcopal cathedral consecrated to St. Michael has survived. Art historians date this building to the 1100s.[66] Since

regrettably abandoned excavations of the cathedral!). The conscientiously compiled archaeological topography, the work of I. Éri, M. Kelemen, P. Németh, S. Tóth and I. Torma (*MRT* 2, 224–256), also contains a full bibliography for each site. The publication and review of the written sources are also standard works: Fraknói–Lukcsics (1896–1907); Békefi (1912) 3–32; Kumorovitz (1953); Gutheil (1977) with a review of his earlier studies.

[64] A. Kralovánszky: Beiträge zum Problem der Ausgestaltung, Chronologie und der ethnischen Bestimmung des sog. Schläfenringes mit S-Ende. *Studia Slavica* 5 (1959) 327–361; *MRT* 2, 251–252. For the original settlers in the area in the

Conquest period, cf. also Heckenast (1970) 42–46; Gy. Györffy: Az Árpád-kori szolgálónépek kérdéséhez (On the question of servant peoples in the Árpádian Age). *Történeti Szemle* 15 (1972) 273–274.

[65] *MRT* 2, sites 51/2, 51/3a and 51/25.

[66] Tóth (1963) 126.

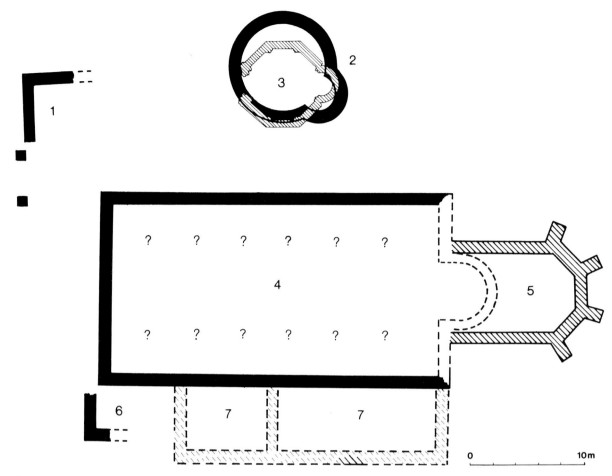

Fig. 7. Veszprém Castle. 1. Walls of the princely (?)–royal (?)–episcopal (?) *palatium;* 2. St. George's chapel 972–997 (?) and after 1018 (?); 3. St. George's chapel, 13th century; 4. St. Michael's cathedral, 11th–14th centuries; 5. enlargement of the chapel, 1380–1400; 6. medieval wall, 11th–13th centuries; 7. St. Ladislaus' and St. Martin's chapels, 13th–14th centuries

recent archaeological excavations and analyses are still unpublished, we can only rely on the observations made during the reconstruction of the cathedral in the early 1900s in establishing the architectural history of the building.[67] In its Romanesque phase, the cathedral was presumably a three-aisled basilica with a round-arched sanctuary and square-ended aisles. The aisles were divided by six pillars on each side. Contemporary descriptions and the still extant walls suggest that the main architectural units were erected of soft red sandstone brought there from the Balaton highlands, while the ascending walls were built of crushed dolomite. Only some of the entablatures and column-caps were carved of limestone. The original location of these carvings could not be determined since these have come to light in a secondary position from under the flooring of the Baroque church. The practically undecorated red sandstone carvings—the column-drums and crowns, the arches connecting the columns—were recovered in their original position in the early 20th century. It was the utilization of two types of building material that had given rise to theories that the parts carved of limestone

had belonged to the cathedral built before 1000 (?), while those built of red sandstone are the remains of the second church which was attached to the cathedral founded by the queen and built in the first third of the 11th century.[68] To all appearances, the Romanesque basilica also had a central crypt and a vestibule in the west. The western towers represent the late Romanesque style, while the still extant enlarged sanctuary and the lower church under it were completed in the last

---

[67] Ádám (1912) 53–129.

[68] Éri (1972) 9; Gutheil (1977) 65–66. According to Tóth (1963) 123–124, the 120×120 cm hard limestone base stones observed by I. Ádám (one of them lay *in situ* 200 cm under the ground level along the line dividing the nave and the side-aisle: Ádám (1912) 95–96) cannot be considered parts of the Romanesque basilica which had been built of red sandstone (from the Balaton highlands) on a higher foundation, and whose surviving walls and pillars are still visible. The builders of a penthouse during the excavation of the St. George chapel—Gyürky (1963) 341–386—have uncovered another pillar footing which lay in a secondary position (Tóth (1963) 122–123). A pillar footing of similar size (112×118 cm) and also of hard limestone was cut away from the foundation of the cellar of the house under 39 Tolbuhin Street, near the cathedral (in 1979). A. Kralovánszky: *RégFüz* I. 33 (1980) 118–119.

Fig. 8. Veszprém Castle. Fresco by Masolino de Panicale, around 1428

5

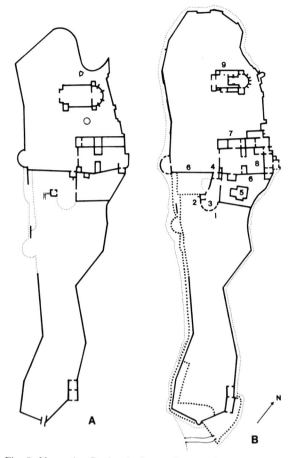

Fig. 9. Veszprém Castle. A. Survey by an unknown military engineer, 1569. B. G. Turco's drawing, 1572. 1. Rondella; 2. outer gate tower; 3. defensive corridor; 4. inner gate tower; 5. military building; 6. outer court; 7. episcopal palace, the quarters of the castellan; 8. inner court; 9. St. Michael's cathedral

years of the 14th century.[69] A survey of 1572 by Turco, a military engineer, shows that the Middle Ages saw several chapels added to the cathedral in the north and south.[70] Regrettably enough, this small-scale drawing

does not enable the realistic reconstruction of either the Gothic or the Romanesque building.[71]

The reconstruction of the building complex located south of the cathedral, the groundplan of which is also shown in this engraving, is likewise problematic. According to Turco's survey this complex, added to the eastern part of the inner castle wall which actually was the bisecting line of the castle, consisted of 17 rooms and 2 courtyards.[72] The northern half of this complex may

[69] According to I. Ádám (1912) 63, the wall of the side-aisles was not attached to the wall of the western towers. The enlargement of the sanctuary and the building of the new lower church took place after the 1380 conflagration, and the new construction was consecrated in 1400 (Fraknói–Lukcsics (1896–1907) II, 324).

[70] Korompay (1957). The St. George chapel built north of the cathedral does not appear in the engraving. We only know of it from the archaeological and historical sources—cp. Gyürki (1963) and *MRT* 2, site 51/la. The chapel of the Holy Ghost, also on the northern side, was definitely extant prior to 1371. J. Holub: *Zala megye története a középkorban. Oklevéltár II, 72 (The history of country Zala in the Middle Ages)*. Manuscript in the Veszprém museum. Veszprém (1933). Békefi (1912) 22. The St. László chapel and the St. Márton chapel, both in the south, were built before 1359 (Fraknói–Lukcsics (1896–1907) II, 182) and 1429 (L. Fejérpataky: A veszprémi káptalan kincseinek összeírása 1429–1437. évekből (The conscription of the treasures of the Veszprém chapter in 1429–1437). *Történeti Tár* (1887) 177), respectively.

[71] We have nevertheless made an attempt at reconstructing these buildings at the request of L. Gerevich. We used a diagram on the scale of 1:500, since the width on the re-drawing coincided with that given in the engraving. However, the length and the orientation were different, and thus our reconstruction is only tentative until the publication of S. Tóth's paper on the excavation of the cathedral.

[72] In view of the fact that the engraving dates from 1572, we have to consider the circumstances discussed in the present paper that establish the owner and the function of the complex. Seeing that the date and the architectural phases of this structure are still unknown it can safely be stated that the L-shaped building added to the eastern precinct of the castle was the core of the complex. This building had seven rooms and a courtyard in front of it; it was defended by a fence in the south and had two buildings added to it in the north and south. Also added to this eastern wing was a structure, presumably supported by cantilever, which may have functioned as a defensive tower and latrine, a fence extending toward the southeast and a side-tower in the corner of the eastern wall of the castle. Another room, the wall of which was contiguous with the southern wall of the 13th century chapel, was added to the northern wall of the inner complex. Consequently, this room cannot be identified with the chapel, provided that the survey and the drawing are reliable (Korompay (1957) 36). The rooms, 6–8 m wide and 8, 9, 12, 14, 16 m long, were hall-sized! The western wing had two large rooms added to it in the north, a courtyard in the south, which was defended by a fence in the west (to which two side-towers were added). The whole building complex was defended in the south and southwest by a round bastion, a fence with gates and military buildings. The core of this castle complex is generally identified with the Árpádian Age royal or queen's palace, mostly on the evidence of a 1757–58 episcopal protocol, according to which "... the area of the episcopal palace, formerly called the royal residence ... inside the gate also included the queen's kitchen". (Veszprém Episcopal Archives, Protocollum Episcopale. 1757–58. 7. Quoted by Gutheil (1977) 67–68). Jenő Major, who kindly read through the present paper, also underlines the significance of this piece of evidence: "... no matter how late the reference to the queen's kitchen is, it should not be left out of consideration since it also makes mention of the royal residence...". In my opinion however, this counter-reasoning cannot be confirmed by data. We know that, similarly to numerous other castles, between 1566 and 1712 the castle of Veszprém was controlled by the king in order to create strategic unity against the Turks and also to cover the expenses of the battles; cf. P. Lukcsics–J. Pfeiffer: *A veszprémi püspöki vár a katolikus restauráció korában (The episcopal castle of Veszprém during the Catholic restoration)*. Veszprém (1933). Accordingly, I would rather link the 1757–58 datum to the 151 years long royal phase which ended 42 years earlier, than to the period 445 years earlier, before 1313! J. Major's assumption that the earliest 'princely' or 'royal' residence can perhaps be located to the territory owned by the nuns in Veszprém Valley definitely merits consideration. I plan to return to this problem in a study to be written jointly with J. Major.

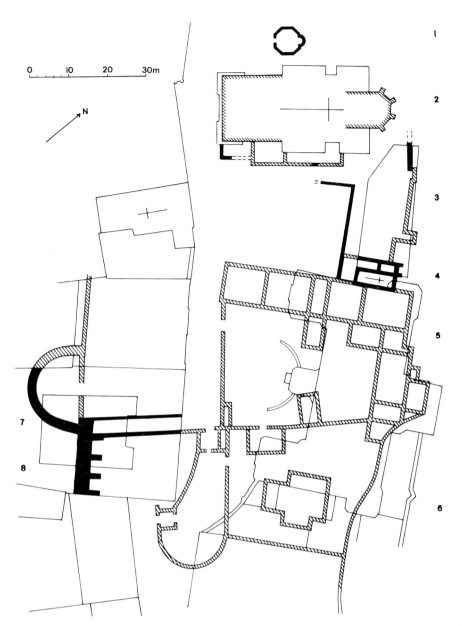

Fig. 10. Veszprém Castle, inner castle. G. Turco's groundplan (1572) with the excavated buildings. 1. St. George's chapel; 2. St. Michael's cathedral; 3. castle wall, 13th–15th centuries; 4. episcopal private chapel, sacristy, room of unknown function and wall, 12th–13th centuries; 5. episcopal *palatium*, 13th–16th centuries; 6. outer military defense works, 15th–16th centuries; 7. rondella, around 1500; 8. castle wall and storage rooms, 15th–16th centuries

presumably be identified with the medieval bishop's palace, and the southern half with its military buildings. The medieval walls may have served as the foundation for parts of the still extant bishop's palace, built in the last third of the 18th century. The more precise dating of the medieval complex, the determination of the architectural periods and the function of the rooms would require further archaeological excavations and analyses of the walls. The cellar of the building was definitely built of Baroque bricks and undatable ashlars (only few of which have survived). The so-called Gizella chapel, added to the palace in the north and the remains of which are still observable, was in all probability part of this palace. However, this chapel cannot be identified

on the military survey. It is likewise questionable whether the survey depicts the whole complex of the palace or only its utilizable parts. The chapel, completed in the first half of the 13th century, was split-level in its original form. The upper level had decayed, only two of the wall pillars survive *in situ*. Today, the chapel is situated between the grand provostal residence which was completed in 1741 and the bishop's palace, the building of which was begun in 1767. The excavations conducted recently in the castle chapel have brought to light the following relics: fragments from the barrel-vaulted sacristy on the upper level; the stone-framed door connecting the sacristy with the sanctuary; remains from the room above the sacristy *(depositorium?,*

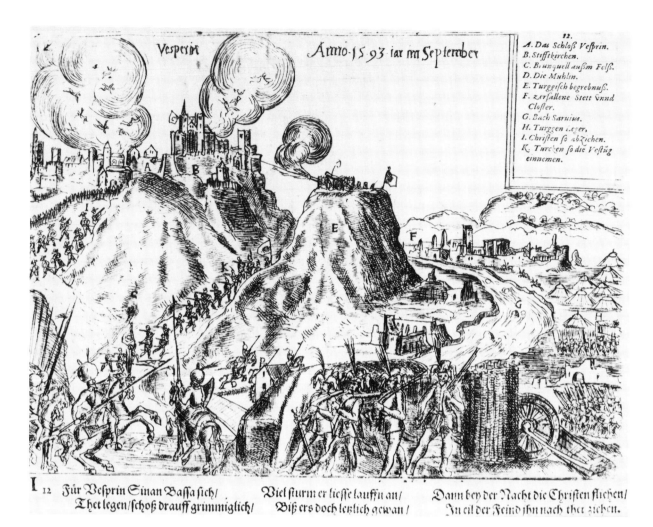

Fig. 11. The siege of Veszprém in 1593. W. P. Zimmermann's engraving, 1605

*oratorium?*); a 14th–15th century stone-framed door near the sanctuary and the remains of two buttresses on the eastern walls of the sacristy and the sanctuary, respectively. The excavations have also recovered the foundation of the lower chapel, built with the *opus spicatum* technique, parts of the spiral staircased tower added to the northern side of the sacristy and the reconstructable fragments of frescoes decorating the southern and western walls of the lower chapel (these depict the four Apostles, Jesus Christ and the Blessed Virgin).[73]

The rotunda, dedicated to St. George and unearthed north of the episcopal cathedral, poses further questions for the researcher of the early Árpádian period (10th–12th centuries). Parallels to this chapel type have been reported from European secular and church centres,

and are generally datable to the period of the conversion to Christianity.[74] On account of its principal axis, which differs from that of the cathedral, the chapel presumably antedates the cathedral. The reconstructible early medieval ground level of the cathedral is flush with that of the chapel. On the strength of its *patrocinium*, the chapel can be assigned either to the last quarter of the 10th century (the Byzantine Christianity of Princess Sarolt) or to the early 11th century (in connection with the St. George relic originating from Ohrid, Bulgaria, and given to King Stephen as a reward for his victorious federal campaign of 1018).[75] It is nevertheless highly probable that the chapel functioned as a *capella regia* and not as an episcopal cathedral. In the 13th century the chapel was rebuilt into an octagonal chapel, the principal axis of which was then parallel with that of the cathedral. In the Late Middle Ages this chapel also functioned as a collegiate church. Following a recon

[73] For results of the 1981–82 excavations, see A. Kralovánszky: Újabb adatok a veszprémi Gizella kápolna középkori és újkori építéstörténetéhez (Contributions to the medieval and modern architectural history of the Gizella Chapel in Veszprém). *Épités és Épitészettudomány* 15 (1983) 273–281.

[74] Gyürky (1963); V. Gervers-Molnár: *A középkori Magyarország rotundái (Rotundas in Medieval Hungary).* Művészettörténeti Füzetek 4. Budapest (1972).

[75] Györffy (1977) 102.

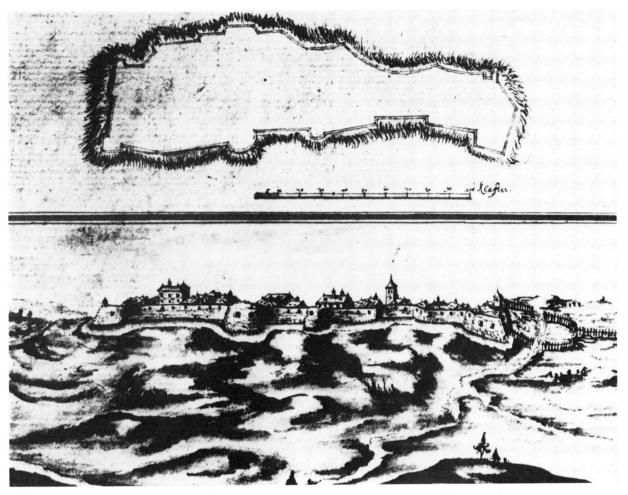

Fig. 12. Veszprém–Castle. Engraving by unknown master, 1667

struction in the second half of the 15th century, this chapel was destroyed sometime in the 16th–17h centuries.[76] Had this chapel functioned as a *capella regia* in its early phase, it would imply that the dwelling of the prince, and later of the king and the bailiff, lay in its immediate vicinity.[77] The excavation of this structure in the north is prevented by the fact that the ground level of the cellar of the 18th century seminary is lower than that of the Árpádian Age structures. Only the archaeological investigation of the street west of the chapel may provide further information in this line.

On the evidence of the written sources, the area of the castle had another church in it, namely the All Saints' church and provostship, which can be located to the southwestern part of the south half of the castle.[78]

There were a number of detached settlements called *angulus* ('szeg', meaning 'nail' in Hungarian) which

became associated with the castle hill, the centre of the estate. These settlements were named after the patrons of their respective churches: St. Nicholas szeg, St. Margaret szeg (from which St. Catherine szeg, named after the patron saint of the Dominican cloister there, seceded), St. Thomas szeg (sometimes also referred to as the village of St. Thomas), Sárszeg, which had no church, and finally St. John the Baptist szeg (Szt. Iván szeg in Hungarian).

The earlier assumption that the parish church of St. John the Baptist was situated east of the outer wall must definitely be considered groundless,[79] since, to all appearances, it must have stood on the hillside overlooking the stream Séd, north of the medieval road linking Fehérvár with Veszprém, on the territory of today's Cserhát district. The presumed site of this church has

[76] Gyürky (1963).

[77] This can be inferred primarily from the Western and South-East European analogies (Aachen, Przemysl, Cracow, etc.).

[78] The first reference of 1307 mentions *castrum Omnium Sanctorum* (J. Nagy–D. Véghely–Gy. Nagy: *Zala vármegye története. Oklevéltár I (The history of Zala county. Archives* I). Budapest (1886) 127–128) on the southern side of the castle hill. A source of 1352 refers to it as a communal chapter: *prepositura ecclesie omnium sanctorum in castro Vesprimiensi.* (G. Fraknói: *Monumenta Romana Episcopatus Vesprimienzis.* Tom. II. Budapestini 1 II, 152).

[79] Gutheil (1977) 121–123.

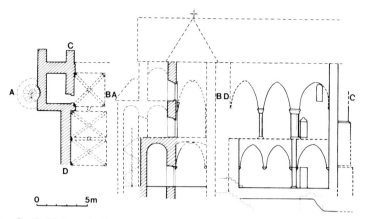

Fig. 13. Veszprém–Castle. Episcopal private chapel (the so-called Gizella chapel), first quarter of the 13th century

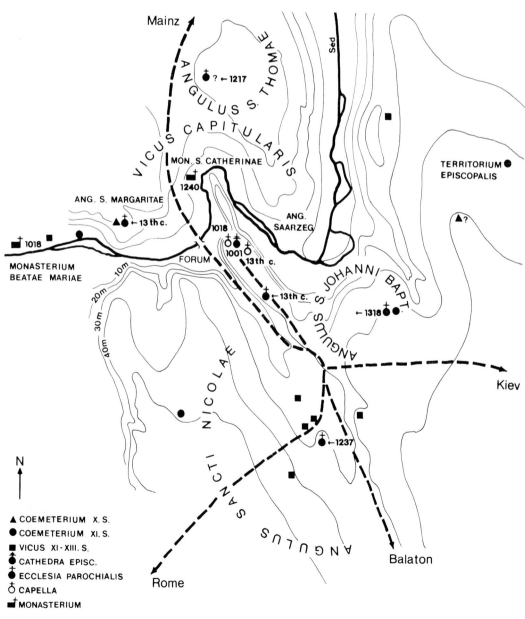

Fig. 14. Reconstructed settlement structure of Veszprém in the 10th–13th centuries

70

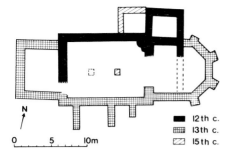

Fig. 15. Veszprém, St. Nicholas' parish church. Excavated
remains, 12th–15th centuries

also yielded inhumation burials, but without grave
goods.[80] In the Middle Ages this area was called St. Iván
szeg after the parish church there.

The parish church of St. Nicholas, which was discovered during the archaeological excavations, stood on a 10
metres high elevation on the continuation of the above-
named road leading to Italy. The first reference to this
church dates from 1237, but in all probability it was built
earlier. The presumed existence of this church in the
late 11th century is neither supported nor contradicted
by the coins of Salamon (1060–1063) and Kálmán
(1096–1116) recovered in 1929–31 and confirmed by the
1978 excavations.[81] Although the stone church was first
erected over the burials, we have no data to prove that
these burials yielded the 11th century coins. Most
Hungarian scholars usually assign the square-ended
type of church to the 13th century,[82] although the
comparable lower church of Tihany abbey in the nearby
Balaton highlands (founded by the king in 1055) may be
taken to indicate an earlier date. On the strength of the
indirect historical evidence, however, we can assign the
church to the 1210s. Supporting this dating are the facts
that its dimensions measured in feet may be associated
with the same measure of length used in the Upper
Rhineland, and that its construction is indicative of a
master with antique and European education. Quite
probably this master can be identified with the Walloon
bishop Robertus. The church stood on the main commercial road linking Fehérvár with Italy. Between
1208–1210 Robertus served as the provost of the royal

basilica in Fehérvár, the town where most of the Latin
and Walloon people in this country had lived. In his
capacity as bishop of Veszprém (after 1210) he must
have had a share in the building of the first episcopal
palace on the castle hill, the so-called Gizella chapel and
the St. Nicholas church (quite remarkably, the churches
at the Latin–Walloon settlements in both Esztergom
and Székesfehérvár were dedicated to St. Nicholas!).[83]
The apparent resettlement by the bishop of this area
may presumably be accounted for by the fact that the
iron furnaces located in the immediate vicinity of the St.
Nicholas church and dated to the 10th–12th centuries
had gradually become obsolete,[84] their importance de-
creased and they were perhaps even closed down. In the
15th century the church was rebuilt, its sanctuary was
extended towards the east, and a charnel house, a tower
and an entrance hall were added to it in the north, west
and south. Then the originally single-naved church was
separated into two aisles by pillars (?) or columns (?)
erected on an east-west axis, obviously simultaneously
with the construction of the six-part arched ceiling. This
method of rebuilding the churches into two-aisled
churches in known to have been common primarily in
the northern areas of medieval Hungary (present-day
Slovakia), in the Szepesség and the Csallóköz on the
Danube, where the 1430s saw the replacement of the
earlier horizontal wooden ceilings with arched ones.
These analogies perhaps also reflect commercial relations between these regions.

The medieval marketplace, the *forum*, was situated at
the northwestern corner of the castle hill on the right
bank of the stream Séd, and was attached to (or
belonged to?) St. Nicholas szeg. Its existence in the
early periods is evinced by the postscript to the royal
charter of Tihany abbey, dating from 1055.[85]

The St. Catherine cloister of the Dominicans was
founded by Bertalan, the then bishop of Veszprém, in
1239. It stood on the left bank of the stream under the
castle hill.[86] The church, consecrated to the Apostle St.
Thomas, first referred to in 1267, may have stood north
of the cloister, on the eastern side of the mound by the
Győr–Vienna road.[87] Its exact location cannot be determined by archaeological means.[88]

[83] K. Éry–A. Kralovánszky: Veszprém–Kálvária domb
(Veszprém–Kálvária hill). *RégFüz* I. 32 (1979) 101–103.

[84] *MRT* 2, sites 51/49, 51, 52d: G. Heckenast–Gy. Nováki–
G. Vastag–E. Zoltay: *A magyarországi vaskohászat története a
korai középkorban (History of iron smelting in Hungary in the
Early Middle Ages).* Budapest (1968) 171.

[85] … *Bezprenensis mercati tributum*: Erdélyi (1902) 14, 330;
Also Gutheil (1977) 187; J. Major (verbal communication)

[86] *MRT* 2, site 51/4a.

[87] *MRT* 2, site 51/5.

[88] A 1370 source refers to the weekly markets held at the
settlement that were controlled by the bishopric of Veszprém:
R. Békefi: *A Balaton környékének egyházai és várai a középkorban (Medieval churches and castles in the Balaton region).*
Budapest (1907) 14. The annual fair, held there on Ascension
Day, is mentioned in a 1503 source: R. Békefi, *ibid.* Another
annual fair, held on St. George's Day, is known to have been
held there in the preceding period (1489: The private archives
of the Veszprém chapter. Veszprém oppidum. 65).

[80] Contrary to the description of site 51/7 in *MRT* 2, I would
locate the presumed site of the church to site 51/31, since this
good-lying area has already yielded Árpádian Age burials. The
parish churches of St. Margaret and St. Nicholas both stood on
the edge of a hill-top, unlike the location indicated in the map
on p. 223 of *MRT* 2, where no burials have yet been uncovered
and where the features of the terrain were rather unfavourable
(hill-side overlooking the castle hill).

[81] The leader of the excavation assigned them to the 11th
century. Gy. Rhé: Új Árpád-kori templommaradványok Veszprémben (Remains of Árpádian Age churches found recently
in Veszprém). *A Veszprém Vármegyei Múzeum Évi Jelentése*
(1932), 1–14.

[82] K. Kozák: A román-kori egyenes szentélyzáródás hazai
kialakulásáról (The development of the Romanesque square-
ended sanctuaries in Hungary). *Magyar Műemlékvédelem* 1
(1961–62) 111–133.

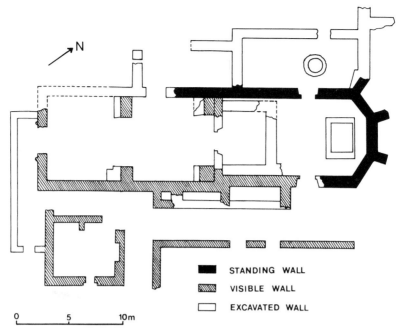

STANDING WALL

VISIBLE WALL

EXCAVATED WALL

0    5    10m

Fig. 16. Veszprém, church of the Dominican cloister dedicated to St. Catherine, 1240–14th century

Margaret szeg, on the above-mentioned road leading to Western Europe, consisted of the following constructions: the St. Catherine cloister and the attached St. Margaret parish church (assigned to the 12th–13th centuries),[89] some 20 prebendal houses (14th–15th centuries), a mill (14th century) and a bath (15th century).[90]

The 'szegs' surrounded the castle hill, the episcopal and bailiff's centre, in a ring. The canonic, and after 1313 the seignioral law subordinated these units to the bishop of Veszprém. The scanty written sources do not provide a sufficient basis at present for determining which of them belonged to the queen, the prince and the bishop in the Árpádian Age (owing to its potentialities and liabilities in the provision of the centre, Nicholas szeg must definitely have belonged to the royal possessions from the very beginning).[91]

The only structure which was demonstrably owned by the king was the Greek—originally 13th century Cistercian—cloister some 1 km west of the castle hill. The founding of this cloister can presumably be associated with the marriage resultant from the joint military campaign of King Stephen and the emperor of Byzan-

tium between 1016–1018. We know that the early feudal rulers often resorted to marriage to strengthen their links with foreign states. The wife of Prince Imre (b. 1007) was a Byzantine princess. This apparently justifies the assumption that King Stephen founded the Greek cloister after 1016–1018, and that subsequently he transferred the legal authority over it from the bishop of Veszprém to the archbishop of Esztergom.[92]

In the case of Veszprém, various ethnic groups that contributed to the flourishing economic and cultural life in the Middle Ages can be assumed, but their presence cannot be proved. We have already mentioned the Greek nuns. In Iván szeg we may presume a related or unrelated Byzantine (?)–Bulgarian (?)–Southern Slav influence, on account of the etymology of the denominating patron's name, and also of his function: the patron of the curriers! (Following the 16th century demolition of the church in Iván szeg, the name of the place was changed to Cserhát: cserzés, 'tanning', a technical term in leather work.[93]) The presence of the two Walloon bishops can be considered a unique phenomenon. There are no surviving personal names—either of officials or of civilians—on the evidence of

[89] MRT 2, site 51/3a-b.

[90] Gutheil (1977) 182–195.

[91] Not improbably only the charters supporting the possessory right of the Veszprém chapter have survived in his private archives. Catherine szeg appears to have been owned by the queen, who in 1275 donated the St. Catherine mill and the Jutas Street in the szeg (Private archives of the Veszprém chapter. Veszprém oppidum 68; Gutheil (1977) 307). In 1370 Szenttamásfalva was owned by the bishop (in villa episcopali sancti Thome martiris, cf. note 87), although in 1489 its market duty was split between the chapter of Veszprém and the magistrate of Buda (cf. note 88). The settlement of the princely people is still open debate.

[92] Gy. Moravcsik: Görögnyelvű monostorok Szent István király korában (Greek-speaking monasteries under King St. Stephen). SZIE I, 408–418; Györffy (1977) 321–323.

[93] Our assumption is that the system of settlements which was designed to provide Veszprém with goods and services— the blacksmiths in Nicholas szeg, the curriers in Iván szeg and the inhabitants of Csatár (shield-maker), 3 km from the castle hill—was similar to that presumed in the region of Esztergom. Cf. Heckenast (1970) 97; Gy. Györffy: Az Árpád-kori szolgálónépek kérdéséhez (On the question of servant peoples in the Árpádian Age). Történelmi Szemle 15 (1972), 287, note 108; Györffy (1970) 97.

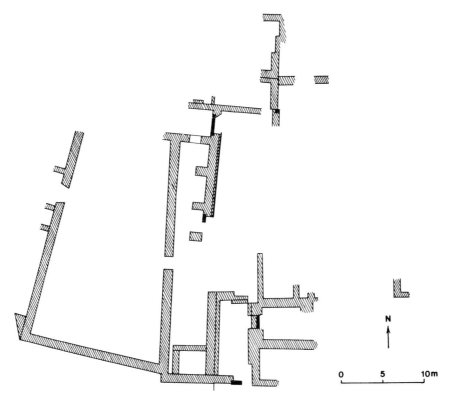

Fig. 17. Veszprém. The groundplan of the excavated remains of the Cistercian cloister in Veszprémvölgy, 14th century

which this ethnic composition could be further specified. According to the written sources, the Hungarians outnumbered by far the other ethnic groups in the area.

In the late 15th century Veszprém had some 1600–2000 inhabitants.[94] If we take the inferred number of inhabitants as a basis for reconstructing the same number in the preceding centuries, then, considering the configurations of the terrain, its habitability, the known archaeological and written data and the comparable areas elsewhere in the country, the 11th century population of the castle hill and the settlements in the outlying grounds of the castle cannot have numbered more than 100–500 and 500–700, respectively.[95]

The archaeological and written sources suggest that even though Veszprém ranked among the most significant administrative settlements during the Árpádian Age (dwelling place of the grand duke, county and episcopal seat), it was considerably less advanced in terms of urbanization (trade, commerce, independent administration of justice, right to elect the parson). This

latter fact may be due to the disadvantageous geographical location on the one hand, and on the other to the narrow-minded and improvident conduct of the local bishopric (which also functioned as the feudal landlord) which neglected the promotion of the craftsmen and merchants. The development of Veszprém practically came to a standstill in this period, and the town remained on the level of market towns during the following centuries.[96]

The present paper could offer only a brief account of the attempts to reconstruct the history of Veszprém. It is hardly to be expected that further written documents will be discovered that could provide additional information. We are nevertheless convinced that by replacing the accidental archaeological research, which had often been conducted by non-professionals, with systematic and planned excavations we could further detail the

[94] Éri (1972) 14; According to V. Bácskai, a butcher in an average Transdanubian market town catered for some 120 people: Magyar mezővárosok a XV. században (Market towns in 15th century Hungary). *ÉTtK* 37 (1965) 50. In 1489 Veszprém had 8 butcher's stalls (Gutheil (1977) 336).

[95] J. Nemeskéri–A. Kralovánszky: Székesfehérvár becsült népessége a X–XI. századokban (The estimated population of Székesfehérvár in the 10th–11th centuries). *Székesfehérvár Évszázadai* 1. Ed. by A. Kralovánszky. Székesfehérvár (1967) 125–138. These numbers are based on this study and also on the early burials in Veszprém.

[96] One of the leading authorities on both the economic and the church history of the period, is of practically the same opinion. Mályusz (1953) 162–172. The following general works are also useful for the medieval history of both Székesfehérvár and Veszprém: B. Hóman: *A magyar városok az Árpádok korában (Hungarian towns under the Árpád Dynasty).* Budapest (1908); A. Pleidell: A magyar várostörténet első fejezete (The first chapter in the history of Hungarian towns). *Századok* 68 (1934) 276–313; E. Mályusz: A magyarság és a városi élet a középkorban (The Hungarians and urban life in the Middle Ages). *Századok* 78 (1944) 36–62; J. Major: A magyar városok és városhálózat kialakulásának kezdetei (The emergence of towns and an urban network in Hungary). *Településtudományi Közlemények* 18 (1966) 48–90.

medieval history of the town. The reassessment of old facts in the light of the new findings could also be conducive to this end.

## SZÉKESFEHÉRVÁR

Of the theories explaining the name of the town (Fehérvár, 'white castle'), that of J. Horváth appears to be the most plausible. According to him, the town *"ob specialitatem nobilitatis sue nomen accepit"* — a quotation from St. Stephen's minor legend, written before 1108 in Székesfehérvár.[97] This theory was further elaborated by Gy. Györffy who assumed that the castle, built of white stone, was named after the advanced building methods typical of the reign of the king.[98] It is to be remarked here that the contemporary written sources refer to the town, named originally Fehérvár in Hungarian, with the Latin, German and Slavic equivalent of this name: Alba civitas, Wzzenburch (= Weissenburg), Baligrata (= Bjelograd, Belgrade). The name Alba Regia was first used in 1235. This name, obviously a reference to the significance attached to the throne in the royal basilica, and also to the practice of crowning the rulers in the town, was later translated into Hungarian, German and Slavic (Székesfehérvár, Stuhlweissenburg, Istolni Beograd).[99]

The royal basilica, where most of our kings and their relatives were buried between 1031–1540 and where the Hungarian kings were crowned and throned between 1038–1527, was founded by King Stephen in the early 11th century as a private chapel *(propriam capellam)*. The royal insignia and the most important charters were also kept in this building. It was here that the official history of the country was compiled.[100] From the second half of the 11th century the annual parliament (in the second half of August), where the king also exercised jurisdiction, had been held on the outskirts of the town.[101] Fehérvár was the denominator of a weight unit *(pondus Albensis)*, and for a decade money was also

minted in the town (1430s).[102] The administrative status of the town was replaced by a sacral role in the mid-13th century, when Buda became the real and ultimate administrative centre of medieval Hungary.[103]

In view of the scanty data on the Roman settlements and burials found on the territory of medieval Fehérvár, most scholars had, until recently, presumed a posthouse on the road connecting Gorsium, 8 km south of the town, with Arrabona (Győr).[104] The excavations conducted between 1965–1972 in the area of the one-time royal basilica brought to light the remains of two different stone structures from the lowest level (min. 5×5 metres and 9×6 metres, respectively). These buildings must definitely have antedated the 11th century basilica. The axis of the sandstone building, erected with *pseudoisodomum* technique, deviates from the principal axis of the basilica by four degrees and the same was noted in the large-size (15×15 metres) crushed-stone building unearthed in the last century in front of the western wing of the medieval basilica.[105] Although no chronologically diagnostic finds have come to light in the area (only Roman roof-tiles and *imbrices* were found), the three buildings can definitely be assigned to the Roman period, since neither in the Migration, nor in the Avar period were there stone structures raised in Pannonia (except for the late 9th century stone churches mentioned by the 9th century *Conversio*). Also supporting this dating is the fact that none of the three buildings can be identified as a Christian church.

Mention must be made here of the theories according to which the emergence of Fehérvár during the second third of the 10th century can be associated with the activity of Szabolcs, considered to have been a prince[106] by present-day research. This assumption is based on two considerations: first, that two settlements named Szabolcs (after the personal name) are known to have lain 20–25 km from medieval Fehérvár. One of these settlements was demolished in the mid-11th century in order to prevent an attack on Fehérvár by its owners, the Csák dynasty, who were also descendants of Szabolcs. Secondly, the princely dwelling place under Géza must have had some precedents. In our view these considerations are no longer acceptable or tenable, since they are contradicted by both the archaeological data and the written sources.[107] It has been pointed out by most

[97] Legenda Minor S. Stephani. *SRH* II, 396; J. Horváth: Székesfehérvár korai történetének néhány kérdése az írásos források alapján (The early history of Székesfehérvár on the evidence of the written sources). *Székesfehérvár Évszázadai* 1. Ed. by A. Kralovánszky. Székesfehérvár (1967) 109–110.

[98] Györffy (1967) 19–20.

[99] *Ibid.*, 19; Rogerius: Carmen Miserabile. *SRH* II, 555; Györffy, (1973) 290: in his opinion "these were introduced after 1240". Györffy (1987) 368.

[100] For an excellent summary of the history of Székesfehérvár drawing upon the full documentary material, see Károly (1898) 372–504; J. Fitz: *Székesfehérvár*. Budapest (1966), and J. Deér: Aachen und die Herrschersitze der Arpaden. *MIÖG* 79 (1971) 1–56; H. Göckenjan: Stuhlweissenburg. Eine ungarische Königresidenz von 11.–13. Jh. *Beiträge zur Stadt- und Regionalgeschichte Ost- und Nordeuropas*. Ed. by. K. Zernack. Wiesbaden (1971) 135–152; cf. also the studies in *Székesfehérvár Évszázadai* I (1967), 2 (1972), and 3 (1978). Ed. by A. Kralovánszky.

[101] For the parliaments held outside Székesfehérvár in the area called Föveny, cf. A. Kralovánszky: Velence község történetéhez (Contributions to the history of the village of Velence). *Alba Regia* 4–5 (1963–64) 230–232.

[102] L. Huszár: Anjou-korai pénzverés Székesfehérvárott (Minting of coins in Székesfehérvár under the Angevins). *Székesfehérvár Évszázadai* 2. Ed. by A. Kralovánszky. Székesfehérvár (1972) 113–122.

[103] L. B. Kumorovitz: Buda (és Pest) "fővárossá" alakulásának kezdetei (The beginnings of the transformation of Buda — and Pest — into 'the capital'). *TBM* 18 (1971) 7–58.

[104] J. Fitz: *Székesfehérvár*. Budapest (1966) 6.

[105] See A. Kralovánszky's excavation report in *ArchÉrt* 98 (1971) 280, and *ArchÉrt* 100 (1973) 277. I wish to thank Ernő Szakál for the definition of *pseudoisodomum*. Cf. also J. Fitz. Notes. *Alba Regia* 12 (1971) 260. Ferenc Fülep also considered the wall to be a Roman structure (verbal communication during his on-the-spot survey in 1971).

[106] Györffy (1970) 210–213

[107] Györffy (1970) 213–214 suggested that Csákvár (Fejér County) served as the summer residence and Pusztaszabolcs as

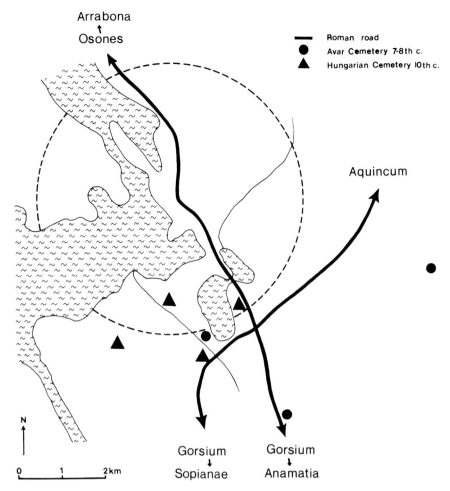

Fig. 18. The Avar and Magyar Conquest period cemeteries around Székesfehérvár, 7th–10th centuries

Fig. 19. Settlements in and around Székesfehérvár in the 10th–11th centuries

75

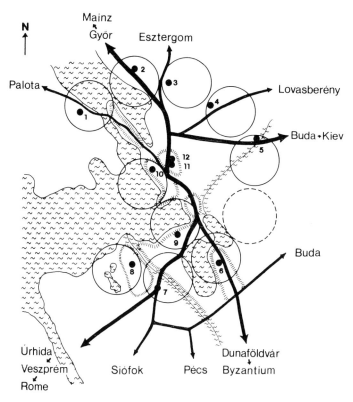

Fig. 20. Cemeteries in and around Székesfehérvár, 10th–11th centuries

historians that toponyms formed of tribal names should be considered indicative of the disintegration of the conquering Magyar tribal society and the subsequent breaking up of the tribal units by the evolving central authority. This process is dated to the second half of the 10th century by historians.[108] The toponyms formed of tribal names that are known from the area of Fehérvár— Kér, Berény, Nyék, Keszi, Ladány—are dated to the last quarter of the 10th century (in relation to the burial of Prince Géza in Fehérvár). The formation of Urhida[109] ('bridge of the prince') and Sárviz, a crossing place southwest of the town, can presumably be assigned to the reign of Géza or his son, King Stephen. The neighbouring settlements with churches of St. George, St. Michael, St. Pantaleion and, presumably, also Cosmas-Damianus are all indicative of an early Byzantine mission and can likewise be assigned to the turn of the 10th–11th centuries.[110] The settlement of Börgönd,

situated in the same area and mentioned by the written sources, can be dated to the early 11th century.[111]

The above-named settlements surrounded Alba civitas in a circle 10 km in radius. This concentration suggests that these settlements were designed to provide for, and also to defend, the prince or king staying in the central town.[112]

The reassessment of earlier and more recent archaeological findings has revealed two other comparable chains of settlements. Ten cemeteries (each associated with a settlement) datable to the turn of the 10th–11th centuries are known within a 2–3 km circle around the highest point of the area. This double ring of settlements can by no means be considered an accidental formation, their development and function must have been closely related to the then current organization of the state and the church. These early settlements could not be identified by name—presumably they did not have one.[113]

The Avar period (7th–9th centuries)[114] and early 10th

the winter residence of Szabolcs. It is most unlikely that there would have been a third residence at Fehérvár, which would have been the most significant of the three had it existed. The fact that in the 1040s Csákvár, called the castle of Szabolcs, was demolished by Endre, Béla and Levente (SRH I, 290) indicates that this was one of the most important fortifications.

[108] I. Kniezsa: Magyarország népei a XI. században (The population of Hungary in the 11th century). SZIE II, 371.

[109] First mentioned in a charter of 1009: Karácsonyi (1891) 58.

[110] Mezey (1972) 22.

[111] Cf. note 109.

[112] Kralovánszky (1972) 1557, 1562.

[113] A. Kralovászky: Székesfehérvár X–XI. századi településtörténeti kérdései (Settlement history of Székesfehérvár in the 10th–11th centuries). Székesfehérvár Évszázadai 1. Ed. by A. Kralovánszky. Székesfehérvár (1967) 35–36. The 10th century cemetery assumed by me has since then been identified and investigated by Gy. Fülöp, RégFüz 1 (1978) 77.

[114] D. Csallány: Archäologische Denkmäler der Awarenzeit in Mitteleuropa. Budapest (1956) 200; A. Kralovánszky: A Pákozd-Börgönd pusztai későavarkori temető (The late

76

century (Conquest period) burials[115] uncovered the area of Fehérvár in the course of archaeological investigations provide a good basis for our theory. The three Avar and four Conquest period burials are all situated south of the medieval town, and are adjusted to the crossing of the roads linking Aquincum with Sopianae and Arrabona with Gorsium in the area between Gorsium and the hilly southern limits of the Sárvíz (see Fig. 18).

The above facts provide an adequate basis for inferring—from the archaeological and topographical data at our disposal—that the Roman roads and their intersections still used in the Migration period and the Conquest period, which lay in an open space that was therefore difficult to defend, were relocated some 4 km north of their original position. The new intersection was situated on the territory of medieval Fehérvár, in front of the former princely fortification,[116] the exact location of which is known from recent excavations there. The fortified dwelling place of the prince stood on top of a 4 metres high, 150 metres long and 100 metres wide elevation in the middle of the medieval *civitas* or *castrum*. It had a four-apsidal central church built of ashlar in the middle,[117] and was surrounded by an approximately 20 metres wide and 10 metres high ditch and embankment, of which only the ditch could be cut through archaeologically. The earlier earth-works including the fill of the area and the formation of a new ground surface prevented the examination of the entrenchment.[118] In terms of its building technique and groundplan, the church in the centre of the fortification has its closest parallels in Byzantium and the Caucasus region, and also in Western, Southern and South-East Europe.[119] We are highly tempted to identify this church with the burial place of Prince Géza (d. 997). (Unfortunately, the vicinity of the church outside the groundplan area could not be excavated—except for a small area to the north—, and thus no traces of the presumed detached or attached palace could be found. A thorough investigation inside the church was likewise hindered by the nine public utilities, as well as by the late medieval and 18th century burials in the area.) The church had St.

Peter as its *patrocinium*.[120] According to the archaeological data and the written sources the church was pulled down in the 1220s–1230s and the new church with the same *patrocinium* was raised to its east by the young King Béla in 1225–1235. In 1235 Béla was crowned in the new church which, following the Mongol invasion, was handed over in 1249 to the Latins settled in the castle from the so-called Buda suburb to the north for use as a parish church.[121] The 10th–11th century potsherds recovered at the site and the stratigraphic sequence were also indicative of the levelling of the ground there: a 40–50 cm thick layer of top-soil had been carried over from the southern side of the elevation to the northern side, thus levelling down the area. The excavations north of the new St. Peter's church (or cathedral, as it is called in the charters) have also uncovered the ground walls of a large-size construction built of crushed stone (the dimensions of these walls could not be established, owing to their continuation under the medieval church). The vicinity of the church has yielded water channels set with mortar, and the remains of a public building assigned to the early Árpádian Age on account of the lack of small articles. The semi-subterranean house divided into two rooms and equipped with a plastered oven and an adjacent 4.5 metres deep, 2 metres long and 2 metres wide pit with vessels, eggs and the remains of sacrificial animals on its bottom found in the area can be associated with the construction of the church between 1225–1235.[122]

Another crushed-stone wall was located north of the central chapel. This wall, added to, and not built together with, the chapel may have functioned as an (original or secondary?) graveyard wall. Supporting this assumption was the east–west oriented building with bent northeastern corner and square eastern termination found added to the northern end of the wall. This building had originally or secondarily functioned as a charnel house.[123] The area of the cemetery had been extended northward from both the central church and the church founded by King Béla IV until the late 15th century when, around 1470, a burgher called Hentel had the town's only, and still extant, late Gothic chapel erected in the graveyard.[124]

At the turn of the 10th–11th centuries, the habitable area on this elevation did not exceed 100×100 or 150×150 metres. Occupying this comparatively small amount of space were the central church, the presumed dwelling place of the prince, and the quarters of the permanent garrison, the temporarily stationed military escort and the accompanying family members. The surface of this area corresponded to that of the contem-

Avar cemetery of Pákozd-Börgönd puszta). *Alba Regia* 2–3 (1961–62 [1963]) 173–179, and the excavation report in *Alba Regia* 11 (1971) 165.

[115] Bakay (1966) and (1968).

[116] First suggested by Fügedi (1967) 32; and in another of his studies: Fügedi (1969) 103–136; his assumptions were later confirmed by his archaeological excavations.

[117] See A. Kralovánszky's excavation report in *ArchÉrt* 99 (1972) 266; and in *Ars Hungarica* 3 (1975) 317; A. Kralovánszky: The Earliest Church of Alba Civitas. *Alba Regia* 20 (1983) 75–88.

[118] The section is shown in Fig. 23. Regrettably enough, the site that was cut through during the laying of cables did not yield any artefacts. The site cannot be assigned to prehistoric times for the lack of archaeological evidence elsewhere in the town.

[119] The expert opinion of Erzsébet Cs. Tompos based on her on-the-spot investigations. Cf. also *Ars Hungarica* 3 (1975) 319; A. Kralovánszky: Baukunsthistorische Angaben zur Frage des Auftauchens des romanischen Kirchentyps in Ungarn. *FolArch* 35 (1984) 111–138.

[120] This can be proved only indirectly, since the *patrocinium* was usually transferred to the new church. Cf. Mezey (1972) 22.

[121] Károly (1898) 671. Fügedi (1967) 39 based his arguments on this 1478 charter, and certain other historical sources.

[122] A. Kralovánszky's excavation report in *Alba Regia* 11 (1971) 166.

[123] A. Kralovánszky's excavation report in *ArchÉrt* 99 (1972) 266.

[124] Károly (1898) 671; Fitz (1955) 68.

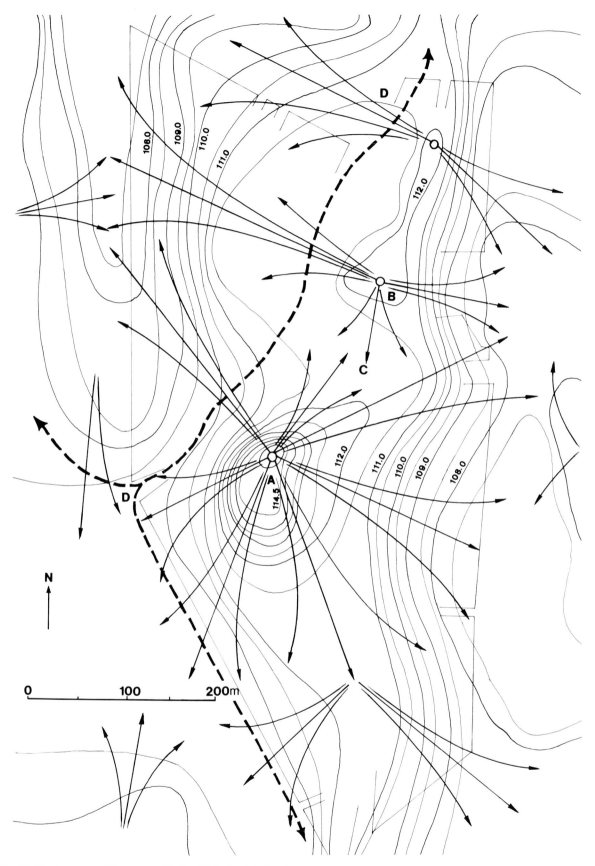

Fig. 21. Contour map of the centre of Székesfehérvár. A. Princely centre; B. *palatium* of the provostship of the Virgin Mary; C. royal basilica of the Virgin Mary; D. position of the town gates

78

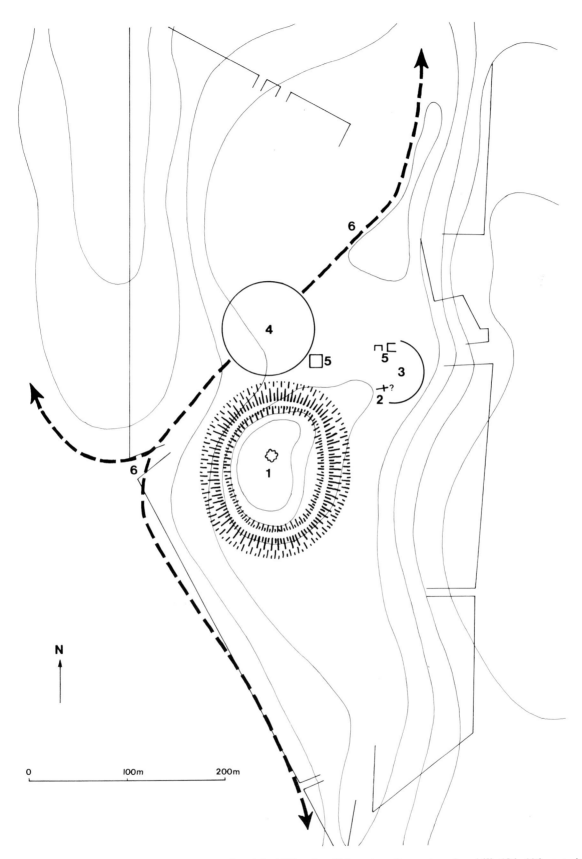

Fig. 22. Székesfehérvár–Centre. 1. St. Peter's church and the hillfort, late 10th century; 2. cemetery chapel (?), 10th–11th centuries; 3. pagan and Christian burials, 10th–11th centuries; 4. marketplace, 10th–11th centuries; 5. remains of Roman buildings; 6. reconstructed roads, 10th–11th centuries

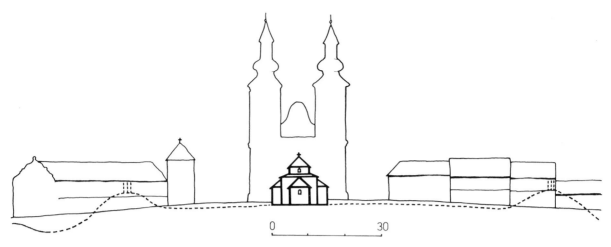

Fig. 23. Székesfehérvár, hillfort and St. Peter's church. North–south section, reconstructed. Late 10th century

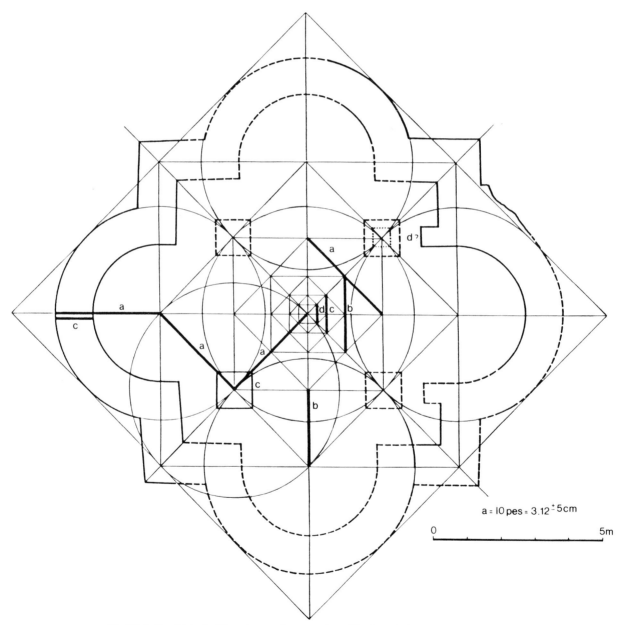

Fig. 24. Székesfehérvár. The scheme of construction of St. Peter's church. Reconstruction

80

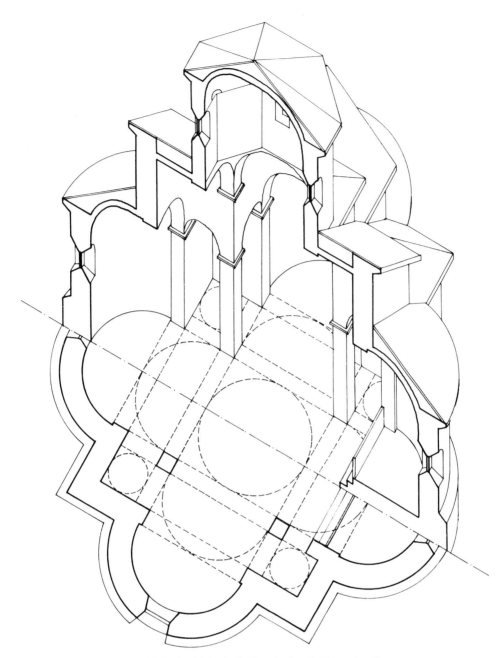

Fig. 25. Székesfehérvár, St. Peter's church. Reconstruction

poraneous imperial and princely dwelling places at Quedlingburg and Wawell.[125]

That the topographical centre of the town had shifted in the early 11th century is obvious considering the location of the 11th century royal basilica and provostship at the foot of the castle hill. The reason for this was that King Stephen could not have his own chapel and provostship (approximately 80×40 and 60×100 metres,

respectively) erected on the mound where his father's dwelling place and stone church had stood (the latter inference likewise contradicts the theories according to which the church where Géza had been buried was built by Stephen as his father's sepulchral chapel).[126]

Lack of space prevents us from a detailed review of the architectural history of the royal basilica, which was unearthed and filled on several occasions in the last century, and was then partly uncovered again in 1936–1938; it was opened to the public, and was finally

[125] H. Wäscher: *Der Burgberg in Quedlinburg.* Berlin (1959); A. Źaki: *Archaeologia Malopolski wczesnosredniewicznej (The medieval archaeology of Little Poland).* Cracow (1974).

[126] D. Dercsényi's kind oral communication, and also Györffy (1977) 102.

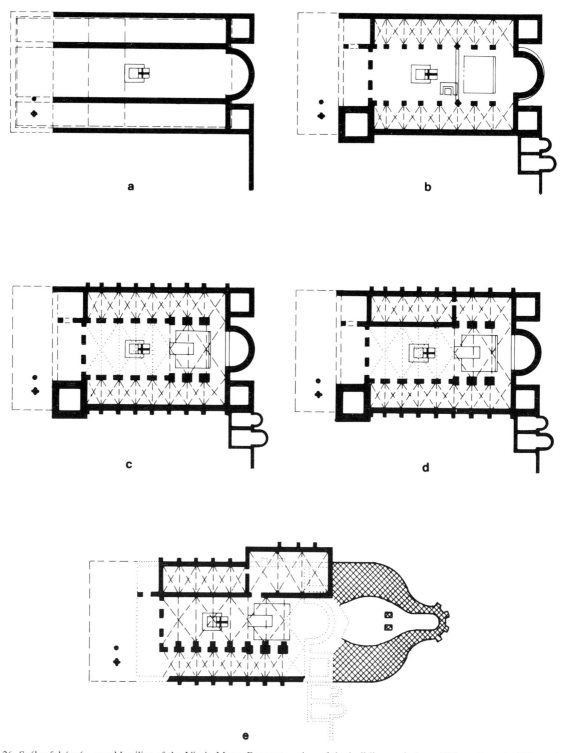

Fig. 26. Székesfehérvár, royal basilica of the Virgin Mary. Reconstruction of the building periods. a. 11th century; b. 12th century; c. 1318–1327; d. after 1349; e. late 15th century

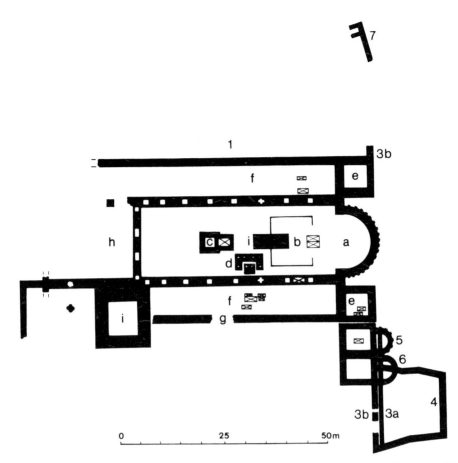

Fig. 27. Székesfehérvár, reconstructed groundplan of the provostship of the Virgin Mary, 1000–1318. 1. Basilica; a. sanctuary; b. choir; c. St. Stephen's crypt and cult place; d. pulpit; e. sacristy, treasury; f. side-aisles; g. assumed southern entrance; h. vestibule; i. podium of the *solium regni;* j. tower; 2. cemetery chapel, and later parish church of the Holy Cross, early 11th century; 3a–b. walls of the provostship, 11th century; 4. building of unknown function, court walls (?), storage rooms (?), 10th–11th centuries; 5. sepulchral chapel, around 1100; 6. sepulchral chapel, around 1200; 7. provostal residence, 11th century

excavated again between 1967–1972.[127] The above-named earliest stone structure and the number of burials antedating the building of the basilica by years or decades suggest that the inhabitants of the castle had used this area as their burial ground. The basilica, huge even on a European scale, was erected on the territory of this cemetery.[128] The date when the construction was begun is still controversial. There are no grounds for rejecting out of hand the close of the 10th century,[129] and

the possibility that work started as a result of the 1003–1004 donation is likewise acceptable.[130] Györffy definitely considers the years 1016–1018 as the date when the necessity of building a basilica there first arose following the inauguration of the road leading to the Holy Land which demonstrably passed through Fehér-vár, following the successful military campaigns in the Balkans.[131] According to the biography of St. Stephen, compiled by bishop Hartvik between 1112–1116, the basilica was still not consecrated in 1038.[132] Without

[127] D. Dercsényi: *A székesfehérvári királyi bazilika (The royal basilica of Székesfehérvár).* Budapest (1942), with an excellent summary and a review of earlier studies.

[128] A. Kralovánszky, *Alba Regia* 8–9 (1967) 253–262.

[129] A. Kralovánszky: A székesfehérvári királyi bazilika alapításának kérdéséhez (The foundation of the royal basilica of Székesfehérvár). *MFMÉ* (1966/67) 121–125.

[130] A. Kralovánszky: A székesfehérvári királyi bazilika alapításának és István királlyá koronázásának kérdéséről (The foundation of the royal basilica of Székesfehérvár and the coronation of King Stephen). *Fejér Megyei Szemle* 3 (1967) 48–54.

[131] Györffy (1977) 317–319.

[132] *SRH* II, 432.

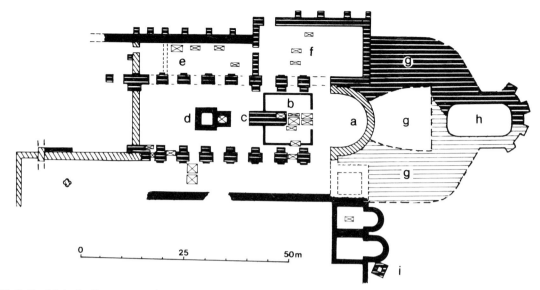

Fig. 28. Székesfehérvár. Reconstructed groundplan of the royal basilica of the Virgin Mary. 14th–15th centuries. a. Sanctuary; b. choir; c. podium of the *solium regni;* d. St. Stephen's crypt and cult place; e. St. Catherine's sepulchral chapel of King Louis the Great, after 1349; f. St. Anne's sepulchral chapel of grand provost Domonkos Kálmáncsehy, after 1475; g. enlargement by King Matthias, after 1475 (?); h. enlargement by King Matthias, the sanctuary of his sepulchral chapel, after 1475; i. tower (belltower?, watchtower?), 15th–16th centuries

challenging the credibility of local tradition, it is none-theless highly improbable that the 1031 burial of Prince St. Imre, demonstrably in this basilica, took place in a still not consecrated church.[133] This possibility is supported by the fact that in 1031 King Stephen and Queen Gizella donated a chasuble to this church (the inscription on the chasuble records this event).[134] Bishop Hartvik's remark may presumably be considered a reference to Stephen's far-reaching plans, mindful of the enormous dimensions of the basilica and the buildings of the provostship. The 11th century church had a circular-ended sanctuary, two square-ended side-aisles on the north and south and two other rooms added to each aisle. The three naves were separated by seven pairs of pillars and terminated in the west by an eighth pair of pillars linked at their points. Lack of sufficient data prevented the precise localization of the presumed *atrium* in the west. All we know is that its western termination must have been flush with the western façade of the still standing episcopal palace.[135] We have found no remains of the high altar, which must have stood at the meeting point of the nave and the circular-ended sanctuary. On the other hand, our excavations have brought to light the tomb of St. Stephen in the centre of the church and the remains of a cultic structure

adjoining it in the west. The choir with the royal tomb in its middle was situated between these two objects, level with the first and third pairs of pillars. The pulpit stood near the southern wall of the nave, between the third and fourth pairs of pillars.[136] The entrance of the patrons is presumed to have stood level with the fifth and sixth pair of pillars, i.e. it may have been perpendicular to the tomb of St. Stephen.[137] Adjoining this Romanesque basilica in the south were two buildings, presumably the sepulchral vaults of aristocrats. Each of these buildings had a nave and a circular-ended sanctuary.[138] The first chapel added to the building at the southeastern corner of the basilica, which had functioned as the treasury and archive, can be dated to 1100, and the second sepulchral chapel adjoining it in the south to the 1200s. Extending under the latter structure is the wall of an earlier building with asymmetric rectangular groundplan, or that of a fence. The function of this wall has not yet been established. This wall, and the two sepulchral chapels, were attached to the wall added to the eastern wall of the basilica and set level with it. We have also uncovered the remains of a double gate in this wall.[139] The demi-cupola of the sanctuary of the Romanesque basilica was tessellated, and the aisles were in all probability covered with open framework or straight timbered ceiling. The flooring was covered with hard limestone slabs. The

[133] For his burial in the basilica, cf. Leg. S. Emerici ducis. *SRH* II, 459.

[134] ANNO INCARNATIONIS CHRISTI MXXXI INDICTIONE XIIV A STEPHANO REGE ET GISELA REGINA CASULA HAEC OPERATA ET DATA ECCLESIAE SANCTA MARIAE SITAE IN CIVITATE ALBA.

[135] Cf. also H. Koller: A székesfehérvári királyi trónszék kérdése (The royal throne at Székesfehérvár). *Székesfehérvár Évszázadai* 2. Ed. by A. Kralovánszky. Székesfehérvár (1972) 7–20.

[136] A. Kralovánszky's excavation reports in *ArchÉrt* 99 (1972) 266–267, and *ArchÉrt* 100 (1973) 277.

[137] S. Tóth's reconstruction. Gy. Kristó–F. Makk–E. Marosi: *III. Béla emlékezete (The memory of King Béla III).* Budapest (1981) Fig. 47.

[138] A. Kralovánszky: Előzetes jelentés az 1965. évi székesfehérvári feltárásokról (Preliminary report of the excavations in Székesfehérvár in the year 1965). *Alba Regia* 8–9 (1967) 253–262.

[139] *Ibid.*

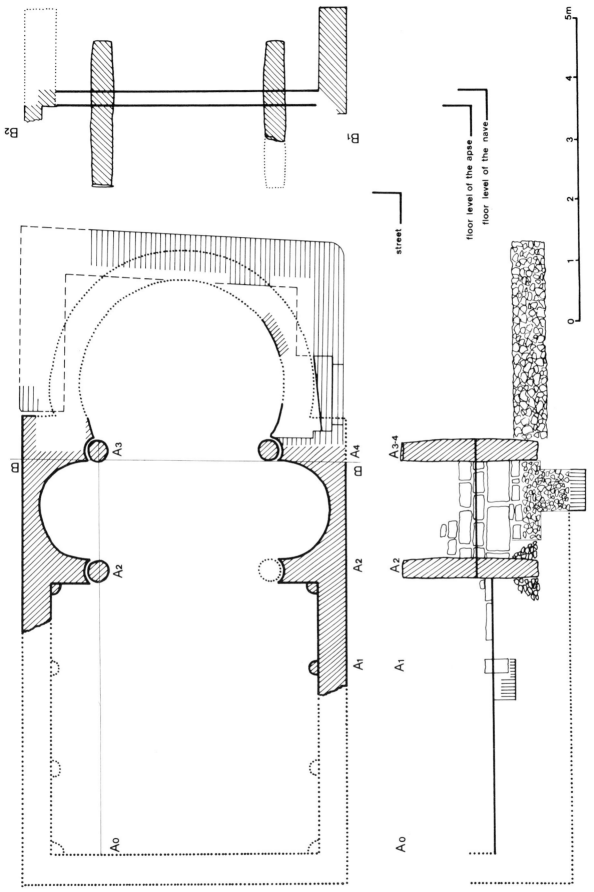

Fig. 29. Székesfehérvár, chapel of the Holy Cross of the provostship of the Virgin Mary, early 11th century–15th century. Groundplan and sections

85

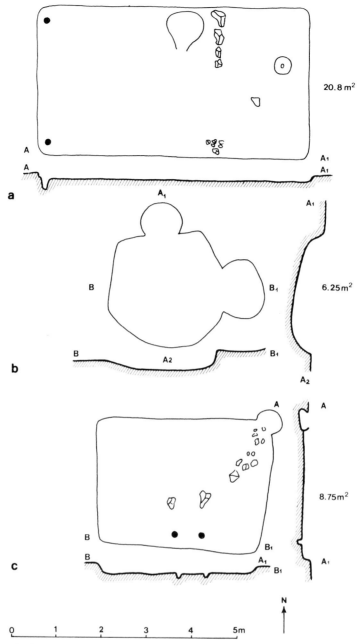

Fig. 30. Székesfehérvár, semi-subterranean huts. a. Near St. Peter's cathedral, 13th century; b–c. Móri street, near the Buda
*suburbium*, 10th–11th century

area of the tomb of St. Stephen and the cultic place was
decorated with a mosaic flooring of white marble and
red brick, representing the colours of the family.[140]

In 1318 King Charles Robert had an arched ceiling
built in the basilica, and simultaneously the pillars were
immured. In all probability it was during this reconstruction that the structure surrounding the choir was enlarged and a large-size podium was erected in the centre
of the western wall of the choir. This podium, presumably the place of the *solium regni*, was furnished with a

canopy.[141] The destruction by fire of the basilica's
roof-timbers in 1327 was presumably followed by minor
alterations.[142] Between 1349–1374 King Louis the Great
had an enclosed sepulchral chapel built in the western
half of the northern side-aisle for himself, his father and
his family.[143] In the late 15th century King Matthias

---

[140] Its photograph is published in Kralovánszky (1972) 1561.

[141] The place of a pillar (?) or column (?) could be observed
in each longitudinal foundation wall.

[142] *SRH* I, 491.

[143] *Monumenta Hungarica* 4 (1960) 78; A. Kralovánszky:
A székesfehérvári Anjou sírkápolna (The sepulchral chapel of

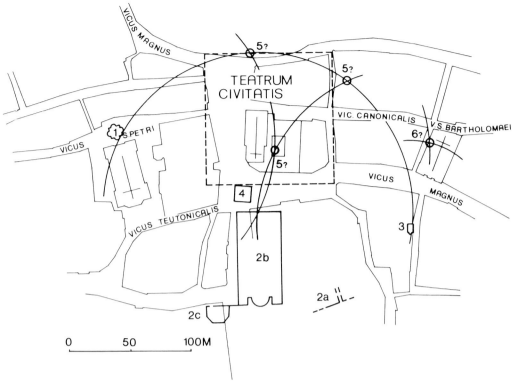

Fig. 31. Székesfehérvár–Centre, reconstruction of the settlement structure in the 10th–15th centuries. 1. St. Peter's church, 10th–13th centuries; 2a. palace of the provostship of the Virgin Mary, 11th–16th centuries; 2b. basilica of the Virgin Mary, 11th–14th centuries; 2c. court of the provostship (?), storage rooms (?), 11th–12th centuries; 3. chapel of the Holy Cross of the provostship of the Virgin Mary; 11th–16th centuries; 4. tower, 3rd–4th–18th centuries; 5. St. Emerich's chapel, 12th–16th centuries; 6. St. Bertalan's chapel (?), 13th–16th centuries; (?)

launched work to extend the building between the partly demolished town wall and the eastern sanctuary of the basilica, but his death prevented him from completing it. His plans involved the construction in the principal axis of the eastern extension (which was approximately 2 metres higher than the original ground level) of his own sepulchra chapel, and also of three chapels in the north and south (the groundwalls of these have survived). The last Hungarian king to be buried in the basilica was János Zápolyai (1540).[144] His burial place can probably be identified with the brick grave in the hollow in the northeastern corner of the podium.[145] In the Late Middle Ages three royal brick graves were built beside the three other Romanesque royal brick graves in the choir. Besides the tomb of St. Stephen, the

burial of King Béla III and his wife, Anne of Antioch, have been found and identified in the basilica. The latter burials were situated near the third pillar in the southern side-aisle. The plundered brick grave which still contained human bones found in the northern side-aisle, level with the sixth and seventh pillars, can most probably be identified with that of King Louis the Great and his two wives.[146] In the late 15th century the provost of the basilica, Domonkos Kálmáncsehi, had a new chapel built between the first and third pillars in the eastern half of the norther side-aisle in honour of St. Anne.[147]

The groundwalls of the Romanesque basilica were built of large-size Roman limestone ashlars and contained various architectonical mouldings. From the

the Angevins at Székesfehérvár). *Művészet I. Lajos király korában 1342–1382.* Ed. by E. Marosi–M. Tóth–L. Varga. Budapest (1982) 165–174.

[144] Cf. E. Marosi: Mátyás király székesfehérvári sírkápolnája (The sepulchral chapel of King Matthias at Székesfehérvár). *Székesfehérvár Évszázadai* 2. Ed. by A. Kralovánszky. Székesfehérvár (1972) 169–184.

[145] Presumably because the podium was no longer used as the setting of the royal throne. The grave that had been built from bricks that differed from Gothic ones both in their colour and in dimensions, was cut into the crushed-stone foundation of the podium.

[146] A. Kralovánszky's report in *Ars Hungarica* 3 (1975) 318. The red marble carvings recovered from this grave were parts of the carvings that were earlier indentified as the tomb of King Louis I and were instrumental for Ernő Szakál's reconstruction: A székesfehérvári Anjou síremlékek és I. Lajos király sírkápolnája. A rekonstrukciók adatai és lehetőségei (The Angevin tombs at Székesfehérvár and the sepulchral chapel of King Louis I. Data and possibilities for reconstruction). *Művészet I. Lajos király korában 1342–1382.* Ed. by E. Marosi–M. Tóth–L. Varga. Budapest (1982) 175–179, cf. P. Lővei: A székesfehérvári Anjou sírkápolna művészettörténeti helye (The art historical significance of the sepulchral chapel of the Angevins at Székesfehérvár). *Ibid.,* 184–203.

[147] Fitz (1955) 69; for the exact location cf. note 143.

87

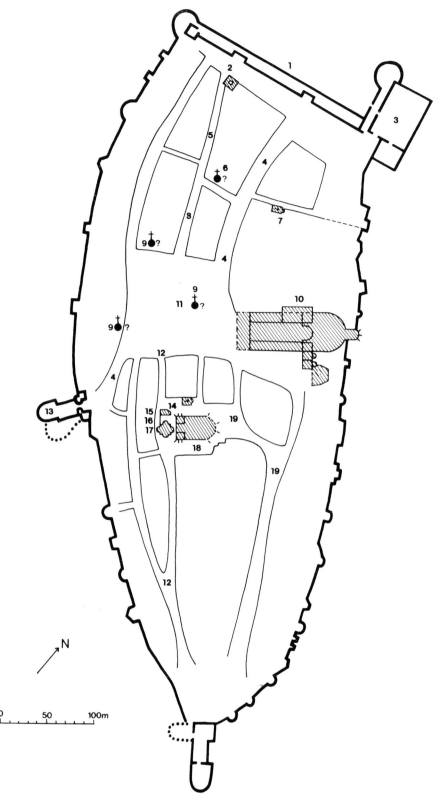

Fig. 32. Székesfehérvár–*Castrum*, topographical reconstruction, 972–1601. 1. Castle wall, 13th(?)–16th centuries; 2. tower (?), salt depot (?), 13th century (?); 3. Buda gate, 13th(?)–16th centuries; 4. *vicus magnus*, 10th–16th centuries; 5. St. Bertalan street (?), 13th century; 6. St. Bertalan's chapel (?), 13th century (?); 7. church of the Holy Cross of the provostship of the Virgin Mary, 11th–16th centuries; 8. Canon street (?), 13th–16th centuries (?); 9. St. Emerich's chapel, 12th–16th centuries; 10. royal basilica of the Virgin Mary, 11th–16th centuries; 11. marketplace, 10th–16th centuries; 12. St. Peter street, 13th–16th centuries; 13. palace gate, 13th(?)–16th centuries; 14. sepulchral chapel of St. Peter's church (built by a burgher called Hentel around 1470); 15. *ossarium*, 13th(?)–16th centuries; 16. stone wall, 10th–12th centuries; 17. St. Peter's church, 972–1225; 18. St. Peter's cathedral, 1235–16th century; Német street (?), 14th–16th centuries

88

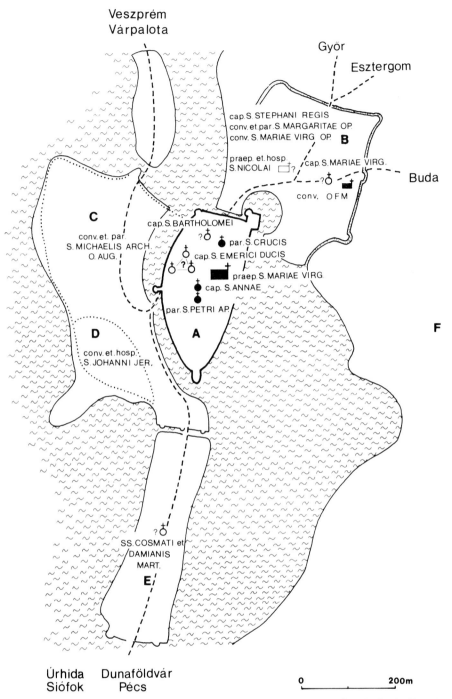

Fig. 33. Topographical reconstruction of Székesfehérvár and its *suburbia*, 11th–16th centuries. A. Castle; B. *civitas exterior;* C. *nova civitas* (?); D. *insula* (?); E. Ingovány; F. *nova villa*

surviving remains of the outer surface of the ascending wall of the northern side-aisle and the recently unearthed lesenes on the northern outer side of the main apse it is infered that the ascending walls were built of soft sandstone and carved ashlar.[148]

[148] Altogether 17 lesenes could be reconstructed on the basis of the 4 which have survived *in situ.*

The uncovered remains of the building complex which had housed the provostship do not offer a sound basis for reconstructing its groundplan and dimensions. According to a French engraving dating from 1601 and considered authentic, the structures built collaterally with the eastern castle wall had yet another building added to them in the west which, together with a presumed fence, formed an enclosed unit with an inner

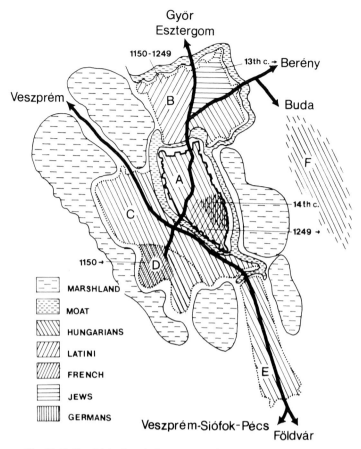

Fig. 34. Székesfehérvár, ethnic reconstruction, 11th–16th centuries

courtyard.[149] In the course of the 1979 excavations we found the demolished remains of a north–south wall. This wall, built of crushed stone and set with yellow gravel, was not perpendicular to the principal axis of the basilica. We also found another 1 metre wide wall which ran parellel with the north–south wall. It was built of long, flat ashlars set on a crushed stone foundation, and had two extensions towards the west. These walls had demonstrably been in use until the end of the 18th century. On the strength of the stratigraphical observations and various small finds recovered there they can be assigned to the Árpádian Age.[150] Further excavations are planned at the site to elucidate the function of this structure.

The excavations in 1972 north of this building complex have brought to light a single-aisled church with three-apsidal ends. This church, built of sandstone ashlars, had crushed stone foundations and terrazzo flooring. It had two conchae at the northern and southern meeting point of the sanctuary and the nave. Each of these conchae were supported by four Roman pillars made of hard limestone. Three of these pillars, used secondarily but according to their original function, have survived *in situ*. The fourth pillar, of which only the place could be observed, was presumably built of sandstone column-drums at the time of the construction of the church. The horseshoe-shaped sanctuary was pulled down in the Middle Ages and was rebuilt as a straight one. A two-stepped entrance was built in its southern wall. The area south of the church has yielded east–west oriented inhumation burials with no grave goods. The church was identified with the parish church of the Holy Cross that is mentioned in a 1419 source as the church of the cemetery of the royal basilica. This church and the above-mentioned St. Peter's church (used as a parish church after 1249) were the only parish churches in the medieval castle. It had probably served the church and secular people in the provostship. On the strength of certain historical, among others form-historical, considerations, this unparalleled church can be assigned to the first half of the 11th century.[151] These parish churches were generally frequented by people who inhabited semi-subterranean huts, and not stone houses.

[149] J. Fitz: Francia metszet Székesfehérvár 1601. évi ostro-máról (The 1601 siege of Székesfehérvár in a French engraving). *Alba Regia* 8–9 (1967–68) 149–154.

[150] I wish to thank Jenő Fitz, the director of the István Király Museum and Imre Kisberk, the Roman Catholic Bishop for their generous support throughout the campaigns.

[151] A. Kralovánszky: Székesfehérvár István király korában (Székesfehérvár under King Stephen). *Alba Regia* 12 (1972) 277–278; K. Éry: An Anthropological Sketch of Árpádian Age Burials at the Holy Crucifix Church in Székesfehérvár. *Alba Regia* 16 (1978) 159–167.

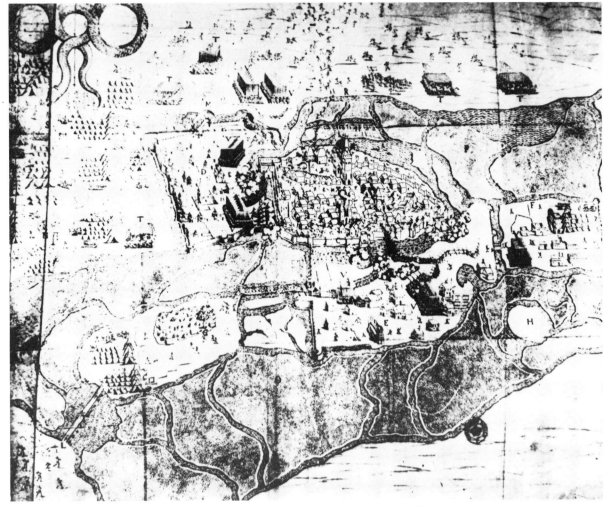

Fig. 35. Székesfehérvár, French engraving, before 1605.

We know that a chapel of St. Imre stood within the medieval *castrum* which had been looked after by the canons of the provostship and which can be traced back to the last third of the 12th century. The chapel, whose location could not be determined, may have stood in the immediate vicinity of the basilica, on the spot where the new Franciscan church and monastery were erected after the Turkish occupation in the middle or at the edge of the medieval marketplace.[152]

A charter dating from the second half of the 15th century refers to a church consecrated to St. Bertalan. Since Bertalan was the patron saint of the salt transporters and, according to 13th century charters, Fehérvár was one of the main salt distributing centres in Transdanubia, we can date the building of this church to the Early Middle Ages. On the evidence of the 15th–16th century charters and other considerations, it must have stood in the northwestern quarter of the inner town.[153]

Facilitating the research into the medieval topography and architectural history of the town are the traces of the medieval streets, 90 per cent of which have survived.[154] An ethnic reconstruction is also possible on the basis of the evidence of the charters (Fig. 34).

[152] Cf. Kovács (1972) 262.
[153] We observed the remains of a thick-walled tower during the construction of the house at the intersection of Ady Endre and Zalka Máté Streets. Cf. Kovács (1972) 267.

[154] Some of these streets were identified by Fügedi (1969) 130 and L. Nagy: Székesfehérvár középkori topográfiája (Medieval topography of Székesfehérvár). *Székesfehérvár Évszázadai* 2. Ed. by A. Kralovánszky. Székesfehérvár (1972) 199–209. I have already published an outline of our theory: Az ezeréves Székesfehérvár (Thousand-year old Székesfehérvár). *Természet Világa* 8 (1972) 340. This possibilily is further supported by the fact that in 1546 the Turks disposed of a number of plots and houses in the castle: A. Velics–E. Kammerer: *Magyarországi török kincstári defterek (Defters of the Turkish treasury in Hungary)*. Vol. II. Budapest (1890) 50. Within the castle, their route was: Sziget gate (Palotai gate), Disznó Street (butcher's stalls were situated in the *Vicus Teutonicalis!*), the cathedral area (the block of the basilica and the provostship), Káptalan Street (southern half of Máté Zalka Street), Zsidó Street (Jókai Street?), Csiszár Street (Ady Endre Street?), Város Street (*Vicus magnus*, today Március 15 Street), Péter Street (*Vicus S. Petri*, today Arany J. Street).

Fig. 36. Székesfehérvár–*Castrum*. Detail of the French engraving

The wall encircling the medieval town is known from a military engineer's record drawn in 1601. It is rather difficult to date to this wall, but in all probability it was already standing in the early 15th century. The excavations conducted at the meeting point of the 17th century 'monastery bastion' and the medieval castle wall could only establish that the wall, built of large ashlars, had a 20×20 cm beam as its foundation, obviously on account of the waterlogged soil. We could not define the function of the wide north–south oriented crushed stone wall which we found on the site during an earlier excavation. This wall had tapered beams, 30–40 cm in diameter, driven vertically into the soil, as its foundation.[155]

The medieval castle wall was enclosed by a moat. The suburs: *Civitas exterior* to the north, *Insula* and *Nova civitas* to the west, *Ingovány* ('Bog') to the south, and *Nova villa* to the east, lay beyond the moat.[156]

The so-called Buda suburb and the island each had a hospital from the late 12th century, which can be associated with the above-described increase in the importance of the commercial and pilgrims' road there. The former hospital belonged to the provostship of St. Nicholas,[157] while the latter to the St. Stephen convent of the Johannines.[158] On the evidence of the archaeological data both hospitals could be located to within 200 metres.[159]

---

From the castle they proceeded towards the Island, then to Ingovány and finally to the Buda suburb. These data, together with the land registers dating from the turn of the 17th–18th centuries and an 1828 map, apparently support the assumption that there was an alley or street which connected the middle of Zalka M. Street with present-day Jókai Street, and thus the northern half of Zalka M. Street may have been named differently than the southern half, which in our opinion was called St. Bertalan Street. A 1478 source mentions an old tower near one of the plots in Bertalan Street. This tower can perhaps be identified with the one mentioned in note 153. Consequently, the church of St. Bertalan may have stood in the capitular district of the town, in the plot of today's Cistercian church, an assumption also supported by the fact that in 1688 Antal Vánossy built the former church of the Cistercians "in the area of a Turkish mosque" (Károly (1891) 202), i.e. there must have been a church there in the Middle Ages.

[155] A. Kralovánszky, *ArchÉrt* 97 (1970) 322.

[156] A more detailed description of the suburbs would require further written or archaeological proofs. Cf. Kovács (1972).

[157] Fügedi (1969) 120–124; Gy. Györffy: A székesfehérvári latinok betelepülésének kérdése (The settlement of the Latins in Székesfehérvár). *Székesfehérvár évszázadai 2.* Ed. By A. Kralovánszky. Székesfehérvár (1972) 41–42.

[158] Mezey (1972). Jenő Major noted that the archishop of Esztergom may have founded a convent of the Johannines on the Island in the mid-12th century since that territory was part of his estate. We have to agree with this assumption since the archbishop of Esztergom demonstrably owned 'palaces' in Székesfehérvár (*CD* VIII/1, 183), and the first building of the Johannines may be plausibly identified with one of these (the archbishop may have resided there on the occasion of royal coronations, marriages or burials).

[159] During the building operations in Honvéd Street we discovered the cemetery of the St. Nicholas provostship, which contained burials without grave goods. The buildings of the Johannines are still being excavated by Gy. Siklósi.

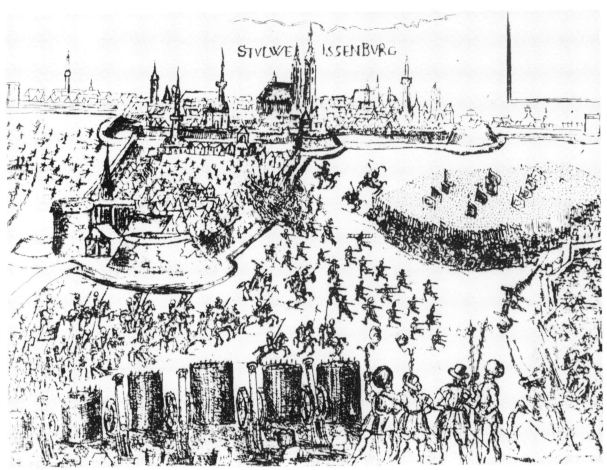

Fig. 37. Székesfehérvár. Engraving by W. P. Zimmermann, before 1605.

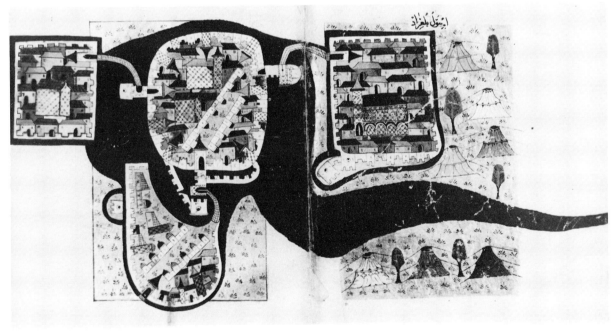

Fig. 38. Székesfehérvár. Matrakci Nasuhs chronicle, around 1543.

93

The 13th–15th centuries saw the construction of the parish church and cloister consecrated to St. Margaret, another Dominican cloister consecrated to the Blessed Virgin, the Franciscan cloister whose patron saint is not known and the chapels of the Blessed Virgin and of St. Stephen in the Buda suburb. Lack of archaeological excavations prevents the definition of their exact location. The written sources reveal little more about this suburb than that its population perhaps included Latin people between 1147 and 1249, and that Jews had also settled there from the 13th century.[160]

Besides the above-mentioned church of the Johannines, the other structures known to have stood on the island west of the castle include the St. Michael parish church and an Augustan cloister. These buildings could not be located either.[161]

The southern suburb, or more precisely village, also had a church. If we identify the settlement of Ingovány with this settlement it follows that the church with one tower depicted in Turkish period engravings was consecrated to St. Cosmas and Damianus.[162]

The suburbs had no defensive stone walls. They were defended by palisaded fences along the edge of the marshland and at the foot of the island-like elevations.

The canonical status of the town was particularly complicated in the Middle Ages. The authority over the basilica and the attached provostship, established as the king's 'own chapel' and consecrated to the Assumption of the Blessed Virgin, was transferred in 1181 from the archbishop of Esztergom to the Holy See in Rome, i.e. it obtained an exclusive jurisdiction over the regionally competent bishopric of Veszprém.[163] Indicative of the Holy See's privileged status is the fact that in the 13th century the papal cardinal legate fixed the number of these canons as 40 persons[164] (in the 14th–15th centuries the chapter of the Veszprém bishopric had 36, while that of the Esztergom archbishopric had 39 canons). According to a 13th century source, the private chapel of the ruling dynasty had possessory right, traceable to the 11th century, over 27 churched villages. By the 1330s this number was increased to 61. Consequently, it must have played an important role in the economy of the country.[165] The Johannines enjoyed a separate legal status: they were subjected to the archbishop of Esztergom as from the foundation of their order. All the other churched settlements in the region—including the St. Peter and perhaps also the St. Bertalan churches in the castle—were subjected to the bishop of Veszprém. The Dominicans, the Franciscans and the Augustans were subjected to the pope through their respective grand chapel or the college of cardinals.

The aim of the present paper was to shed light on the similarities between the birth and early-period development of Veszprém and Székesfehérvár, and also on their economic and social potentials that led to their divergent development. These circumstances served primarily to the advantage of Székesfehérvár. The evidence offered by archaeological investigations and its collation with the results of European settlement historical research proved to be instrumental in elucidating the history of these two towns. Further investigation undeniably calls for further intensive archaeological research in both towns, since the written sources apparently cannot provide further clues on the history and art of Veszprém and Székesfehérvár—two towns which had played a decisive role in the evolution and development of the state and the church of Hungary.[166]

REFERENCES

Adám, I. (1912): A veszprémi székesegyház (The cathedral of Veszprém). Veszprém.
Bakay, K. (1966): Gräberfelder aus den 10-11. Jahrhunderten in der Umgebung von Székesfehérvár und die Frage der fürstlichen Residenz. I. Alba Regia 6–7, 43–88.
Bakay, K. (1968): Gräberfelder aus den 10–11. Jahrhunderten in der Umgebung von Székesfehérvár und die Frage der fürstlichen Residenz. II. Alba Regia 8–9, 57–84.
Békefi, R. (1912): Veszprém a középkorban (Veszprém in the Middle Ages). Veszprém múltja és jelene. Ed. by K. Hornig. Veszprém, 3–32.
Erdélyi, L. (1902): A pannonhalmi főapátság története (History of the Pannonhalma Abbey). Budapest.
Éri, I. (1972): Veszprém. Budapest.
Fitz, J. (1955): Székesfehérvár középkorához (The medieval history of Székesfehérvár). Fehérvár 1, 66.
Fraknói, V.–Lukcsics, J. (1896–1907): Monumenta Romana episcopatus Wesprimensis I–IV. Budapest.
Fügedi, E. (1967): Székesfehérvár középkori alaprajza és a polgárság kezdetei Magyarországon (The medieval groundplan of Székesfehérvár and the emergence of burghers in Hungary). Településtörténeti Közlemények 20, 31–45.
Fügedi, E. (1969): Der Stadtplan von Stuhlweissenburg und die Anfänge des Bürgertums in Ungarn. Acta Historica 15, 103–136.
Gutheil, J. (1977): Az Árpád-kori Veszprém (Veszprém in the Árpádian Age). Veszprém.
Györffy, Gy. (1958): A magyar nemzetségtől a vármegyéig, a törzstől az államig. (From clan to county, from tribe to country). Századok 92 (1958) 12–87, 565–615.
Györffy, Gy. (1967): Székesfehérvár feltűnése a történeti forrásokban (Early references to Székesfehérvár in histori-

[160] J. Fitz: Székesfehérvár. Budapest (1966): Fügedi (1969).
[161] ZsO, 759.
[162] Kralovánszky (1972) 1563. G. Fehér jr.: A magyar történelem 16. századi török ábrázolásai (16th century Turkish depictions of Hungarian history). Székesfehérvár Évszázadai 3. Ed. by A. Kralovánszky. Székesfehérvár (1977) 57.
[163] According to Györffy (1977) 319 the Holy See only "protected" but "did not obtain ownership of" the nullius, independent church in the 12th century. Mezey (1972) 28 takes the opposite view.
[164] 1234. CD IV/I, 215.
[165] Mezey (1972) 25.

[166] We plan to return to various questions not surveyed in the present paper in another study. For a survey of recent results see A. Kralovánszky: Neuere Angaben zur mittelalterliche Siedlungsgebiet von Székesfehérvár. Paper read at the 2nd British–Hungarian Conference on the history of medieval towns, Budapest (1982), and Neuere Siedlungs- und Baudaten aus dem 10. Jahrhundert. Paper read at the conference Hungarians and Slavs Along the Danube in the 10th century. Linz (1983).

cal sources). *Székesfehérvár évszázadai* 1. Ed. by A. Kralovánszky. Székesfehérvár, 19–25.

Györffy, Gy. (1969): A magyar egyházszervezés kezdeteiről (The beginnings of church organizations in Hungary). *MTA II OK* 18, 214–219.

Györffy, Gy. (1970): A honfoglaló magyarok települési rendje (The settlement system of the Magyar tribes in the Conquest period). *ArchÉrt* 97, 191–242.

Györffy, Gy. (1973): Budapest története az Árpád-korban (History of Budapest in the Árpádian Age). *Budapest története az őskortól az Árpád-kor végéig.* Ed. by L. Gerevich. Budapest, 217–294.

Györffy, Gy. (1977): *István király és műve (King Stephen and his work).* Budapest.

Györffy, Gy. (1987): *Az Árpád-kori Magyarország történeti földrajza (The historical geography of Árpádian Age Hungary).* II. Budapest 363–384.

Gyürky, K. (1963): Die St. Georg-Kapella in der Burg von Veszprém. *ActaArchHung* 15, 341–386.

Heckenast, G. (1970): *Fejedelmi (királyi) szolgáló népek a korai Árpád-korban (Princely (royal) servants in the early Árpádian Age).* Értekezések a történettudomány köréből 53. Budapest.

Karácsonyi, J. (1891): *Szent István oklevelei és a Szilveszter bulla (Charters of St. Stephen and the Sylvester Bull).* Budapest.

Károly, J. (1898): *Fejér megye története. Székesfehérvár története (History of Fejér County. History of Székesfehérvár).* Székesfehérvár.

Komjáthy, M. (1973): A veszprémvölgyi alapítólevél kibocsáj-tójáról (The issuer of the Veszprém valley deed of foundation). *LevKözl* 42, 33–49.

Korompay, Gy. (1957): *Veszprém.* Budapest.

Kovács, P. (1972): Megjegyzések Székesfehérvár középkori topográfiájának kutatásához (Research into the medieval topography of Székesfehérvár). *Alba Regia* 12, 261–267.

Kralovánszky, A. (1972): Az ezeréves Székesfehérvár korai története (The early history of millennial Székesfehérvár). *Élet és Tudomány* 33, 1556–1563.

Kumorovitz, L. B. (1953): *Veszprémi regeszták (Veszprém abstracts), 1301–1387.* Budapest.

Mályusz, E. (1953): A mezővárosi fejlődés (The emergence of market towns). *Tanulmányok a parasztság történetéhez Magyarországon a XIV. században.* Ed. by. Gy. Székely. Budapest, 128–191.

Mezey, L. (1972): Székesfehérvár egyházi intézményei a középkorban (Church institutions in Székesfehérvár during the Middle Ages). *Székesfehérvár Évszázadai* 2. Ed. by A. Kralovánszky. Székesfehérvár, 21–34.

Pauler, Gy. (1893): *A magyar nemzet története az Árpád-házi királyok alatt (History of the Hungarian nation under the Árpád Dynasty).* Budapest.

Tóth, S. (1963): A veszprémi székesegyház középkori kőfarag-ványai (Medieval stone carvings from the cathedral of Veszprém). *VMMK* 1, 115–141.

Vajay, Sz. (1967): Géza nagyfejedelem és családja (Grand Duke Géza and his family). *Székesfehérvár Évszázadai* 1. Ed. by A. Kralovánszky. Székesfehérvár, 63–100.

Wertner, M. (1892): *Az Árpádok családi története (History of the Árpád Dynasty).* Nagybecskerek.

# THE DEVELOPMENT AND TOPOGRAPHY OF SOPRON IN THE MIDDLE AGES

IMRE HOLL

The comparison of information gained from the town plan, the historical sources and the results of archaeological investigations show that Sopron does not belong to the group of towns of Hungary for which, similarly to the western *civitates* (even if with differring characteristics),[1] a possible course of development was stimulated by the existence of separate commercial settlements of artisans and *latini* added to an episcopal see or a regal castle. In the 13th and 14th centuries this latter part of these settlements grew continuously, and often became the actual town centre, moreover, they also became separated from the castle topographically (e. g. Esztergom, Vác, and to a lesser degree, Győr and Pécs). Although the historiography of Sopron often assumed a similar process, the excavations of the past two decades have yielded a different picture.

Here, too, the forerunner was a Roman settlement which at the close of the 1st century rose to the rank of town (Scarbantia), parts of which were given up as a consequence of the increasingly frequent raids; its centre was surrounded by a town wall at the beginning of the 4th century. Some of the still inhabited stone houses were demolished in the 3rd century and were used to build a town wall covered with ashlars 3 m thick. The wall had a regular plan with 39 towers, two of which were gatehouses on the northern and southern side. Following the decline in the 5th century (after the destruction at an unknown date), the town was abandoned for some time. Excavations have not discovered traces indicative of settlement or finds from the late Migration period so far. This stratigraphical level was formed by Roman debris, black humus and peat. (This abandonment may provide an explanation for the German name of the settlement: Ödenburg.[1a])

The state forming Hungarian royal power organised the country into a network of counties, each with its own seat and the fortress of the *comes* (governor of the regal castle). The *castrum Suprun* had thus evolved at the beginning of the 11th century. Similarly to other county seats, it was named after its first *comes*. The archaeological excavations of the past two decades have clarified the location of the fortress of the *comes* and the fortification system. The fortification wall was constructed of massive wooden trunks arranged in a chamber construction, bolstered with earth to a width of 20 m and a height of at least 5 m. Analogies to this fortification type are known from Central Europe from the 10th–11th centuries, the best examples being from the Kiev principality and the town of Kiev itself.[2] The earthen bank was supported by the inner side of the Roman town wall and it not only followed its line, but also used its surviving 2–3 m high remains as an outside cover. On the basis of the recovered pottery, its construction can be dated to the 11th century, which corresponds to the historical process. Little is known of the life of the *comes* inside the castle. Traces indicative of houses built around a framework of wooden posts with wattle and daub walls have only been observed in three spots so far.[3] We know that the fortress of the *comes* had two gates: the northern one over the spot of the former Roman gate, the eastern one on a new spot, since the medieval road leading southeast deviated from the former Roman road. On the testimony of local

---

[1] The dualism of *civitas* and *burgus* was first discussed by Rietschel, Rörig, Pirenn, Ganshof and Ennen (1897–1953). The legal status of the Hungarian towns listed here differed from their western contemporaries and their topography also differed. For a comparison and an analysis of divergences, see Fügedi (1969) 101–118, esp. 108. Fügedi termed the towns of the 11th–12th centuries 'towns of the nomadic type' ('Städte asiatischen-nomadischen Typs') owing to their differing traits. L. Gerevich: Die mittelalterlichen Städte im Zentrum Ungarns. *Vor- und Frühformen der europäischen Stadt im Mittelalter* I–II. Göttingen (1974) 258ff, does not accept this term.

[1a] Former research explained the name Ödenburg by suggesting the existence of an earlier hillfort ('Burg') north of the settlement, the existence of which has not yet been proven. K. Mollay; *Scarbantia, Ödenburg, Sopron.* Budapest (1944). After excavating the Roman town wall we realized that this name probably denotes the deserted Roman town.

[2] For the discovery of the earthwork see Tomka (1976) 391–410. For the Roman town see K. Sz. Póczy: Die Anfänge der Urbanization in Scarbantia. *ActaArchHung* 23 (1971) 93–110.

[3] Tomka (1976). See also Gömöri (1976) 421–422.

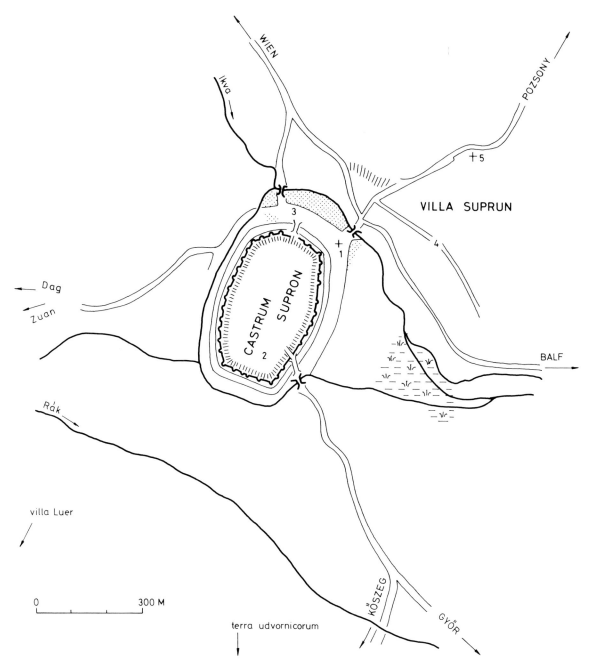

Fig. 1. Sopron. The fortress of the *comes* and its environment in the 11th–12th century. 1. Church of the Holy Virgin, marketplace; 2. Salt market — Salzmarkt; 3. Smiths' street — Schmiedgasse, suburb; 4. Fishermen's street — Fischergasse; 5. St. Michael parish church

topographical data, the house of the *comes* probably stood within the northern gate, and the salt market ('Salzmarkt') was near the other gate in the southeastern part of the fortress.[4]

Immediately in front of the northern side of the fortress there probably lay the small settlement of the smiths bound to the performance of various duties; that of the fishermen was northeast of the fortress, beyond the brook. Both places are indicated by the profession names (preserved as street names), since at the beginning of the 15th century — to which the earliest written

[4] K. Mollay discussed several topographical issues in his history of Sopron, published in *Sopron és környéke műemlékei (Monuments in and around Sopron)*. Ed. by D. Dercsényi. Budapest (1956²). This study, however, was written prior to the archaeological investigations, and thus reached differring con-

clusions on several topographical questions such as the location of the fortress of the *comes*.

97

Fig. 2. The town walls (R: Roman town walls, remains of the earthwork ditch, II: 1330–1340)

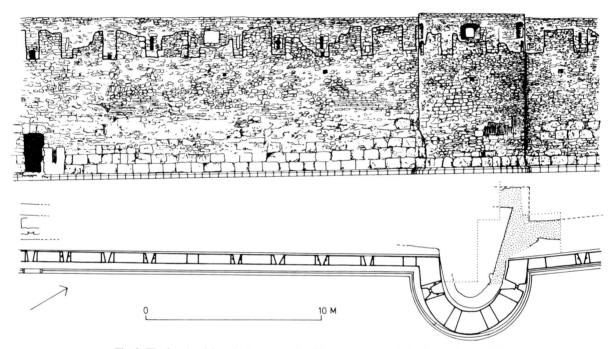

Fig. 3. The façade of the middle town wall, with the pediment of the Roman town wall

records can be assigned — men of these professions no longer lived in these quarters. Further on, to the northeast of the fortress stood the parish church of St. Michael (first mentioned in 1278) of the village settlement (*villa Suprun*, 1156, 1199).[5]

Several smaller villages lay in the close environs of the county seat. Evidence for ironworking and smithies have been reported from two of them.[6]

The town plan would indicate that the marketplace lay beside the northeastern side of the fortress and the church of the Blessed Virgin (mentioned from 1278) that once stood there was the church of the fortress. Its position was also favourable in view of the inhabitants of neighbouring settlements who frequented the market and the merchant stalls. The study of the routes taken by the long-distance roads through Sopron (several of which correspond to the Roman roads) reveals that although they conspicuously lead to the *castrum*, they pass under it. This phenomenon can perhaps be explain-

[5] Earlier investigations gave various reasons for the location of the parish church in the suburb (deliberate separation from the fortress of the *comes*, former and/or orthodox Christian tradition, transference of the church, etc.). See Házi (1939). J. Major: Hozzászólás a "Sopron és környéke műemlékei" c. könyvhöz (Comments on the volume "Monuments in and around Sopron"). *Településtudományi Közlemények* (1953) 94–112 (with a critique of the relevant topographical issues). For comments, see Gy. Nováki: A soproni Várhely ásatásának története (The history of the excavations at Sopron–Várhely). *Soproni Szemle* 9 (1955), and Mollay (1956) 34–42. Mollay thought *villa Supron* to have been the first settlement built on the plain which was later fortified. See Mollay (1956) 42–43. For an explanation for the simultaneous use of *villa* and *castrum*, see B. Surányi: Az Árpád-kori Sopron topog-

ráfiájának kérdéséhez (The topography of Sopron in the Árpádian Age). *Történelmi Szemle* (1961) 220–223.

[6] Gömöri (1976) 412–420. Finds of the 10th century were recovered from the smithies. The population of certain neighbouring villages known only by their name today were obliged for services and provision of the fortress.

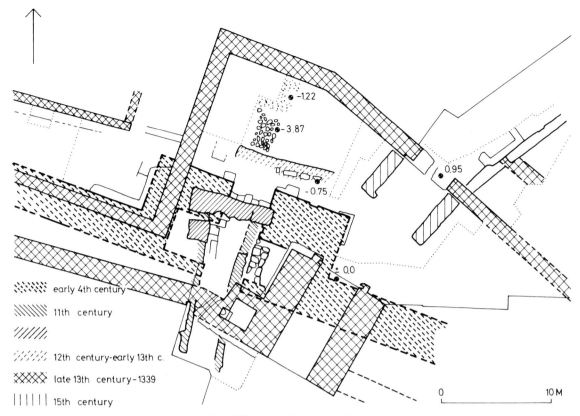

Fig. 4. The building periods of the northern town gate

ed by the defence system: unlike the Roman towns which were open to roads, medieval fortresses were closed to roads, but they nonetheless controlled the traffic (Fig. 1).[7]

It is thus fairly obvious that the location of the *castrum* of the county seat was primarily influenced by the favourable topographical position, the road network and the Roman town walls which were well suited to defensive purposes.

The archaeological and historical investigations of the past 20 years have revealed that the early topography of Sopron shares numerous similarities with that of other county seats and centres: a fortress and a set of more or less related settlements.[8]

These seats had undergone a significant development by the middle of the 13th century. The ultimate result was the emergence of independent medieval towns (also

in the legal sense of the word). At the same time, topographical development often took diverse paths.[9]

The development of Sopron is not known in detail due to the scarcity of the evidence; nonetheless, major tendencies can be reconstructed from the building activity of the 13th century (1247: the settlement of Johannite knights in the northern suburb; the building of the funerary chapel of St. James near the parish church in the middle of the 13th century). Accordingly, the suburbian settlement appears to have grown considerably.[10]

[7] I. Holl: Sopron im Mittelalter. *ActaArchHung* 31 (1979) 105–149. Here I gave a detailed analysis of the topography of late medieval towns.

[8] Such as Győr, Pécs, Székesfehérvár. The small settlements sometimes had their own churches or a monastery. For Veszprém, see P. Németh: Az első magyar egyházmegye kialakulásának kérdéséhez (The emergence of the first Hungarian diocese). *Székesfehérvár Évszázadai* 1. Ed. by A. Kralovánszky. Székesfehérvár (1967), 117–123. Smaller settlements were mentioned with the name *szeg* or *vicus* (occasionally Weiler, Gasse, Dorf).

[9] Regarding subsequent development, we must emphasize the increase in trade and the settlement of Walloons, Flemings, Lotharingians and, to a lesser degree, Germans and Italians. The major trade routes are outlined by coin finds: *via* Carinthia and the Rhineland from the turn of the 12th and the 13th centuries; *via* Vienna from the end of the 13th century. See I. Gedai: Székesfehérvár közép- és törökkori pénzleletei (The medieval and Turkish period coin finds from Székesfehérvár). *Székesfehérvár Évszázadai* 2. Ed. by A. Kralovánszky. Székesfehérvár (1972) 191–193; I. Gedai: Fremde Münzen im Karpatenbecken aus den 11–13. Jh. *ActaArchHung* 21 (1969) 105–148. For topographical issues see Fügedi (1969).

[10] There is no data for the composition of the population in the 13th century; one event, however, definitely proves the social significance of artisans: a tanner called István *(Stephanus pelliparius)* and his brothers chose to remain loyal to the Hungarian king, and therefore the treacherous *comes* Peter had them murdered when he surrendered the *castrum* to the

Fig. 5. Sopron in the Late Middle Ages. 11. Church of the Holy Virgin; 12. Franciscan monastery; 13. St. George's church; 14. the synagogues; 15. St. Michael's parish church; 16. St. James' chapel; 17. Johannite church; 18. chapel of the Holy Spirit; 19. chapel of Maria-Magdalena; 20. marketplace; 21. Salzmarkt; 22–24. marketplaces; 25–28. baths; 29. hospital

After the Tartar raids (1241), royal policy changed in several respects. The construction of feudal and regal castles was coupled with the issue of a series of town privileges. A characteristic trait of the settlement policy was to increase the population of independent towns, e.g. by resettling the inhabitants of neighbouring settlements. Beside economic strengthening, the military and

defensive objectives are also apparent: the defense of the former regal fortresses was undertaken by the burghers.[11] The fact that the Austrian prince, Frederick

[11] Direct data concerning resettlement: Zagreb (1242), Buda (1246?), Esztergom (1249), Székesfehérvár (1249), Győr (1271), Sopron (1277). In Esztergom the resettlement of the inhabitants within the walls of the regal and episcopal castle on the hill did not prove to be long-lasting; in Buda, on the other hand, the former inhabitants of Pest settled in the newly established town. The defensive objectives are apparent since the places of resettlement in Zagreb, Buda and Esztergom lie on hills.

Bohemian king in 1273. This event is recorded in the diploma of 1279. I. Lindeck-Pozza: *Urkundenbuch des Burgenlandes.* II. Graz (1965) 134.

Fig. 6. Sopron in 1700. The sketchy engraving still reflects the medieval topography. (17. St. Michael's parish church)

II, and the Bohemian king, Ottokar, aspired to occupy the western part of the country accelerated the growth of fortresses into towns.[12]

Following the attainment of the rights of township (1277)[13] the serfs of the regal castle and the *hospites* became burghers, hence the reconstruction of the walls and other constructions were now undertaken by them. They were aided by the surrender of regal incomes and various donations.[14] It should be noted that instead of

establishing a burghers' town of new structure and layout, this involved the preservation of the town nucleus; the fortress of the *comes* became the inner town which adhered to the boundaries of the Roman town and its fortifications. By relinquishing the duty incomes between 1330 and 1344 the king increased the support of the building of fortifications: the burghers again planned the triple wall ring following the Roman layout. Excavations have proved that not only the Roman walls, but also 34 of the 39 towers were retained. The surviving part of the Roman wall constituted its outer surface and in lower parts the Roman ashlars were also reused. A pediment following the protrusions of the towers crowned the walls. This wall was the main fortified ring. The northern town gate with a new gatehouse was built beside the previous two gates. (Five successive building periods were observed here during the excavations.[15])

The inner wall ring was erected over the destroyed earthwork ditch of the fortress, behind the middle fortified ring. Between the two walls there extended a 6–7 m wide *zwinger*. The third town wall was a fairly low

[12] Ottokar also occupied Moson, Sopron and Győr; Sopron was captured three times between 1268–76.

[13] Privileges were granted to them already by the middle of the century, but the diploma itself is lost. In 1250 there were negotiations between the Johannite knights and the *burgenses* of the castle, and there is evidence for towers surrendered to the castle serfs *(civibus in saepedicto castro)*. Mollay (1956) 48–50.

[14] 1277: ... *consideratisque antiquis operum consumtionibus et fracturis in eodem castro nostro Supron, ad reparationem ... concessimus.* CD 5/2, 397. 1297: ... *murorum eiusdem ciuitatis confraccionem ex nimia antiquitate, et operis vetustatem vidissemus. AUO* V, 171. *...pro renovatione civitatis. Ibid.* Since nothing was known about the Roman town walls and the location of the fortress of the *comes* until the 1959 campaign, the interpretation of the diploma was also obscure. The term *vetustissimus murus* was also applied to the Roman town walls of Vienna in 1280: H. Ladenbauer-Orel: *Der Berghof.* Vienna (1974).

[15] The survival of the location of the gate, but the alteration of its form was also customary elsewhere. B. Cunliffe: Excavations at Porchester Castle, Hants 1969–1971. Fourth interim report. *The Antiquaries Journal* 52 (1972) 78–80, Porchester.

101

outer wall, preceded by a 25–35 m wide shallow moat encircling the town. This triple defensive wall ring surpasses most Central European fortifications, even those considered to have been most developed at that time. (Thus, for instance, Bern was protected by a double ring from 1345; Regensburg's second ring was built in 1383 and Warsaw's even later.) The reason for this may have been that the European towns having a sophisticated fortification system protected a larger territory and had no financial resources to protect it with walls. The closest analogy to and the model of the fortification system in Sopron was the town wall of Constantinople, built by Theodosius in 412, though obviously on a much grander scale.

The burghers of Sopron probably insisted on their town walls because of their high technical level and the enormous human labour invested in it. They have since then been maintained, but not enlarged. Even after the introduction of firearms, only the crenelles and the gates were modernized (first half of the 15th century); and three bastions were later added as gun emplacements (1614–41). Beyond the maintenance of the fortification of the central part, there were no financial resources to protect the suburbs.

## LATE MEDIEVAL TOPOGRAPHY

In Sopron the suburbs were a focal issue of settlement from the very beginning. Several successive royal decrees (1283–1328) forbade, but could not prevent the settlers from abandoning their houses built within the town walls, and moving to the suburbs.[16] The spacious suburb undoubtedly attracted numerous craftsmen and agriculturalists (wine growing) from the very start. This is why the parish church (rebuilt in the latter half of the 14th century) remained there. The convent of the Johannite knights endowed with the right of duty taxation, lying on the road to Vienna, also defended this outer settlement. The Chapel of the Holy Spirit (the parson's domestic chapel) was also built here (1421). At the same time, the Franciscan monastery was built in a rather unusual spot, in the marketplace, within the walls (c. 1280). Only one other Christian church (St. George's, built after 1380) and two succeeding synagogues were built within the walls.

Except for two small marketplaces (Main Square — 'Platz' and Salt Market — 'Salzmarkt'), the large marketplaces (Corn Market, Wood Market, Cattle Market — 'Kornmarkt', 'Holzmarkt', 'Viehmarkt') form a concentric circle around the town. The names of the main routes and streets leading to them are without exception mentioned in the abundant records from the beginning of the 15th century and are thus of aid in reconstructing the town plan. The unchanged survival of plot boundaries and streets has been proven at several spots by

architectural investigations and excavations.[17] The small inner town was inhabited by the wealthier strata of the population (merchants, wealthy artisans) in the shelter of the walls; nonetheless, 75% of the inhabitants lived in the suburbs by 1379.

Except for various churches, the town did not abound in public buildings. In the 14th century there were already 4 baths (1 in the inner town, 3 by the brook); but there was no town hall. In 1422 a patrician house was surrendered for this purpose, and still later, another, finally, a third patrician house was also rebuilt as a town hall. The various guild and religious societies had no common halls either, meetings were usually held in the house of the guild master in office.[18] Churches mostly also served communal, representative purposes. They were built entirely from burghers' donations, and most of their altars were supported by guilds and various societies (Fig. 5).[19]

We shall conclude this brief survey of the medieval town with the evidence yielded by the excavations.[20]

Among the goods reaching the town through foreign trade, a biconical glass vessel perhaps manufactured in a southern, possibly an Italian workshop, and an iron lock with inlay decoration, made in Russia, can be dated to the 13th century. At the same time, Austrian pottery wares had also begun to be imported, and their import increased significantly by the end of the 13th century; it was continuously present through the 14th–16th centuries, even if in lesser number. Of luxury goods, stoneware cups from the Rhineland (Siegburg) and glass beakers from Venice can be proved to have been used by rich patricians during the 15th and the 16th centuries.

## REFERENCES

Gömöri, J. (1976): Die Erforschung der Burg der Gespanschaft von Sopron. *ActaArchHung* 28, 421–422.
Fügedi, E. (1969): Die Entstehung des Städtewesens in Ungarn. *Alba Regia* 10, 101–118.
Házi, J. (1939): *Sopron középkori egyháztörténete (The medieval ecclesiastic history of Sopron)*. Sopron.
Mollay, K. (1976): Sopron a középkor végén (Sopron at the close of the Middle Ages). *Soproni Szemle* 10, 34–42.
Tomka, P. (1976): Erforschung der Gespanschaftburgen in Komitat Győr-Sopron. *ActaArchHung* 28, 391–410.

[17] For medieval patrician houses see F. Dávid: Gótikus lakóházak Sopronban (Gothic houses in Sopron). *Magyar Műemlékvédelem* 5 (1967–1968/1970/) 95–123.

[18] Only four religious societies acquired guild halls (in 1454, 1510 and 1511), but they were not representative buildings either, being rather like suburban patrician houses.

[19] A part of the religious societies also conceal guilds: Corpus christi society (*zecha Corporis Christi*, 1433), smiths; guild of the Blessed Virgin, blacksmiths; society of the apostle St. James (*zecha Beati Jacobi, z. carnificum*, 1433), butcher guild. They usually used their funds to buy vineyards. Házi (1939) 287–304.

[20] For the excavation of the town walls and the finds, I. Holl: Sopron középkori városfalai I–IV (The medieval town walls of Sopron). *Arch. Ért.* 94 (1967) 155–183; *ArchÉrt 95 (1968)* 188–205; *ArchÉrt* 98 (1971) 24–44; *ArchÉrt* 100 (1973) 180–207. No mention is made in the written sources about the imported goods recovered in the course of the excavations.

[16] 1283: ... *quidem ex eis derelicto castro nostro Supruniensi in rure continue resideret ... et magna pars ipsius castri per hoc vacua haberetur.* I. Lindeck-Pozza: *Urkundenbuch des Burgenlandes.* II. Graz (1965) 1283.

# URBANISATION IN THE EAST-CENTRAL PART OF MEDIEVAL HUNGARY

## A. KUBINYI

*In memoriam Jenő Major*
*(1922–1988)*

The majority of the towns of medieval Hungary were situated in Transdanubia or in the border regions — present-day Slovakia and Transylvania. On the territory between the Danube and Transylvania — the geographic region of the Great Hungarian Plain — towns were represented by only one free royal town, Szeged, and some bishop's residences — that is, if we discount Pest on the left bank of the Danube opposite the capital, Buda. However, the bishop's residences in the Great Hungarian Plain were not the legal equals, nor had the appearance of the royal towns. But in the second part of the Middle Ages we find a large number of 'market towns' on this territory that did not enjoy full town status and were called *oppida* in the sources. The lack of an urban development and the almost complete absence of settlements with full town status is difficult to understand, even more so because — as I have shown elsewhere — the southern part of the Great Hungarian Plain was of major commercial importance, especially in the period preceding the Mongol invasion of 1241, a fact which greatly influenced the development of Szeged. In later times, the export of cattle and, in the case of various settlements, the trade in Syrmian wine led to the spectacular development of market towns *(oppida)*, some of which — though lacking full town status — could boast a prosperity rivalling that of the free towns.[1]

Most scholars, however, especially students of geography and ethnography, distinguish a special type of town on the Great Hungarian Plain. Gy. Prinz defined this type as the irregular radial settlement type and quoted analogues from Turkestan.[2] The same type was interpreted differently by I. Györffy, an ethnographer. He perceived a quality in the groundplans of the agricultural towns of the Great Hungarian Plain: The peasants originally had two lots: the dwelling house was erected on the inner lot and the outbuildings (e.g. stalls, sties) on the outer ('sty gardens'). In his opinion this so-called 'garden', 'sty garden' town type was a survival of the winter quarters of the earliest Hungarian settlers.[3]

Most studies dealing with urban planning,[4] urban geography[5] and urban history[6] use the term 'Alföldstadt' or Alföld town to define this type and stress its Hungarian nature originating from the Middle Ages, disregarding serious objections since over half a century, from Konrad Schünemann, a German town historian, who has an expert knowledge of the Hungarian academic literature and sources.[7] Gy. László, an archaeologist, pointed out that the connection between the 'garden towns' and the first Hungarian settlers cannot be proved. He linked this settlement type to the Avars, and thus dated it before the Hungarian Conquest.[8] However, in the light of recent research we must reject this theory. The settlement type described by Prinz and Györffy undoubtedly existed in the 18th century, but there is no evidence for its existence in the Middle Ages. The possibility that this town type appeared at the close of the 15th century when the export of cattle increased significantly cannot be excluded.[9] The investigations at Hajdúböszörmény

[1] Kubinyi (1980) 423–444.
[2] Prinz (1922) 3–5.
[3] Györffy (1942) 153–215; I. Györffy: *Magyar falu, magyar ház (Hungarian village, Hungarian house)*. Budapest (1943) 97–108.

[4] Egli (1962) 243ff.
[5] R. E. Dickinson: *The West European City. A Geographical Interpretation*. London (1962) 414–415.
[6] K.-D. Grothusen: *Entstehung und Geschichte Zagrebs bis zum Ausgang des 14. Jhs.* Wiesbaden (1967) 12, 52, 54.
[7] K. Schünemann: *Die Entstehung des Städtewesens in Südosteuropa*. Breslau–Oppeln (n.d.) 16–32.
[8] László (1944) 70–76, 223.
[9] Cf. I. Szabó: *A középkori magyar falu (The Hungarian village in the Middle Ages)*. Budapest (1969) 148–156; Maksay (1971) 9, 96–101. Cf. L. Solymosi: A tanyarendszer középkori előzményeinek historiográfiája (The historiography of the mediaeval antecedents of the detached farms network). *A magyar tanyarendszer múltja*. Ed. by F. Pölöskei–Gy. Szabad. Budapest (1980) 71–96. After accepting my opinion that the system of double inner plots on the Great Hungarian Plain dates from a later period, Jenő Major, who kindly read my paper, noted the relatively early occurrrence of this system in the towns situated outside the Great Hungarian Plain. He considers the suburban manors in Sopron, which at the turn of the 13th–14th centuries usually meant a plot in the inner town, to be representatives of this system, adding that this was far from common since it was basically the privilege of the rich. This interesting observation would deserve a separate study. This system can also be noted in Buda, in the mining towns and elsewhere. The literature usually cites these data in connection

reflect the changes in interpretation. The concept of the 'Alföldstadt' was based on the groundplan of this town — published by Prinz,[10] Györffy,[11] László[12] and Egli[13] —, but now even the ancient origin of this town is challenged. The monograph on the history of the town dates the appearance of the 'garden' settlements to the 15th century.[14] The study on the architecture of Haj-dúböszörmény is more circumspect as regards 'gardens',[15] but it is clear that originally Hajdúböszörmény was a one-street settlement from which a rib street pattern developed in the 13th century and which began to disintegrate only in the second half of the 15th century.[16]

There are new theories, too, which — at least before the emergence of towns in the legal sense in the 13th century — advocate the existence of a Hungarian town type that differs from the Western European ones. In his discussion of Arabic sources E. Fügedi mentions an Asian type,[17] and Gy. Györffy, who disputes this, points out that even nomadic societies knew a town type which is also to be found in Hungary.[18] Unfortunately, archaeological evidence for this Asian or nomadic town type is very slender for the time being, which is why L. Gerevich correctly rejects these theories and notes that in Hungary — lying at the economic and cultural borderland of Europe — there co-existed several types of settlements which included also an 'Alföld type' and an 'Alföld-fringe type'.[19]

In this essay I am going to survey these settlements. Can we assume the existence of a special nomadic or Asian type? What characterizes the town plans of this region? To what extent does the so-called 'market town' *(oppidum)* differ from real towns on the one hand, and from villages on the other? Is it possible to trace chronological or developmental differences? One of the difficulties to be faced is that, with the exception of some churches, this territory has been neglected in terms of archaeological investigations in towns and, except for a few settlements, the written records were destroyed in Turkish times. As a consequence, our conclusions may have only hypothetical value. Owing to the nature and paucity of sources there remained only one course for defining the Alföld and Alföld-fringe towns, namely, to single out settlements about which more is known, and to describe their groundplan — in the hope that common traits would perhaps be found. In short, I hope I can outline at least the main types (Fig. 1).

THE EARLY TOWN TYPE

*(1) Eger*

On the edge of the Alföld, in one of the valleys of the southern Bükk mountains, stands the centre of one of the oldest bishoprics of Hungary founded by St. Stephen in the first ecclesiastical division of the country (before 1009).[20] The episcopal cathedral of Eger, and probably the bishop's residence too, were built on the 25 metres high Castle hill situated east of the Eger stream. However, the cathedral and bishop's residence from the time of St. Stephen have not yet been found. Archaeological evidence only exists for the Romanesque cathedral, built from the second half of the 12th century.[21] The town developed gradually under the bishop's castle on both sides of the Eger stream, but did not, for a long time, form a single integrated settlement. Unfortunately it is only possible to reconstruct conditions at the close of the Middle Ages and this reveals quite a strange picture. We must note that the town had originally been protected by a rampart, mentioned for the first time in the 16th century, that was replaced by stone walls only in the second half of the 16th century. At that time the town had four gates.[22] According to the State Tax Registers of 1494 and 1495 — whose testimony is corroborated by 16th century sources —, the territory later encircled by the wall was divided into six districts, each with its own magistrate, implying an independent municipal organization. Of these the town proper, called *civitas* or *theatrum* in the sources (obviously because it incorporated the market square), Szt. Miklós utca (St. Nicholas street), Olasz utca (Italian street), Szabadhely (Free Place) and Újváros (New town) be-

with Rörig's 'Unternehmerkonsortium' theory (cf. A. Kubinyi: *Die Anfänge Ofens*. Osteuropastudien der Hochschulen des Landes Hessen. Reihe I. Giessener Abhandlungen zur Agrar- und Wirtschaftsforschung des europäischen Ostens. Vol. 60. Berlin (1972) 29, 95–97, 101). The house in the centre of the town and the related manor in the suburbs (or a serfs' village) owned by the local patrician can practically be considered the equivalent of the two inner plots characteristic of the 'field-garden' settlement form. This in turn indicates that the comparable phenomena observed in the market towns on the Great Hungarian Plain can be associated with the enrichment of the local leaders, in other words, the occurrence of this system indicates the emergence of a burgher mentality in the market towns. Accordingly, it can be linked to the 15th–16th century enrichment of the cattle-dealers.

[10] Prinz (1922) Pl. IV. 14.

[11] Györffy (1942) Pl. V.

[12] László (1944) 71.

[13] Egli (1962) 244, and note 191.

[14] Gy. Módy: Hajdúböszörmény és környéke a XIII. századtól a hajdúk letelepedéséig (Hajdúböszörmény and its environs from the 13th century until the settlement of the Heyducks). *Hajdúböszörmény története*. Ed. by I. Szendrey. Debrecen (1973) 58ff.

[15] I. Kathy–K. Sz. Kürti: *Hajdúböszörmény építészete–képzőművészete (The architecture and art of Hajdúböszörmény)*. Hajdúböszörmény (1979) 21. A work recommended to me by my friend, J. Major.

[16] *Ibid.*, 27-29 and the maps.

[17] E. Fügedi: Középkori magyar városprivilégiumok (Privileges of the medieval Hungarian towns). *TBM* 14 (1961) 20–23.

[18] Gy. Györffy: Budapest története az Árpád-korban (History of Budapest in the Árpádian Age). *Budapest története I.* Ed. by L. Gerevich. Budapest (1973) 219–247.

[19] L. Gerevich: Die mittelalterliche Städte im Zentrum

Ungarns. *Vor- und Frühformen der europäischen Stadt im Mittelalter* II. Ed. by H. Jankuhn–W. Schlesinger–H. Steuer. Göttingen (1975²) 258ff.

[20] Györffy (1977) 179–183.

[21] *HMM* II, 77, 137.

[22] Pataki (1972) 16.

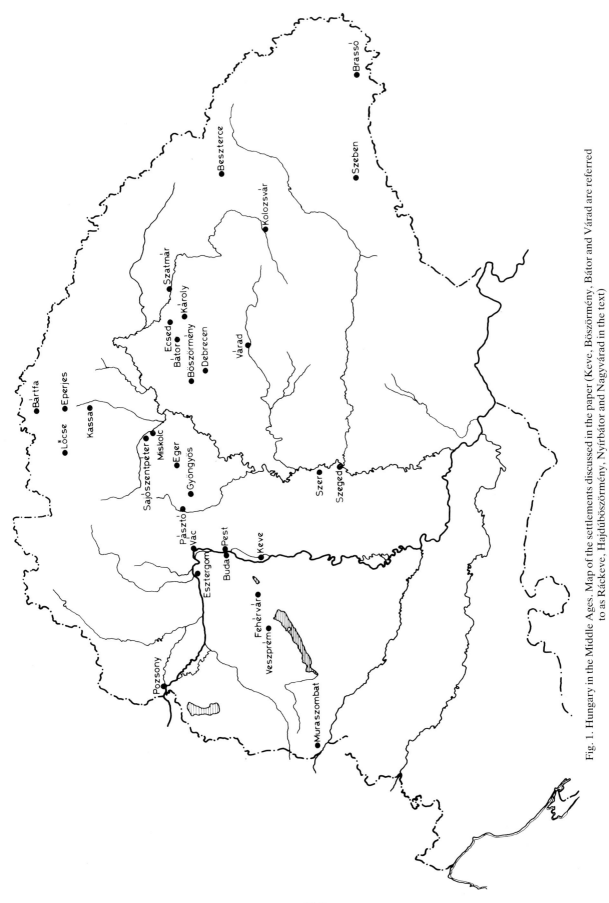

Fig. 1. Hungary in the Middle Ages. Map of the settlements discussed in the paper (Keve, Böszörmény, Bátor and Várad are referred to as Ráckeve, Hajdúböszörmény, Nyírbátor and Nagyvárad in the text)

longed to the bishop. The 'Free Place' was — according to the sources — so called because it had the privilege of tax exemption, whereas the 'New town' — *Nova civitas* in Latin — suggests a later settlement. The sixth district, i.e. Harangozó utca (Bell ringer street) was in 1494 owned by the bishop's vicar. Of the settlements beyond the town wall, a part of the village of Almagyar was later incorporated within the town wall. This belonged to the cathedral chapter, similarly to Tihamér, but Cegléd, for example, which also lay beyond the walls, belonged to the bishop. The size of the Eger settlements based on the average number of the serfs' tax items was as follows in 1494 and 1495:

Table 1. A comparison of the Eger settlements in 1494/95

| Quarter | Average number of serfs' houses | Percentage |
|---|---|---|
| Town (market) | 87 | 25.2 |
| St. Nicholas street | 7 | 2 |
| Italian Street | 30 | 8.7 |
| Free Place | 57.5 | 16.6 |
| New town | 4.5 | 1.3 |
| Bell ringer Street | 16 | 4.6 |
| Total inside the walls | 202 | 58.4 |
| Almagyar | 23.5 | 6.8 |
| Tihamér | 93.5 | 27 |
| Cegléd | 27 | 7.8 |
| Total outside the walls | 144 | 41.6 |
| Total for the Eger settlements | 346 | 100 |

It is clear that the most densely inhabited settlement was Tihamér, left outside the walls in the 16th century. The exact location of the settlements is not entirely clear, but we must note that there were other districts which I did not include because they had no separate municipal organization and consequently were most probably situated among the above. Perhaps the street called *Capitulum* (Chapter Row) forming part of the Market district but inhabited by cathedral prebends does not appear in the tax rolls (Fig. 2).[23] However, the Eger agglomeration consisted not only of these settlements. That is to say, apart from the settlements mentioned so far, there were in the Eger valley half a dozen others that had almost merged and lay within four kilometres to the north and twelve kilometres to the south of Eger: Felnémet in the north, Kistálya, Nagytálya, Kismaklár, Nagymaklár and already in the 15th century 'puszta' (deserted) Andornak in the south. In 1494 and 1495, 117.5 tax items were listed for Felnémet and 194 for Tálya and Maklár together.[24] Thus

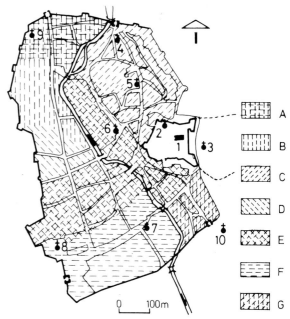

Fig. 2. Eger in the Middle Ages. A. St. Nicholas Street, B. Open area, C. Olasz street, D. New Town, E. Town (market), F. Harangozó Street, G. Almagyar. 1. Cathedral, 2. St. Peter's church, 3. St. Stephen's church, 4. St. Jacob's church, 5. church of the Blessed Virgin, 6. St. Catherine's church, 7. St. Demeter's church, 8. St. Michael's church, 9. St. Nicholas's church, 10. St. László's church.

in the Eger valley, on a very narrow territory less than 16 km in length, there were 657.5 taxi tems. This suggests a major population concentration since — according to I. Szabó's estimates — at the turn of the 15th–16th centuries there were two households per tax item and five persons per household on the average, which would yield a total population of 6575.[25] This should, however, be regarded as a minimum number[26] to which we must add the clergy and monks of the bishop's residence and the servants of the prebends and the bishop, so that the real population of the agglomeration was probably 10,000 persons, whose majority lived in the Eger settlements.

The exact process of the Eger agglomeration is not entirely clear. On the territory of the town there are six sites from which 10th and 11th century finds have been recovered, including two 10th and two 11th century cemeteries.[27] The majority of the legally independent districts of Eger developed around a church, as did the

[23] Kandra (1888) 439–441, 444–447. For the location of the districts see Kovács (1965) 73-92. We have adopted his classification, although his identifications often differ from ours. Cf. Pataki (1972) 13–17.

[24] Cf. Kandra (1883) 439–441, 444–447.

[25] I. Szabó: Magyarország népessége az 1330-as és az 1526-os évek között (The population of Hungary between 1330–1526). *Magyarország történeti demográfiája*. Ed. by J. Kovacsics. Budapest (1963) 77, 92.

[26] Recent studies prefer a coefficient assuming a household of 8 to 10 members. R. Müller: A középkori településtörténet kutatásának problémái (Problems in the research of medieval settlement patterns). *A településtörténeti kutatás módszertana*. Ed. by R. Müller. Veszprém (1973) 63.

[27] Nagy (1978) 11-14. Cf. also its review by B. Kovács in *Archivum. A Heves Megyei Levéltár Közleményei* 8 (1979) 126.

non-independent ones.[28] The *patrocinium*s of these churches are also instructive. The cathedral was consecrated to St. John the Evangelist. Beside its northern wall stood the original collegiate church named after King St. Stephen, which was destroyed at the time of the Mongol invasion, and was later rebuilt in Gothic style. Farther to the east, in the outer part of the late medieval castle in an originally independent district and on a promontory *(De promontorio Agriensi)* stood St. Peter's church. This was built in the 13th century at the latest, had parochial rights and was a collegiate church.[29] St. James' church lay in the northern part of the town, near one of the later town gates. According to a 1240 deed this church was originally built as a hospice for invalids and paupers, but at this time we find it in the hands of the secular clergy. One district belonged to it but this did not have an independent organization and was probably part of the neighbouring 'Italian Street' hamlet.[30] The dedication suggests a pilgrim character and as Hungarians also visited Compostella in the 12th–13th centuries, the name is understandable.[31] To the south of St. James' church, perhaps already in the Italian Street, stood a Franciscan monastery, mentioned already in 1260, serving as the centre of a place of custody.[32] It is possible that the Franciscans — who were usually banished to the edge of the town — acquired such a central position in this case because they received a church which had previously served another purpose. This is proven by the name of the patron saint, the Blessed Virgin, because this was the only church in Eger named after her, although this dedication is widespread in early Hungary. We do not know the age of St. Catharine's chapel, situated in the 'Chapter Row' district.[33] The parish church of 'Bell ringer' Street, St. Demeter's, is mentioned in 1297 for the first time.[34] The parish church of the town itself was named after St. Michael. This church lay further away from the market square, to its southeast, and was mentioned for the first time in 1310.[35] In the northwestern corner of the town stood the monastery of the monks of the Augustinian order, first mentioned in 1346 and named after St. Nicholas. He also gave his name to a district of Eger which had a hamlet of its own.[36] This fact again suggests that the existence of a parish preceded the building of a monastery in this case too. The church of St. Ladislas of Almagyar, equipped with a hospice, was built or rebuilt in 1331.[37] The parish of Tihamér was named after Cosmas and Damianus.[38]

Accordingly, there may have been at least nine churches (dedicated to John, Stephen, Peter, James, Mary, Demeter, Michael, Nicholas and Cosmas-Damianus) within about a two, or two and a half kilometre radius of Eger before the Mongol invasion of 1241.

The number of saint's names reflecting eastern rites is most conspicuous, suggesting that the Magyar tribes who settled here, and the 'Kabar' tribes who joined them adopted Byzantine Christianity.[39] The settlements that grew up around the churches, merged only slowly, with the free areas partly filled in by a conscious settlement of population groups. The 'New Town' obviously reflects this process, as does the 'Free Place' district and, if the modern town maps are to be trusted, also the regularity of the street network.

The villages lying farther from the town also offer interesting conclusions. Let us take as a starting point one of the Eger settlements, namely the 'Italian Street'. In the Hungarian of the Middle Ages the name 'Olasz' (Italian) was used for all people of Latin origin, at first primarily for Walloons.[40] The name of the hamlet certainly refers to the Latin inhabitants, but perhaps so does the name 'James' of the church too. Indeed, the available evidence shows that in the Eger valley there lived Latins with a particular organization. As early as the first half of the 14th century the *Comes Vallis Agriensis* is said to have attacked, with all his guests and Gauls *(cum... universis hospitibus et Galicis)*, the entourage of the chief of the royal mint.[41] The Walloons of Eger Valley came from the Liège area and spoke that dialect even in the 15th and 16th centuries. They are said to have moved to Hungary in the 11th century, but it has also been suggested that they arrived after the Mongol invasion.[42] We believe that this settlement process must have preceded the 13th century for the later settlers had

---

[28] Cf. note 23.

[29] *HMM* II, 132, 146, 156.

[30] Kovács (1965) 79–83. He draws a distinction between the districts in St. James and Olasz Streets.

[31] For the cult of James, cf. *Lexikon für Theologie und Kirche*[2]. V. k. Freiburg (1960) 834; S. Bálint: *Ünnepi kalendárium (Festal Calendar)*. Vol. II. Budapest (1977) 77–88.

[32] Kovács (1965) 80–81. Jenő Major drew my attention to the theories which assume a settlement called Felmagyar on the northern side of the castle on the analogy of Almagyar. In his opinion the Franciscan church (or, more precisely, its predecessor) may have served this settlement, which may originally have included Almagyar. Major identifies these two settlements, each bearing a tribal name, with the earliest core of the *suburbium* of Eger. His theory is highly plausible.

[33] Kovács (1965) 81.

[34] Kovács (1965) 84.

[35] Kovács (1965) 86.

[36] Kovács (1965) 86.

[37] Kovács (1965) 83. Cf. also Pataki (1972) 15.

[38] Cf. note 37. Jenő Major notes that since the thermal springs at Eger belonged to Tihamér, the church there was understandably named after the two healing saints, Cosmas and Damianus.

[39] B. Kovács: Magyarok és palócok. Adatok a Palócföld IX–XI. századi településtörténetéhez (Hungarians and Palots. Contributions to the 9th–11th century settlement history of the Palots Region). *EMÉ* 7 (1969) 166–167; Nagy (1978) 13–14.

[40] Székely (1964) 2–19.

[41] M. G. Kovachich: *Formulae solennes styli*. Pesthini (1799) 20.

[42] A summary of the earlier literature is given by Székely (1964) 5, 38–39. For the period after the Mongol invasion see G. Bárczi: A legkorábbi vallon–magyar érintkezésekhez (On the earliest Walloon–Hungarian contacts). *Századok* 71 (1937) 393–416; F. Bakó: Maklár. Településnéprajzi tanulmány (Maklár. A settlement ethnographical study). *EMÉ* 2 (1964) 288–289; E. Fügedi: Das mittelalterliche Königreich Ungarn als Gastland. *Die deutsche Ostsiedlung des Mittelalters als Problem der europäischen Geschichte*. Vorträge und Forschungen 18. Sigmaringen (1975) 488, note 45.

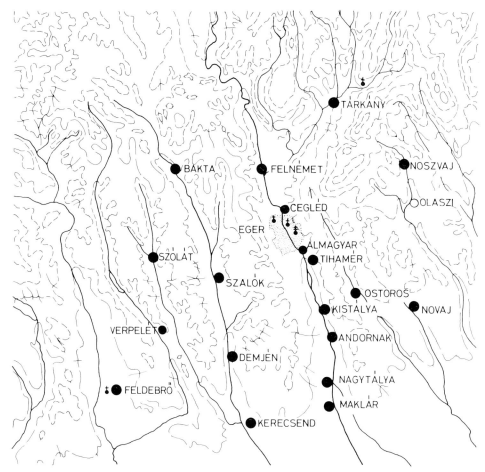

Fig. 3. Eger and its surroundings in the Middle Ages

very important so-called *hospes* privileges, evidence of which cannot be shown for the earlier settlers.[43] This is further supported by a village called 'Olaszi' near Noszvaj, about 10 kilometres north of Eger.[44] The first mention of this settlement dates to 1275, but since it had already been destroyed by that time, it must therefore have existed before the Mongol invasion and must have been connected with the neighbouring Walloon settlement of the Eger Valley. As a matter of fact, one of the settlements of the Eger Valley, Tálya, preserved its French name (Taille, 'clearing').[45] On the other hand, Felnémet (Németi, 'village of the Germans'), situated north of Eger is indicative of German settlers.[46] Consequently, it would appear that the Eger Valley agglomeration was founded by the bishops before the Mongol invasion through settling Walloon and German groups. Thus the Hungarian and foreign settlements alternated with each other (cp. the cemeteries and Byzantine church names of the 11th and 12th centuries) (Fig. 3).[47]

In short, Eger represented quite a distinct type of settlement pattern. On the territory of the town, and to its north and south in the Eger Valley, about a dozen places enjoying certain privileges could be found in a relatively small area. This territory was engaged primarily in viticulture and had to import grain, as a result of which the Eger Valley became the market centre of a larger area[48] — a development boosted by the importance of the bishop's residence as a centre of consumption. However, the unification of the regionally dispersed agglomeration did not occur until the end of the Middle Ages. In this way the development of Felnémet, Tálya and Maklár, as well as the independence of the

[43] For the privileges cf. Kubinyi (1975) 529–554.

[44] Székely (1964) 15.

[45] L. Kiss: *Földrajzi nevek etimológiai szótára (Etymological dictionary of geographical names)*. Budapest (1978) 627; Soós (1975) 327. The *patrocinium* of the church (St. Egyed) is also indicative of the Walloons.

[46] Kubinyi (1975) 546–547. Walloons may also have lived there besides the Germans. Soós (1975) 202.

[47] Andornak in Eger valley can be derived from the personal name of Andronicus. L. Kiss: *Földrajzi nevek etimológiai szótára (Etymological dictionary of geographical names)*. Budapest (1978) 55.

[48] K. Faragó–J. Major: A magyar középvárosok kialakulása és fejlődése az első világháborúig (The evolution and development of the medium-sized Hungarian towns until World War I). *Településtudományi Közlemények* 28 (1979) 10.

108

settlements inside and beyond the town walls, and also the *divide et impera* policy of the ecclesiastical landlords hindered the more extensive urban development of Eger.[49]

## (2) Vác

Another bishop's residence also on the fringes of the Great Hungarian Plain, Vác, represents a completely different type of settlement. It was also founded by St. Stephen in the late years of his reign (†1038).[50] One of our sources, however, while narrating a miraculous event, links the foundation of the town to King Géza I (1074–1077). This passage, an interpolation with a view to the interests of St. Peter's chapel, attributes the building of the cathedral named after the Holy Virgin and the stone chapel dedicated to St. Peter to this king. The interpolator obviously wanted to grant this church the rights of the royal churches.[51] The lists compiled by Pope Boniface IX in 1389, 1399 and 1400 of the churches which were exempted from the jurisdiction of the diocese and were directly subjected to the Archbishop of Esztergom definitely include the Vác church.[52] This church is usually identified with the parish church of St. Michael in the 'German town' of Vác, thus dating it to the period preceding the foundation of the bishopric.[53] However, the 'German town' was founded only in the mid-13th century.[54] Since the church of Vác is not mentioned in other lists of privileged churches, its exemption was most probably only a legal claim.[55] Indeed, the jurisdiction of the bishop over three of the churches in the town is sufficiently borne out by the surviving evidence,[56] while the church of St. Peter is the only one we know to have even dared an interpolation in the chronicle in order to coerce its exemption. Consequently, the exempted church in Vác listed without its *patrocinium* can only have been the church of St. Peter. In fact this church could well have antedated the formation of the bishopric (and of the town). It lay outside the town, in the 'fields', presumably not far from today's Hétkápolna, on a mound approximately 500 m south of the site of the bishop's castle (and the town).[57] A 10th century cemetery was found in its vicinity.[58] The title of the church (St. Peter) is also indicative of its relatively early foundation.[59] The first settlement in Vác is assumed to have been somewhere in the vicinity of the church of St. Peter, and the congregation is thought to have moved north only after the formation of the bishopric. The church retained its parochial jurisdiction well into the 14th century, although by that time no settlement was subjected to it. It is nevertheless possible that this church had managed the parochial affairs of the 'Hungarian Town' until the building of St. Margaret's church later.

The bishop's castle and the cathedral of Vác were erected on a mound north of Hétkápolna, on the bank of the Danube. The Annales Yburgenses mention Wazenburg in 1074.[60] In 1075, King Géza I donated a goldsmith to the Garamszentbenedek abbey in the Naszály forest near Vác.[61] Confirming this donation is a document from 1209, in which the Pope speaks of the goldsmiths of Vác.[62] The — still unpublished — excavations conducted in the castle have brought to light Romanesque carvings, pottery, a rich assemblage of Renaissance artefacts and the remains of the castle walls. Most significant among the Romanesque stone carvings recovered from the cathedral is a sculpted human head. The fragment of a Limoges cross is also

[49] For the negative role played by the church landowners in the history of the town, cf. E. Mályusz: A mezővárosi fejlődés (The development of market towns). *Tanulmányok a parasztság történetéhez Magyarországon a 14. században*. Ed. by Gy. Székely. Budapest (1953) 160–172.

[50] Györffy (1977) 327–328.

[51] J. Gerics: Krónikáink szerepe a középkori jogéletben. A váci egyházalapítás krónikás hagyományainak kritikájához (The role of the chronicles in medieval legal matters. A review of the chronicle traditions of the founding of the church at Vác). *LevKözl* 33 (1962) 3–12.

[52] F. Zimmermann–C. Werner–G. Müller: *Urkundenbuch zur Geschichte der Deutschen in Siebenbürgen.* Vol. III. Hermannstadt (1902) 254, 255; *Monumenta Vaticana historiam regni Hungariae illustrantia.* I. 4. Bullae Bonifaci IX. Budapest (1889) 199. This was confirmed in 1454 by Pope Nicholas V. Lukcsics (1938) Vol. II, 328, no. 1340.

[53] L. Mezey: A váci püspökség kialakulása (The formation of the Vác bishopric). *Váci Egyházmegyei Almanach.* Ed. by J. Bánk. Vác (1970) 18. 30, and note 45.

[54] Cf. below.

[55] M. Jankovich: Buda-környék plébániáinak középkori kialakulása és a királyi kápolnák intézménye (The evolution of medieval parsonages around Buda and the royal chapels). *BudRég* 19 (1959) 72, 75.

[56] The 1480 letter of orders sent to the 18 parsons of the Vác diocese starts the list with the parish church of St. Margaret in the 'Hungarian Town' of Vác. This is followed by St. Michael's parish church in the 'German Town' and the church of the Holy

Cross in the castle. *Dl,* 18331. The data on St. Peter's church proves even less. The emissary of the Vác chapter in 1341 as the ecclesiastical body entrusted with notarial functions was the rector of St. Peter's church, who may well have had other prebendal benefices. *Magyar Történelmi Emlékek II. Oklevelek Hontvármegyei magán-levéltárakból (Hungarian historical relics II. Charters from private archives in Hont County).* Published by Ferenc Kubinyi. Budapest (1888) 162.

[57] Cf. F. Chobot: *A váczi egyházmegye történeti névtára (Historical register of the Vác diocese).* Vol. I. Vác (1915) 77.

[58] I. Stefaits: A váci járás őstörténetének régészeti kérdései (Archaeological problems in the prehistory of Vác district). *StudCom* 3 (1975) 18. Let us add here that a 7th–8th century Avar period cemetery has also been discovered south of Vác, approximately 1 km west of Hétkápolna. S. Tettamanti: Előzetes jelentés a Vác–Kavicsbányai avar temető feltárásáról (Preliminary report on the excavation of the Avar cemetery at Vác–Kavicsbánya). *StudCom* 1 (1972) 45–52.

[59] K. Magyar: A somogyvári apátság Péter-titulusának forrásáról. Adatok a korai magyar egyházszervezés kérdéséhez (On the origins of the Péter *titulus* of the Somogyvár abbey. Data on early church organizations in Hungary). *Levéltári Évkönyv. Somogy megye múltjából* 6 (1975) 24–27.

[60] A. F. Gombos: *Catalogus fontium historiae Hungaricae.* Vol. I. Budapest (1937) 215.

[61] *Codex diplomaticus et epistolaris Slovaciae.* Ed. by R. Marsina. Vol. I. Bratislava (1971) 56.

[62] *Ibid.,* 118.

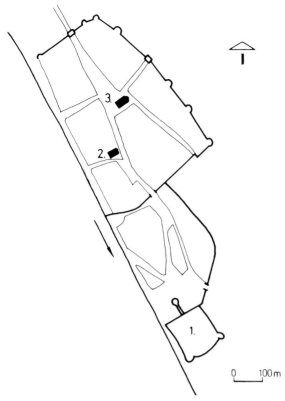

Fig. 4. Vác in the Middle Ages. 1. castle, 2. St. James' church, 3. St. Michael's church

cording to a register dating from the Turkish period, the church was surrounded by a moat (or, to be more precise, by the moat encircling the 'Hungarian town'), and also by mills, flood-locks, ponds and kitchen gardens.[68] The first reference to the church dates from the first half of the 14th century.[69] On the evidence of its *patrocinium*, its foundation can most probably be assigned to the 12th century. Around 1131–1132 King Béla II transferred the twentieth part of the income of the Vác bishopric, otherwise the legal due of the king, to the 'Church of St. Margaret', i.e. to the collegiate chapter of Dömös.[70] The construction of the royal church at Dömös was completed in the 1130s,[71] and it is highly possible that the Vác church was dedicated to the favourite saint of the royal family at about the same time. It is conspicuous that the parish church lay outside the settlement. The erection of the church, presumably on a small mound or elevation, may thus have preceded the completion of construction in the *suburbium*, and it may have originally served some other function than that of a parish church. The 'Hungarian Town' itself was definitely standing by the time of the Mongol invasion of 1241. According to the chronicler of the invasion, the population sought refuge in the church (the cathedral) and its fortified palaces after the occupation of the town, but these palaces were soon also captured and burnt down by the Mongols. In other words, the bishop's palace also fell to the invaders.[72]

The town of Vác with the bishop's palace and the 'Hungarian Town' that evolved from the *suburbium*, is comparable to a number of western episcopal capitals. Its location on the Danube underscores the importance of this central waterway.[73] The period following the Mongol invasion saw the evolution of the third township, the 'German Town' or the *civitas theutonicalis*. It is first mentioned in 1319 in connection with St. James' monastery of the Augustinians, founded by the bishop of Vác on the limits of the 'German' and 'Hungarian' towns.[74] Since the location of this monastery is known, the 'German town' probably lay north of the 'Hungarian town', on the bank of the Danube. The parish church of St. Michael stood in the southern end of the triangular marketplace of the 'German town'. Marketplaces of

worthy of note.[63] Certain finds suggest the existence of yet another parish church in the castle (dedicated to the Holy Cross), but the date of its construction could not be defined.[64] The area of Vác castle — 2.8 ha — corresponds to that of other early bishop's castles, and implies that it may well have served as a home for other dignitaries besides the bishop and the chapter.[65]

The *suburbium* was situated north of the castle, on the bank of the Danube. If we accept the later maps as authoritative, the roads had led to a wide open space in front of the castle gate (Fig. 4).[66] The *suburbium* later developed into the *civitas hungaricalis,* and the church of Margaret presumably served as its parsonage.[67] Ac-

[63] F. Kőszegi's report in *RégFüz* I. 16 (1963) 90. I. Stefaits's report in *RégFüz* I. 18 (1965) 82-83; D. Dercsényi–P. Granasztói: *Vác.* Budapest (1960) 21. Fig. 4; *Vezető a váci Vak Bottyán Múzeumban (A guide to the Vak Bottyán Museum of Vác).* Ed. by I. Stefaits. Vác (1971) 7.

[64] Cf. note 56.

[65] Cs. Csorba: Pest városfalának vázlatos története (A brief history of the town walls of Pest). *BudRég* 24:1 (1976) 363. For the houses in the castle cf. below.

[66] D. Dercsényi–P. Granasztói: *Vác.* Budapest (1960) 33, Fig. 17.

[67] Most scholars identify the parsonage with the cathedral of the Blessed Virgin in the castle. However, this view is erroneous. Szarka (1948) 26, 33; L. Mezey: A Pray-kódex keletkezése (The birth of the Pray codex). *Magyar Könyvszemle* 87 (1971) 118, correctly considers it a parsonage.

[68] L. Fekete: A törökkori Vác egy XVI. századi összeírás alapján (Vác in the Turkish period as reflected by a 16th century register). Budapest (1942) 85, nos 375–377.

[69] *Monumenta Vaticana historiam regni Hungariae illustrantia. I. 1. Rationes collectorum pontificiorum in Hungaria.* Budapest (1887) 409.

[70] *Codex diplomaticus et epistolaris Slovaciae.* Ed. by R. Marsina. Vol. I. Bratislava (1971) 75.

[71] L. Gerevich: A kora-gótika kezdetei Magyarországon (The beginnings of early Gothic art in Hungary). *MTA II OK* 23 (1974) 156.

[72] *SRH* II, 565.

[73] L. Gerevich: Hungary. *European Towns. Their Archaeology and Early History.* Ed. by M. W. Barley. London–New York–San Francisco (1977) 432–434; A. Kubinyi: Diskussionsbeitrag. *Die Stadt am Fluss.* Ed. by E. Maschke–J. Sydow. Sigmaringen (1978) 199.

[74] F. Knauz: *Monumenta ecclesiae Strigoniensis.* Vol. II. Esztergom (1882) 768.

comparable dimensions (1:2,6) are primarily known from Austria, from the areas north of the Danube and in Bohemia, in towns established in the 13th century.[75] Accordingly, the foundation of the 'German town' can most probably be dated to the second half of the 13th century. In the Late Middle Ages the 'German town' was enclosed by a town wall. Certain parts of this wall, including the northwestern tower, are still standing,[76] while other parts have been brought to light in the course of archaeological excavations.[77] The 'Hungarian town' was defended only by a rampart and a moat.[78] The Hospital of the Holy Spirit stood outside the town walls, in the northern suburb in the continuation of the main street of the town (Nagy Street), running parallel to the Danube[79] (Fig. 4).

The appearance of the late medieval town can be fairly accurately reconstructed from a Turkish register dating from 1570. This register lists not only the owners of the houses, but also the names of the streets, the neighbours, the material used in the buildings, the number of storeys within the buildings and also their age.[80] Regrettably enough, the publisher of this document identified the street names incorrectly, even though there are no apparent difficulties in this.[81] Disregarding now the houses defined as new (i.e. those which were obviously not medieval), the breakdown of the structures in the town by quarter and material is shown in Table 2. (Unfortunately most of the houses in the former 'Hungarian town' were later taken over by the Turkish population, thus the data on these structures are incomplete.)

The relatively low number of stone structures and of multi-storeyed houses suggests that the appearance of Vác cannot be considered urban in the 'western' sense of the word. The arrangement of the one- and multi-storeyed stone structures is still more typical. In the 'German town', most of these houses were erected in

the marketplace or in Great Street crossing it. Of the houses in the marketplace 81.8 per cent were built of stone (54.4 per cent had more than one storey). In Nagy Street, 59.1 per cent of the houses were stone structures. Since this street extended into the suburb, this ratio may have been higher in the section within the town walls. Half of the buildings in Zsidó (Jewish) Street were built of stone, while in the other streets this ratio was only 9.1 per cent. It would appear that in the 'Hungarian town' the stone structures and the multi-storeyed houses lay in the southern extension of Nagy Street. In short, the appearance of late medieval Vác was, by and large, similar to that of the modern towns in the Great Hungarian Plain. It had an urban core with two- or three-storey buildings, or at least with stone structures, while the streets in the outskirts were rather country-like. From an economic point of view, however, Vác can definitely be accorded an urban status.[82]

As regards the late medieval administration of Vác, both town parts had their own magistrate and council, although in some cases they conducted joint proceedings under the leadership of one of the magistrates. Manorial power was exercised by the bishop, or by the chapter in one sector of the 'Hungarian town'. As inhabitants of a manorial town, the burghers of Vác were serfs legally, a circumstance which considerably hindered the later development of the town.[83]

### (3) Szeged

In contrast to Eger and Vác, both situated on the fringes of the Great Hungarian Plain, the town of Szeged was a settlement typical of the Great Hungarian Plain. It differed from the other two inasmuch as it was not an episcopal see. Its status as a free royal town was confirmed by the king in the Late Middle Ages, and it was classed among the five or six most populous and, at the same time, wealthiest towns in the country. In contrast to the other Hungarian towns, the population of Szeged was entirely Hungarian — it never had a

Table 2. Breakdown of the houses in medieval Vác by quarters

| Quarter | Multi-storeyed houses | Stone | Hedgerow | Unknown | Total |
|---|---|---|---|---|---|
| **(a) Number** | | | | | |
| Castle | 3 | 8 | 22 | 2 | 35 |
| 'Hungarian town' | 4 | 17 | 18 | 48 | 87 |
| 'German town' | 14 | 41 | 65 | 7 | 127 |
| Total | 21 | 66 | 105 | 57 | 249 |
| **(b) Percentages** | | | | | |
| Castle | 8.5 | 22.9 | 62.9 | 5.7 | 100 |
| 'Hungarian town' | 4.6 | 19.5 | 20.7 | 55.2 | 100 |
| 'German town' | 11.0 | 32.3 | 51.2 | 5.5 | 100 |
| Total | 8.4 | 26.5 | 42.2 | 22.9 | 100 |

[75] E.g. Waidhofen/Thaya: W. Rausch: Österreichs Grenzstädte im Norden der Donau. Linz (1971) 15; Weitra: ibid., 10–11; Horn: Österreichisches Städtebuch. Vol. 4. 2. Die Städte Niederösterreichs. Vienna (1976) 101–112, Fig. VII; Cheb: Pamet mešt. Meštské pamétkové rezerváce v Českých Zemých (Memory of cities. Memorable cities in Czechoslovakia). Prague (1975) 72, 84; Hradec Králové: ibid., 60, 70; Slavonice: ibid., 300, 312.

[76] D. Dercsényi-P. Granasztói: Vác. Budapest (1960) 164.

[77] K. Kozák's report in RégFüz I. 28 (1975) 141–142.

[78] Cf. also A. Kubinyi: A középkori Vác 1526-ig (Medieval Vác until 1526). Vác története. Ed. by V. Sápi. Szentendre (1983) 49–76.

[79] Szarka (1948) 34–35.

[80] Published by L. Fekete: A törökkori Vác egy XVI. századi összeírás alapján (Vác in the Turkish period as reflected by a 16th century register). Budapest (1942).

[81] Cf. note 78.

[82] A. Kubinyi: Das Wirtschaftsgebiet der Stadt Vác im Mittelalter. Grazer Forschungen zur Wirtschafts- und Sozialgeschichte 3. Graz (1978) 33–43.

[83] Kubinyi (1975) 550.

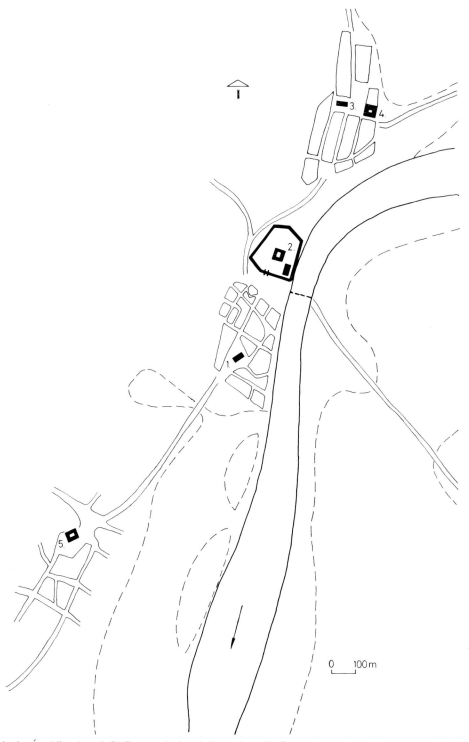

Fig. 5. Szeged in the Árpádian Age. 1. St. Demeter's church, 2. castle, 3. St. George's church and the market, 4. St. Nicholas' church (the Dominican monastery), 5. St. Peter's hospital, the later Franciscan church

considerable number of foreign (Latin or German) inhabitants. The economic significance of the town, apparent as early as the Árpádian Age, can be linked to its favourable geographical location. The town lies near the confluence of the rivers Maros — flowing from Transylvania — and Tisza, which has a north to south course. The salt from Transylvania, transported here by ships on the Maros, was stored, distributed and forwarded even as far as Zagreb from the royal salt-depots. The town also played a significant role in early Hungarian–Byzantine relations, since one of the main commercial routes leading to Byzantium passed through the Tisza valley and Szeged. In the Late Middle Ages the town became one of the cattle exporting centres of Hungary; the Szeged cattle-dealers drove their herds from the Great Hungarian Plain to inner Austria and North Italy through Slavonia.[84]

The first reliable data on the Szeged castle date from 1321. Its stone and brick walls must have been built after 1241, although it is assumed to have had a palisaded castle as a predecessor. The basic area of the castle was considerably large compared to other castles in Hungary (over 5 ha).[85] Its area was larger than that of the bishop's castles (cf. Vác) or of most of the so-called bailiff's castles.[86] The castles built after the 13th century usually covered an even smaller area — most of these were feudal castles. Accordingly, we can agree with scholars who assume that the walls of the later Szeged castle were preceded by a pre-Mongol invasion rampart. Its large basic area can perhaps be explained by the fact that this complex also housed the royal salt-depot. At the same time, the castle must have had a comparatively dense population.[87] The large number of high-quality Romanesque stone carvings recovered in the course of the demolition of the castle in the past century suggests that the castle complex also included a church before the Mongol invasion. This assumption, that has been challenged,[88] was accepted by the author of the monograph on the churches of Szeged.[89] Considering that the town of Szeged had been the residence of an archdeacon, and that these residences were usually established in the vicinity of the castles in the early Árpádian Age, it is more than probable that the church of the archdeacon lay within the castle complex.[90] Our sources indicate the existence of a Gothic church in the castle in later periods. The remains of this church survived into the 18th century, but have disappeared since then. Consequently, the assumption that this church was erected

over the ruins of the old church that was destroyed during the Mongol invasion cannot be confirmed. The late medieval church was consecrated to St. Erzsébet (Elizabeth), and in all probability it belonged to the first Franciscan monastery.[91]

The town of Szeged was founded on the higher ground within the marshland along the river Tisza. The town proper, named Palánk in modern times after the palisaded rampart-like defences of the castle, was a suburb-like settlement south of the town. The Great Road of Buda leading to Transylvania passed through the open area between Palánk and the castle, and the salt loading area lay to the north of the castle. The parish church of St. Demeter was erected in the marketplace of Palánk, the plan of which resembled an isosceles triangle (Fig. 5).[92] The town of Palánk, the predecessor of present-day Szeged, functioned as the inner town in later times. The dating of its church is still controversial. Cs. Sebestyén, the leader of archaeological excavations there, originally dated the first square-ended church to the turn of the 12th–13th centuries but, on the evidence of the unusual size of the bricks, he later assigned it to the first half of the 11th century. This latter date must definitely be considered incorrect.[93] However, this date was also accepted by Sándor Bálint on account of the *patrocinium* indicating a Byzantine rite.[94] Conversely, Kozák dated this first church to the mid-13th century in view of its square-ended choir, although he did reject the possibility that a smaller church with an apsidal termination had preceded this building.[95] Had the church of St. Demeter been indeed erected as late as the mid-13th century, there would be no grounds for identifying it with the earlier church of the archdeacon, and would support the early date of the castle church. Nevertheless, we are of the opinion that the church of the archdeacon can be identified with the church of the castle. Moreover, there is no evidence supporting the dating of square-ended churches to later periods.[96] On the evidence provided by the excavations, the first building of St. Demeter's church was converted into a three-aisled church sometime in the early 14th century,

[84] Kubinyi (1980) 423–438.

[85] K. Cs. Sebestyén: *Szeged középkori vára (The medieval castle of Szeged)*. Szeged (1928) 3–5; Györffy. (1963) 902; G. Entz: *Kőtár (Stone relics)*. Szeged (n.d.) 11; Kubinyi (1980) 425. For the basic area of the castles, cf. Cs. Csorba: Pest városfalának vázlatos története (A brief history of the town walls of Pest). *Bud Rég* 24 (1976) 363.

[86] The basic area of those situated on the fringes of the Great Hungarian Plain was between 1.2–3.9 ha. Gy. Nováki: Die topographischen Eigentümlichkeiten der ungarischen Burgen im 10-11. Jahrhundert am nördlichen Randgebiet der grossen Tiefebene. *ActaArchHung* 28 (1976) 362. Of the Transdanubian bailiff's castles, Győr (also an episcopal see) had a basic area of 3 ha, Moson covered an area of over 4.5 ha, while Sopron was considerably larger (9.5 ha), although this area also included the later town. P. Tomka: Erforschung der Gespanschaftsburgen im Komitat Győr-Sopron. *ActaArch Hung* 28 (1976) 392, 399, 403.

[87] Kubinyi (1980) 426.

[88] G. Entz: *Kőtár (Stone relics)*. Szeged (n. d.) 7–11.

[89] Sebestyén (1938) 7–14; cf. also K. Kozák: A szegedi Szent Dömötör templom építéstörténetének kérdései (The architectural history of St. Demeter's church in Szeged). *MFMÉ* (1966–67/2) 149.

[90] Kubinyi (1980) 426; Bálint (1970–71) 206–207. Bálint identifies the church of the archdeacon with St. Demeter's church.

[91] Cs. Sebestyén (1938) 17–26; Bálint (1975) 25–27. This old tradition would imply that the Franciscans had taken possession of an earlier church. It would otherwise be rather uncommon to presume that the Mendicant friars had settled in the castle rather than in the vast suburbs of Szeged.

[92] Györffy (1963) 900–904.

[93] Cs. Sebestyén (1938) 36.

[94] Bálint (1970–71) 207–209; Bálint (1975) 10–11.

[95] K. Kozák: A szegedi Szent Dömötör templom építéstörténetének kérdései (The architectural history of St. Dömötör's church in Szeged). *MFMÉ* (1966–67) 148.

[96] Churches with square-ended sanctuary are known to have been built in Hungary and in other European countries prior to the mid-13th century, for example in Austria: M. Schwarz: *Romanische Architektur in Niederösterreich*. St. Pölten–Wien (n.d.) 10. A comparable church datable to the late 11th century was uncovered by Méri in the vicinity of Szeged. I. Méri: Árpád-kori népi építkezésünk feltárt emlékei Orosháza határában (Folk architecture from the Árpádian Age uncovered in the vicinity of Orosháza). *RégFüz* II. 12 (1964) 4–9. I would like to point out here that K. Kozák's recent theory, according to which the church of St. Demeter can be associated

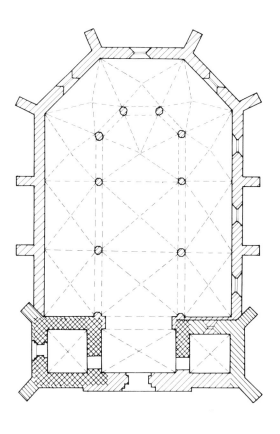

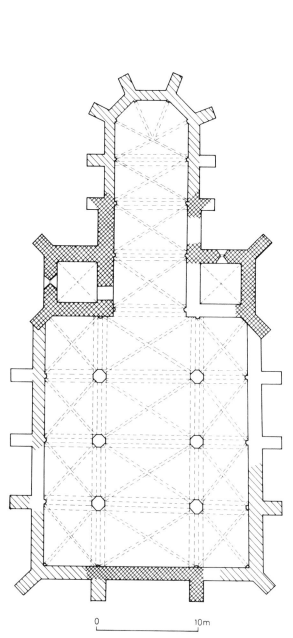

Fig. 6. Groundplan of St. Demeter's church. 1. The 14th century church with the incorporated remains of the Árpádian church, 2. the new church built in the second half of the 15th century and the ruined tower from the Árpádian Age

and at the end of the century a new choir and a sanctuary terminating in three sides of an octagon were added to it. The 15th century saw newer constructions. The old church was pulled down and a new church with an

ambulatory was erected to its east on the same spot where the old sanctuary had stood. However, the tower beside the old sanctuary was left untouched (Fig. 6).[97]

Palánk, or the town of Szeged proper, was the only settlement on the Great Hungarian Plain that was granted the privileges of a royal town in the mid-13th century.[98] The town presumably became entitled to hold weekly markets at a fairly early date. In all probability

with the Order of the Knights of St. John of Jerusalem is rather unconvincing. L. Kozák: Téglából épített körtemplomaink és centrális kápolnáink a XII–XIII. században (12th–13th century brickwork round churches and central chapels in Hungary). *MFMÉ* (1976–77/1) 81, note 65.

[97] Cs. Sebestyén (1938) 34–61.
[98] Kubinyi (1980) 429–430.

114

these markets were held on Mondays.[99] We have no data confirming the town's entitlement to hold annual markets. It was only in 1499 that Lathran Street in Szeged was granted such an entitlement (for St. Lucy's Day, Dec. 13), and also the right to hold weekly markets Thursday through Saturday. This annual market is called '*barum vásár*' in a somewhat later source suggesting the annual Szeged livestock market (*barum*, 'livestock').[100] Since Lathran Street, or to be more exact, Latorján Square can be identified with the open space between Palánk and the castle near the Tisza ferry, this economically important area soon became the site of the new settlement and its marketplace.[101] Palánk was not enclosed by walls. Various scholars date the palisade (*palánk*, 'palisade') after which the town was named to the reign of King Sigismund,[102] but there is no evidence supporting this assumption. The available evidence indicates the existence of a moat surrounding the town right until the days of Turkish rule.[103]

The centre of the third core of the town was situated approximately 500 m north of the castle. This settlement, named Felszeged ('Upper Szeged'), Felsősziget ('Upper Island') (cf. the higher ground in the marshland on which Szeged was built) and later Felsőváros ('Upper town'), was erected on one large and several small areas of higher ground. Its parish church was consecrated to St. George. A late 17th century view shows a two-aisled church, but its form and the fact that the southern aisle was longer than the northern aisle suggests that the church was three-aisled with an apsidal termination. In the 19th century a school was erected which was pulled down in 1905.[104] The Dominican monastery of St. Nicholas, founded in 1318, stood not far from the church, on the edge of the marshland.[105] In all probability this monastery was built on the ruins of the Benedictine abbey of St. Nicholas, mentioned in a source dating from 1225, which was destroyed during the Mongol invasion of 1241.[106] Modern maps indicate that the most important north to south read leading through the town passed between the two churches and widened into a

rectangle at that point.[107] Even if the shape of the square cannot be traced to the Middle Ages, the marketplace of Felszeged can still be considered as having been in this area. The *superior forum*, mentioned around 1327–30,[108] can be located to this area in spite of the fact that the permission to hold weekly markets (on Thursdays) in Felsősziget dates from 1431 only. The permission was granted to the Felsősziget quarter — *locus* — of the town of Szeged,[109] suggesting perhaps that it had been an autonomous part of the town. Mention must also be made of the fact that the *patrocinium* of all three churches in Palánk and Felszeged was especially popular in Eastern Churches.[110]

The centre of the fourth part of the town was situated approximately 1.5 km south of the castle, and 1 km from St. Demeter's church. A source dating from 1422 mentions that Alszeged, the antecedent of Alsóváros, had its own appointed judge and council.[111] On the evidence of the 18th century maps the plan of this quarter differed from that of the other two town parts. The plan of Alszeged resembled that of the so-called garden suburbs.[112] Interestingly enough there is no data on its parsonage even though it is known to have had its own council. Alszeged too was established before the Mongol invasion. Most scholars unanimously identify Alszeged with the Szeged *terra* and port donated by Queen Euphrosyne to the Johannites of Székesfehérvár before 1183, and assume that St. Peter's Hospital and the Alszeged church had been founded by the Johannites.[113] On the strength of the carved stone fragments recovered from the site the church is assigned to the first half of the 13th century, i.e. to the period preceding the Mongol invasion.[114] The Johannites presumably lost their properties in this region after the invasion and the

[99] On the strength of the *superior forum* mentioned in Szeged in 1327–30, there may also have been an *inferior forum* there. I. Petrovics: Oklevelek Szeged középkori történetéhez (Charters on the medieval history of Szeged). *Acta Universitatis Szegediensis de Attila József nominatae. Acta Historica* 66 (1979) 62. The Monday markets are mentioned in a 1407 source: *ZsO* II/2, no. 5649. A 1456 reference: Reizner (1900) 50–51.

[100] Reizner (1900) 89–90.

[101] Cs. Sebestyén (1938) 29. In his opinion Palánk had had no market precisely on account of the 1499 permission to hold markets.

[102] Cs. Sebestyén (1938) 29.

[103] Kubinyi (1980) 431.

[104] Cs. Sebestyén (1938) 71–79. G. Entz: *Kőtár (Stone relics)*. Szeged (n.d.) 13. He associates the Romanesque stone fragments found in the castle with this church.

[105] Bálint (1975) 22–25.

[106] K. Juhász: Ein unbekanntes Benediktinerstift in der Stadt Szeged. *MIÖG* 69 (1961) 359–362; Bálint (1970) 203–205; Bálint (1975) 7–9. My friends Gy. Kristó and I. Petrovics called my attention to the fact that the abbey cannot be definitely associated with Szeged.

[107] On the evidence of an 18th century map: Cs. Sebestyén (1938) 71.

[108] Cf. note 99.

[109] Reizner (1900) 31. It would appear that only the royal permission dates from 1431, or that markets had been held on other days as well.

[110] For details cf. the earlier literature: Kubinyi (1980) 427.

[111] Csánki (1890) Vol. I, 677; cf. also note 2; Reizner (1900) Vol. III, 28.

[112] Cs. Sebestyén (1938) 85; cf. also note 3. Jenő Major has pointed out that my observations on the medieval groundplan of Szeged were in part based on the map published in Gy. Györffy's book. Since there are other possible reconstructions of the groundplan, my conclusions cannot be definitely substantiated. Major considers the groundplan of Alsóváros to have been regular. To complicate matters, István Petrovics published a study not long after the completion of this paper — A középkori magyar városfejlődés és Szeged (The development of medieval Hungarian towns and Szeged). *Fejezetek a régebbi magyar történelemből*. Vol. I. Ed. by Ferenc Makk. Budapest (1981) 117–134. Petrovics's suggestions differ from my conclusions on several points, even though I agree with some of his suggestions, which I nonetheless consider open to debate. After the publication of the volume on the medieval history of Szeged, I plan to return to the subject again, but until then I hesitate to modify my opinion.

[113] E. Jakubovich–D. Pais: *Ó-magyar olvasókönyv (Old Hungarian texts)*. Pécs (1929) 59; Györffy (1963) Vol. I, 901ff; Bálint (1975) 7; etc.

[114] G. Entz: *Kőtár (Stone relics)*. Szeged (n.d.) 14.

settlement subsequently grew into an independent town; in the mid-15th century it was incorporated into Szeged. In 1458 King Mátyás confirmed the right of presentation of the townsmen of Szeged over the St. Demeter and St. George parsonages and the St. Peter and St. Elizabeth Hospitals.[115] The building was replaced by the still existing church (Fig. 7) and monastery of the Blessed Virgin, erected by the Observant Franciscans. Legate Cardinal Cesarini's decree of 1444 ordered the transfer of the Franciscan monastery in Szeged to the Observants, an order that was never carried out. Consequently, the Observant John of Capistrano had to stay with the commander of the castle during his 1455 visit to Szeged.[116] While in 1458 the king confirmed the town of its right of presentation over St. Peter's Hospital, in early 1459 the right to hold weekly markets (on Wednesdays), and also to set up four butcher's stalls was granted to the square in front of the monastery of the Virgin Mary.[117] The hospital may have passed into the hands of the Observants in this period, but St. Elizabeth's monastery still belonged to the Conventual Franciscans. The royal donation at the same time meant the foundation of a marketplace in front of the new monastery, indicating that Alszeged did not have one in the preceding periods. During the restoration of the church in the 1930s, Cs. Sebestyén made rather interesting observations. He established that the brick aisle of the church dates from the early or mid-14th century, i.e. it antedates the sanctuary. On the other hand, the sanctuary, which terminates in three sides of the hexagon, the adjoining tower and the sacristy can be assigned to the last decade of the 15th century, i.e. to a period which also has written evidence for the construction of the monastery. The church, which to all appearances, was originally three-aisled was rebuilt as a single-aisled building in this period.[118] This would imply that the still extant nave cannot be identified with the early 13th century church whose Romanesque carvings came to light during restoration.[119] The new edifice of St. Peter's Hospital, erected in the 14th century, was surprisingly large, and may therefore have also served as the parsonage of the independent settlement of Alszeged.[120] This title was lost after the unification of the town. The old church of St. Peter was used by the Observants from the mid- until the late 15th century, but with a new *patrocinium,* from the very beginning. At the end of the century a new church and monastery were erected, and the nave of the old church was incorporated into it.

The town of Szeged is known to have had several other church institutions, but the location and age of these buildings cannot be established. One of these institutions was the nunnery of the Holy Ghost of the Premonstratensians, which was presumably located in Felsőváros.[121] The above mentioned royal decree also mentions St. Elizabeth's Hospital. Little is known of the history of this building, except for the fact that in 1449 two burghers, János the tailor and János Mizsér, paid for the renovation of St. Elizabeth's chapel and an adjoining building, thus making them suitable for providing for the poor and accommodating one priest.[122] But this building had nothing in common with St. Elizabeth's monastery of the Conventual Franciscans.

In short, Szeged represented a rather unique type of town. According to an oft-quoted French travelogue from the first half of the 15th century the town had only one street, but it was one mile long. The road connecting Alszeged with Felszeged that led through Palánk was indeed fairly long (3.5 km). However, a register from 1522 lists 29 streets in the town.[123] This rich and densely populated town (with approximately 8000 inhabitants), which had no defensive structures around it, was rather village-like in its appearance, even though the 18th century groundplan of Palánk and Felszeged are definitely indicative of settlements not resembling a village. That the first stone structures in the centre of the town were erected in the Late Middle Ages is suggested by the contemporary charters and the Renaissance door and window frames.[124]

The village of Tápé, on the banks of the river Tisza about 2 km from Felszeged, was annexed to Szeged in 1247 by a royal decree.[125] The village that was destroyed during the Mongol invasion was resettled and has since remained in the possession of Szeged.[126] It should also be recalled that a number of monasteries were erected in the environs of Szeged. Besides the Benedictine abbey in Szeged built before the Mongol invasion, there was the abbey of St. Philip in Szőreg, a village southeast of Szeged on the opposite bank of the Tisza and Maros river. The first reference to the latter abbey dates from the late 12th century.[127]

---

[115] Reizner (1900) Vol. IV, 54. The earlier studies interpreted this charter erroneously. For the correct interpretation cf. Z. Somogyi: *A középkori Magyarország szegényügye (Poor relief in medieval Hungary).* Budapest (1941) 88, note 2.

[116] Bálint (1975) 28.

[117] Reizner (1900) Vol. IV, 56.

[118] Cs. Sebestyén (1938) 95–111.

[119] Cf. note 114. The original St. Peter's church may have stood in the vicinity. Cf. Bálint (1970) 202, note 16.

[120] Hospital churches as parsonages: Z. Somogyi: *A középkori Magyarország szegényügye (Poor relief in medieval Hungary).* Budapest (1941). The two Franciscan churches were erected on the ruins of earlier churches. This practice was not unusual in the case of the monasteries of the Mendicant order, cf. H. Koller: Hochmittelalterliche Siedlungsplanungen und Stadtgründungen im Ostalpenraum. *Forschungen zur Geschichte der Städten und Märkte Österreichs.* Linz/Donau (1978) Vol. I, 32.

[121] Bálint (1975) 42–63.

[122] Lukcsics (1938) Vol. II, no. 1058.

[123] Kubinyi (1980) 431. It is highly improbable that the outlay of the town would have changed so markedly in less than a century. Cf. K. Schünemann: *Die Entstehung des Städtewesens in Südosteuropa.* Breslau–Oppeln (n.d.) 22.

[124] Kubinyi (1980) 438; G. Entz: *Kőtár (Stone relics).* Szeged (n.d.) 18.

[125] Reizner (1900) Vol. IV, 3.

[126] The 1522 register of tithes mentions Tápé and Szentmihály, southwest of Szeged, together with Szeged. S. Bálint: *Az 1522. évi tizedlajstrom szegedi vezetéknevei (Surnames in the 1522 register of tithes in Szeged).* Budapest (1963) 44–45.

[127] K. Dávid: *Az Árpád-kori Csanád megye művészeti topográfiája (The artistic topography of Csanád County in the Árpádian Age).* Művészettörténeti Füzetek 7. Budapest (1974) 28-30.

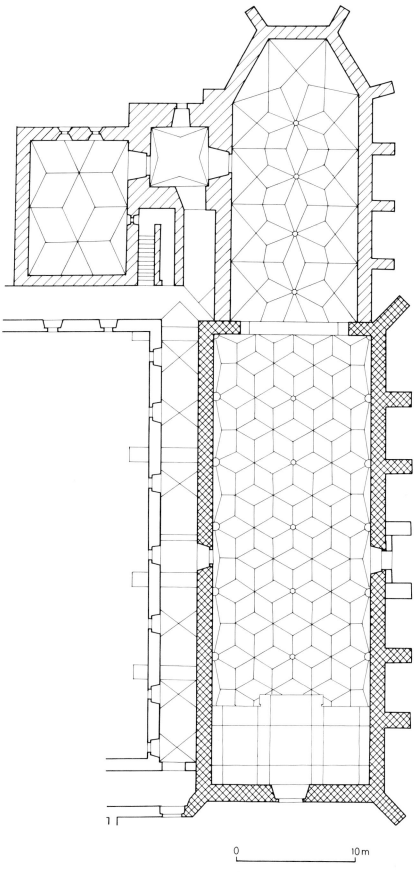

0　　　　　　　　　10 m

Fig. 7. Groundplan of the Franciscan church at Szeged. The nave probably dates from the 14th century

117

The monastery of the wealthy Dorozsma clan lay northwest of Szeged at a similar distance to the others. It is first mentioned in 1237. On the evidence of the Romanesque stone found on the site, the monastery had been erected in the last quarter of the 12th century at the earliest.[128] Remarkably enough, both church institutions were situated on one of the most important roads which connected Buda with Transylvania.

### (4) The early town type

Besides the differing features, the development of the above discussed three towns shared a number of common traits. First, the name of the town referred not only to the original nucleus but also to considerably large *suburbia*, i.e. the town had more than one nucleus. In other words, there was a number of settlements close to each other. These settlements usually lay around a church, and had a castle in their centre (Eger: market, St. Nicholas Street, Olasz Street, Bell ringer Street; Vác: the first settlement that can be assumed around St. Peter's church, the 'Hungarian town', the 'German town'; Szeged: Palánk, Felszeged, Alszeged). Second, the merging of these small settlements in all three towns took place after the mid-15th century. Interestingly enough, the first town to become legally unified was Szeged, even though its geographical environment was the least suited to this (there was only one road connecting the small settlements that were built on the higher ground). The unification of Vác can also be dated to the period before the Turkish occupation. In the early 14th century the 'Hungarian' and 'German' towns of Vác were still not united, as suggested by the fact that the Augustine monastery was built in an open area between the two towns, on the main road running parallel with the Danube. The absorption of the settlement near St. Peter's church and the fact that the parish church of the 'Hungarian town' was left outside the area defended by the rampart were nevertheless signs of the town's concentration. Although the two towns never became legally united, in some cases they both accepted the authority of a common judge. The amalgamation of the settlements at Eger also took place sometime in the Late Middle Ages, with the open areas between giving ground to new quarters (Szabadhely, Újváros). The 16th century saw the erection of the town wall, but the town was still not unified by law. It is also worthy of note that until the mid-16th century none of these towns had a defensive stone wall. The only exception to this was the 'German town' of Vác, which was established fairly late, in the mid-13th century. The majority of the buildings in Vác and Szeged were visibly rural — only in the Late Middle Ages did the first urban buildings appear in the centres of the towns (stone constructions, often multi-storeyed).

Szeged, the most populous and prosperous of the three towns, was the first to acquire a fully unified legal status. This may — at least partly — be due to the fact that this was the only royal, and from the late 15th century free royal, town. The development of Szeged indicates that the geographical position of the settlements affected their original isolation only secondarily. Despite the more favourable location of the settlements at Vác and Eger, they never became legally united. This isolation cannot be accounted for by the different landlords holding properties in the area. For example the bishop of Eger owned several independent quarters in the town. This complex process of agglomeration can least be observed in Vác, where the settlement around St. Peter's church was abandoned at a fairly early time, and the 'German town' was established only in the second half of the 13th century. In other words, only the castle and its suburb, the predecessor of the 'Hungarian town', had existed before the Mongol invasion. It must also be recalled that while the Latin and German *hospites* had settled in Eger and its agglomeration already preceding the Mongol invasion, the presence of *hospites* in Vác dates to after the invasion, and there were practically no foreign *hospites* in Szeged. Consequently, the similarities cannot be ascribed to the presence of the *hospites*. There are other similarities between Eger and Szeged. For example both towns had a number of *patrocinia* common in the eastern rites (Eger: Demeter, Nicholas; Cosmas-Damianus in neighbouring Tihamér; Szeged: Demeter, Nicholas, George), interesting only in terms of the frequency of these titles. The Nicholas *patrocinia* suggest a flourishing local trade, irrespective of possible Byzantine influences.[129] It must be added that the environs of Eger and Szeged were dotted with monasteries.

Regrettably enough, we still know very little about the medieval street network and the Árpádian Age buildings in these three towns. These questions could be answered by further archaeological excavations. The 18th century maps offer a glimpse of the late medieval appearance only, although these should be viewed with reservation owing to the Turkish occupation inbetween. An insight into the life of these towns during the early periods can only be gained from archaeological research.[130]

The three towns — especially Eger and Szeged — were thus agglomerations of small settlements, and their concentration into legally unified towns was a relatively slow process. We have to add that this process was not restricted to this country part alone. The emergence of most of the episcopal sees in Hungary was the end-result of a similar development and the unification of various urban nuclei can in some cases only be noted after the Middle Ages. In Veszprém, Transdanubia, this can in

[128] Györffy (1963) Vol. I, 894; *Árpád-kori kőfaragványok (Stone carvings from the Árpádian Age)*. Székesfehérvár (1978) 184.

[129] Major (1966) 74–75; K. Blaschke: Nikolaipatrozinium und städtische Frühgeschichte. *Zeitschrift für Rechtsgeschichte, Kan. Abt.* 53 (1967) 273–337; Bálint (1975) 7–9.

[130] The late medieval groundplan of the town is not necessarily identical with that of an earlier period. Cf. B. Schwineköper: Die Problematik von Begriffen wie Stauferstädte, Zähringerstädte und ähnlichen Bezeichnungen. *Südwestdeutsche Städte im Zeitalter der Staufer*. Ed. by E. Maschke–J. Sydow. Sigmaringen (1980) 112–114.

part be attributed to the morphology of the terrain (hills and valleys), even though the bishop's castle in Veszprém was likewise surrounded by churches and monasteries.[131] The same can be said of Nagyvárad (Oradea), the significant market town on the eastern fringes of the Great Hungarian Plain, where the independent settlements, each having a church in the centre, developed on islets in the river Körös that flowed round the bishop's castle. The population of Nagyvárad included Latin *hospites,*[132] but they were not represented in Veszprém. Neither town had defensive structures. However, the fact that these towns did not become unified cannot be attributed simply to the geographical environment (cf. the developments in Eger and Szeged). This progress was most probably blocked by the church landowner since landed interests could best be protected in a town not unified by law.[133]

There was thus a settlement type in medieval Hungary which featured a number of small detached settlements at a relatively early date (the 11th century in the case of the episcopal sees). These settlements were usually clustered around a church or a monastery, and surrounded the castle in the nucleus of the town. Traces indicative of trade, marketplaces, and early specialized craftsmen's settlements have also been discovered.[134] It has been shown that some of these settlements were still not unified into towns by the end of the Middle Ages. Mention must be made here of Jenő Major's observation that the 11th–12th century Hungarian marketplaces were surrounded by craftsmen's or merchants' settlements at a distance of approximately 2–3 km, but sometimes 5 or even 10 km. These settlements were very small villages, but "taken together, they can well be considered to have been the detached quarters of a town. The medieval town itself was in fact no more than a concentrated cluster of these separate settlements."[135] Major correctly noted that these agglomerations represented detached cores of the social division of labour (for the time being only in space), but since his conclusions were based on the study of one type of marketplace only, his analysis did not include the agglomeration of settlements surrounding churches built near castles, where the concentration of the churches had led to an increase in consumption.

In the past two decades, researchers abroad came to

more or less comparable conclusions. Herzog, the art historian, established that the 10th century German towns under the reign of King Otto were likewise areally detached. He was the first to note the 'ring of churches' surrounding the nucleus of the town, besides the castle and the 'merchant' settlements.[136] This layout, however, was not widespread throughout Europe.[137] The emergence of enclosed towns, of urban settlements and towns proper, can be assigned to the second half of the 11th–early 12th centuries.[138] Herzog's theory was further elaborated by Koller, a historian, who also cited additional evidence.[139] Koller pointed out that in several cases the name of an originally extensive area was adopted by the settlements established in them.[140] A town could evolve either from the concentric expansion of the town core or from the union of a number of separate settlements.[141] Koller also noted that the early urban settlements consisted of rather humble houses, but he did not link this to poverty. Churches were generally ornate, while the houses were not. The practice of erecting the houses side by side was also a later development.[142] This does not apply to the towns in France, whose emergence can be dated to an earlier period and were the results of a different process.

Koller's observations fully match our knowledge of the development of the late medieval Hungarian towns discussed in the above. Since the majority of the small settlements surrounding the churches predate the Mongol invasion, their development roughly coincides with, or is only slightly later than, the period discussed by Herzog and Koller. The emergence of the legally unified towns and the disappearance of the earlier settlement type is assigned to the second half of the 12th century by Koller, thus to a somewhat later period than suggested by Herzog.[143] (There is a general consensus that fortified towns became widespread in the 12th–13th centuries.[144]) It can thus be established that the initial 11th–12th century phase in Hungarian urban development can be likened to that in 10th–11th century Germany. This can most clearly be demonstrated in the case of Szeged and the episcopal towns. However, their subsequent development came to an abrupt halt and their birth in the Late Middle Ages was preceded by a long period of stagnation. The wave of urbanisation in 13th century Hungary (the development of legally unified towns) affected only the settlements in Transdanubia, Upper Northern Hungary and Transylvania, bypassing the

---

[131] J. Gutheil: *Az Árpád-kori Veszprém (Veszprém in the Árpádian Age).* Veszprém (1977) 182–212. One of the districts evolved in the vicinity of St. Nicholas' church.

[132] Györffy (1963) Vol. I, 681–689; Kubinyi (1980) 439–440. The town of Nagyvárad also had a St. Nicholas *vicus,* with a market in it. Major (1966) 73.

[133] E. Mályusz: A mezővárosi fejlődés (The development of market towns). *Tanulmányok a parasztság történetéhez Magyarországon a 14. században.* Ed. by Gy. Székely. Budapest (1953) 164–166, 168–172.

[134] Cf. the goldsmiths in Naszály, near Vác. Cf. note 61. For the craftsmen in Veszprém and the St. Nicholas districts, see A. Kubinyi: Die Anfänge des städtischen Handwerkes in Ungarn. *La formation et le développement des métiers au Moyen Age (V^e–XIV^e siècles).* Ed. by L. Gerevich–Á. Salamon. Budapest (1977) 142.

[135] Major (1966) 68.

[136] E. Herzog: *Die ottonische Stadt.* Berlin (1964) 227–252.

[137] *Ibid.,* 253–254.

[138] *Ibid.,* 255–256.

[139] Koller: Hochmittelalterliche Siedlungsplanungen und Stadtgründungen im Ostalpenraum. *Forschungen zur Geschichte der Städten und Märkte Österreichs.* Vol. 1. Linz/Donau (1978) 4, 25–38.

[140] *Ibid.,* 8–11.

[141] *Ibid.,* 15.

[142] *Ibid.,* 37.

[143] *Ibid.,* 46–57.

[144] B. Schwineköper: Die Problematik von Begriffen wie Stauferstädte, Zähringerstädte und ähnlichen Bezeichnungen. *Südwestdeutsche Städte im Zeitalter der Staufer.* Ed. by E. Maschke–J. Sydow. Sigmaringen (1980) 121–122.

Great Hungarian Plain and some of the episcopal towns. Even though Szeged in the Great Hungarian Plain appears to be an exception, the agglomeration of the settlements there took place as late as the 15th century, despite the franchise of town granted earlier. This clearly implies that no Asian or nomadic town types, or towns characteristic of the Great Hungarian Plain only, can be presumed. The evolution of urban nuclei in 11th–12th century Hungary is comparable to that of non-Hungarian towns in the same period. The towns in, or on the fringes of, the Great Hungarian Plain differed from the settlements in other parts of the country inasmuch as their development was interrupted by a centuries-long stagnation, and that they caught up with the stage of development of 12th century German and 13th–14th century Hungarian towns only much later.

### THE PROBLEM OF MARKET TOWNS

#### (1) Town and market town

As mentioned above, the settlements in Hungary included not only the towns proper but also the so-called market towns *(oppida)*, enjoying more or less urban liberties. In the Late Middle Ages, only the inhabitants of the free royal towns could exercise civil liberties, while the burghers of the other towns or town-like settlements were considered serfs by law. The free royal towns were subjects of the king and all, except Szeged, were defended by walls.[145] The burghers of the manorial *liberae civitates* — most of which had defensive structures — were granted considerably more privileges, but were still considered serfs in terms of the feudal state.[146] Hungarian scholars use the term market town *(oppidum)* collectively for denoting the franchised settlements which were not free royal towns, and whose burghers were therefore serfs. From an economic point of view, some of these settlements that would not qualify as towns (Stoob calls them 'Minderstädte'),[147] must have functioned as towns, since it is unimaginable that vast regions in the country would have lacked towns. The only free royal town in the Great Hungarian Plain was Szeged, and there was no such town in southern Transdanubia. We cannot consider the town of Pécs in this sense since it had not been granted this franchise. Several criteria have been proposed for identifying those enjoying a full urban function among the numerous market towns. One of these criteria is whether the settlement had had a monastery of the Mendicant order.[148] Other criteria include the number of inhabitants with foreign university degrees, or the role of the settlement in the market system of a larger region.[149] It has recently been suggested that one of these criteria should be the contemporary definition of a settlement (e.g. whether a settlement, a market town by law, was called *civitas*).[150] A decade ago I suggested another possible criterion, namely the analysis of the layout and the architecture of the settlement. In my paper I also pointed out that this criterion calls for archaeological investigations.[151] Regrettably enough, the past decade was not marked by significant progress in the archaeological investigation of the market towns. Nevertheless, I shall in the following focus on whether any urban features can be discerned in the medieval architecture of the major market towns in, or on the fringes of, the Great Hungarian Plain. Even though I shall now primarily concentrate on this one criterion, I would like to emphasize that only the complex analysis of all the above criteria can help in distinguishing between towns and market towns. Data permitting, the population number, the ratio of urban crafts, the breakdown and differentiation of the handicrafts, etc., can also be instrumental.

The market town (a non-fortified town in its literal sense)[152] is not a specifically Hungarian phenomenon. It is readily comparable with the Bavarian-Austrian 'Markt'.[153] Similar, not always fortified towns but ranking below than the town proper in a legal sense are also known elsewhere in Europe.[154] Thus, in our discussion of this settlement type in Hungary, we can quote

[145] Kubinyi (1977) 164–183; A. Kubinyi: Zur Frage der Vertretung der Städte im ungarischen Reichstag bis 1526. *Städte und Ständestaat. Zur Rolle der Städte bei der Entwicklung der Ständeverfassung in europäischen Staaten vom 13. bis zum 15. Jahrhundert.* Ed. by B. Töpfer. Berlin (1980) 215–246. With a detailed survey of earlier studies.

[146] E. Ladányi: Libera villa, civitas, oppidum. Terminologische Fragen in der ungarischen Städteentwicklung. *AnnUniv Bud* 18 (1977) 27–29; Kubinyi (1980) 216.

[147] H. Stoob: Minderstädte. Formen der Stadtentstehung im Spätmittelalter. *Vierteljahrschrift für Sozial- und Wirtschaftsgeschichte* 46 (1956) 1–28.

[148] E. Fügedi: La formation des villes et les ordres mendiants en Hongrie. *Annales, Économies, Sociétés, Civilisations* (1970) 966–987.

[149] Kubinyi (1977) 167–178.

[150] Ladányi: Libera villa, civitas, oppidum. Terminologische Fragen in der ungarischen Städteentwicklung. *AnnUnivBud* 18 (1977) 2–43; G. Érszegi: Középkor (The Middle Ages). *Sárvár monográfiája.* Ed. by F. Horváth. Szombathely (1978) 193–200; A. Kubinyi: Hozzászólás Sárvár monográfiájához (Comments on the Sárvár Monograph). *Vasi Szemle* 33 (1979) 577–580.

[151] A. Kubinyi: A XIV–XVI. század várostörténeti problémái és a régészet (The problems of 14th–16th century urban history and archaeology). *RégFüz* II. 14 (1971) 46.

[152] Kubinyi (1977) 176.

[153] German sources refer to it as 'Markt', e.g. Sopronkeresztúr (1429): J. Házi: *Sopron szabad királyi város története (The history of Sopron, a free royal town).* Vol. I/2. Sopron (1923) 393; Csepreg (1451): *ibid.*, Vol. I/3. Sopron (1924) 321; etc.

[154] H. Stoob: Minderstädte. Formen der Stadtentstehung im Spätmittelalter. *Vierteljahrschrift für Sozial- und Wirtschaftsgeschichte* 46 (1958) 1–28. The undefended towns were dominant in England: M. Beresford: *New Towns in the Middle Ages. Town Plantation in England, Wales and Gascony.* New York–Washington (1967); C. Platt: *The English Mediaeval Town.* London (1976) 27–45; H. L. Turner: *Town Defences in England and Wales.* London (1971) 16, 91. English researchers generally note that it was primarily the royal, and not the manorial town that had been defended. For example only eight out of 46 towns under ecclesiastical lordship had had defensive structures.

comparable towns from outside Hungary. The recently published excellent survey of the 'Markt's in Upper Austria must be singled out in this respect. The following passage contains a noteworthy observation concerning the groundplan of these towns: "man kann klar erkennen, dass nur der Marktplatz — wenn keiner vorhanden ist, dann eben sein Fehlen — das Bild eines Marktes bestimmt hat und bestimmt. Es gibt in einem gewöhnlichen Markt keine Nebenstrassen oder gar eigene Marktviertel. Der den Platz umschliessende Häuserblock mit den an den Rückfronten anschliessenden Burgrechtsgründen bildete die spezifische Siedlungsform Markt, im Unterschied zu der mehrstrassigen Stadt."[155] In other words, a settlement with a marketplace and more than one street is considered a town in Upper Austria. We have to add that the type of 'town' with one street, or with a marketplace but without a street is common in other countries too, e.g. in England.[156] The usefulness of this criterion in the investigation and definition of Hungarian towns needs to be examined. For example, the above-quoted market town of Hajdúböszörmény at first only had one street (but was not, at that time, a market town), later it became a town with cross-streets and finally it showed a parallel street pattern.[157]

### (2) Gyöngyös

Gyöngyös which is usually called a 'Great Hungarian Plain type' town lies at the foot of the Mátra Mts on the fringes of the Great Hungarian Plain.[158] The original settlement followed a bend of the Nagy stream flowing in a north to south direction in the east, although part of the settlement extended also to the western bank of the stream. The town had a cross-road plan: the parish church stood at the intersection of four streets. The medieval Solymos Street (today Petőfi Sándor Street) ran in a north to south direction, and terminated in the Solymosi gate in the north. The continuation of this street to the south was the widening Piac (Market) Square (today Main Square), from where the parallel

Rózsa and Móricz Zsigmond Streets branch out. The southern termination of the north to south main road is Jókai Street (formerly Csapó Street), which had a gate at its end. The north–south road crosses the east–west main road in the northern end of Main Square. Kossuth Lajos Street, and its continuation, Lenin Street in the east were together called Bene Street in the Middle Ages, and it terminated at the Bene gate in the east.[159] The continuation of this street on the western bank of the stream was the medieval Tó or Tót Street (today Vachott Sándor Street).[160] References to the above-mentioned gates date from modern times only. But Gyöngyös had never had town walls, only a ditch and a hedgerow fence defended it.[161] This settlement type (rib street pattern and a ditch delimiting the settlement in a semicircle) appears to be typical — we shall see that Miskolc was similar to this. Hajdúböszörmény, too, had a street grid, but there it was only a secondary phenomenón (Fig. 8).

The town of Gyöngyös had definitely existed by the mid-13th century. In the second half of the 13th century it was in the possession of the Csobánka branch of the Aba family of noble rank, and belonged to their castle at Bene.[162] The ruins of this castle, that was probably built in the second half of the 13th century, can be seen on top of a 471 m high hill, 6.5 km northeast of the town.[163] In 1301 the members of the Csobánka family divided Bene and Gyöngyös among them, dividing the village (villa) of Gyöngyös into three parts.[164] The charter suggests that the cruciform street pattern with a church at the intersection had already existed, and also that the western street had crossed the stream. The source locates the Corpus Christi chapel, erected by László Csobánka, to the western bank of the stream. The medieval names of two of the four streets are also instructive. These names indicate the direction where they led. Solymos Street led to the north, to the village of Solymos, whilst Bene Street led to the east, and turned north outside the town to Bene castle. The studies on the settlement history of Gyöngyös agree that the north to south street running parallel with the stream (the northern side of which is Solymos Street) was the original nucleus of the settlement.[165] This can most probably be accepted. This was the site of the widening street market. An 1855 map shows that the street section near the forking of present-day Jókai Street into Rózsa and Móricz Zsigmond Streets widened towards the north until the intersection with the east–

[155] W. Katzinger: Die Märkte Oberösterreichs. Eine Studie zu ihren Anfängen im 13. und 14. Jahrhundert. *Forschungen zur Geschichte der Städten und Märkte Österreichs.* Linz/Donau (1978) Vol. I, 98-99.

[156] M. Beresford: *New Towns in the Middle Ages. Town Plantation in England, Wales and Gascony.* New York–Washington (1967) 106: Olney; 107: Harewood; 109: South Zeal; 110: New Alresford—with some of the streets that run parallel with the market street and had houses in them obviously dating from a later period; 113: Bretford; 114: Newton Poppleford; 115: Colyford; 116: Bridgetown Pomeroy; 120: Grampound; 122: Alnmouth; 139: Henley in Arden. Most of these were founded as boroughs. Cf. also C. Platt: *The English Mediaeval Town.* London (1971) 27–30. Comparable small towns are now being excavated in England, cf. M. Aston–T. Rowley: *Landscape Archaeology. An Introduction to Fieldwork Techniques on Post-Roman Landscapes.* Newton Abbot–London–Vancouver (1974) 96–102, 140–141.

[157] Cf. notes 15–16.

[158] *HMM* III, 25.

[159] *Ibid.,* 176, 60, 123, 129, 140–141.

[160] *Ibid.,* 191.

[161] *Ibid.,* 15.

[162] A charter of 1261 mentions the neighbouring village of Gyöngyöspüspöki. The presumed differentiation between Püspöki and Gyöngyös suggests that Püspöki must have evolved into an important settlement by that period. *RegArp* II/1. no. 2123. Cf. also Dezséri Bachó (1942) 41–65.

[163] *HMM* III, 155–157; Fügedi (1977) 107; P. Engel: *Királyi hatalom és arisztokrácia viszonya a Zsigmond-korban (Relations between the royal power and the aristocracy under King Sigismund).* Budapest (1977) 97.

[164] *AO* I, 3–6.

[165] Dezséri Bachó (1942) 49–50.

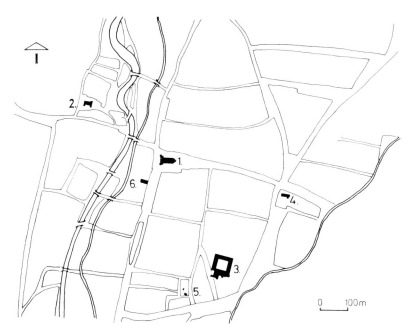

Fig. 8. Gyöngyös in the Middle Ages. 1. St. Bertalan's parish church, 2. Corpus Christi (later St. Orban's) church, 3. Franciscan monastery and church, 4. St. Elizabeth's church, 5. chapel of the Holy Ghost (house of Beginas), 6. medieval house

west street near the parish church dedicated to St. Bertalan. The church is mentioned in the 1301 charter of division. Its original form in not known. In the late 15th century it was rebuilt into a huge late Gothic hall-church. The two towers on the western front were added to the three-aisled church during the Baroque period. The church features a bronze baptismal font from around 1500, and its treasury, which has preserved the medieval equipment, is one of the richest collections of medieval relics (Fig. 9).[166] Solymos Street, running north of the church, was as narrow as the southern end of the street. Parallels of this town type with one street widening into a marketplace in the middle are also known outside Hungary.[167] This system was changed for several reasons. After the building of Bene castle it became necessary to provide communication with the centre of the estate. It is conspicuous that the road leading to Bene did not branch off from Solymos Street leading to the north, but turned off at a right angle toward the east from the north-to-south road at the church, and turned north only after leaving the area occupied by the later town. This section of the road runs almost parallel with Solymos Street. One reason for this was that the neighbouring village of Solymos to the north did not belong to the Bene estate. There was also another, more important reason. The main road connecting Buda, in the centre of the country, with

Poland through the town of Kassa (Košice) reached the foot of the Mátra hills at Gyöngyös, from where it proceeded towards northeast. The most significant towns on the road between Buda, Pest and Kassa were Gyöngyös, Eger and Miskolc.[168] The merchants arriving in Gyöngyös from Pest turned east immediately after leaving the marketplace. The widening funnel-shaped termination of Bene Street leads into the north–south street at the church. The fourth street in the crossing, the western continuation of Bene Street crossing the stream, Tó Street, does not follow the direction of Bene Street but leads westwards to the vineyards, starting from the northwestern corner house in Bene Street. This corner house of the *comes* Benedek played a prominent role in the partition of the estate in 1301.[169] The above-named Corpus Christi chapel, dedicated in later times to St. Urban, the patron saint of vine, was built on the northern side of Tó Street, on the opposite bank of the stream.[170]

Consequently the gridded street system of Gyöngyös cannot be considered a primary arrangement, although it definitely existed as early as 1301. The Csobánka family lost their hold over Gyöngyös in 1323, and a royal decree of 1327 donated the town to the Szécsényi family. In later times the property rights were shared by a number of major landowners.[171] In the 15th century Bene castle was demolished and Gyöngyös became the centre of the estate (estate parts).[172] While in the

[166] *HMM* II, 62–114. Jenő Major rejects my suggestion that Gyöngyös perhaps had a market as early as 1301. (The partition gave the later market street to the youngest child, without further explanation.) Should his assumption prove to be correct—which is not altogether improbable—this would imply that the widening of the street was completed shortly afterwards, but definitely prior to the acquisition of the town status.

[167] Cf. some of the examples listed in note 156.

[168] Kubinyi (1977) 176.

[169] The so-called Iron Crown house. *HMM* III, 145; *AO* I, 3; Dezséri Bachó (1942) 50.

[170] *HMM* III, 44–52.

[171] Dezséri Bachó (1942) 65–84.

[172] *HMM* III, 155–156; P. Engel: *Királyi hatalom és arisztokrácia viszonya a Zsigmond korban (Relations between the royal power and the aristocracy under King Sigismund).* Budapest (1977) 97.

122

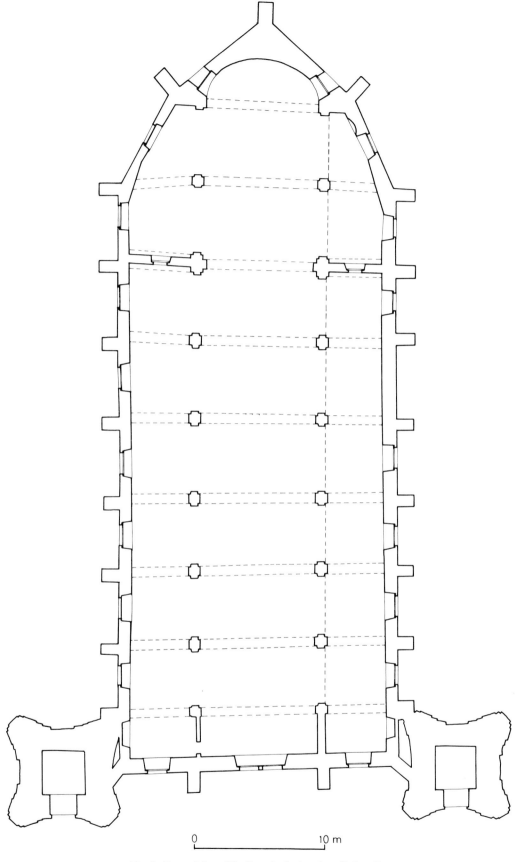

0            10 m

Fig. 9. Groundplan of St. Bertalan's church at Gyöngyös

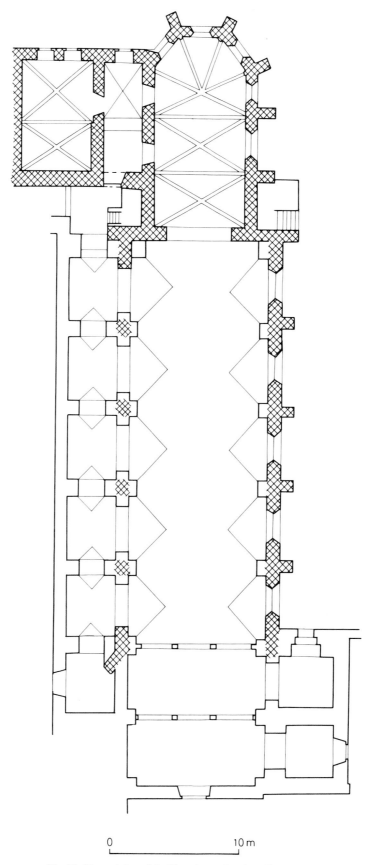

0          10 m

Fig. 10. Groundplan of the Franciscan church at Gyöngyös

124

possession of the Szécsényi family Gyöngyös began to develop into a market town. A royal decree of 1334, granted at the request of Tamás Szécsényi, entitled Gyöngyös to build defensive walls around the town (a similar title was also granted to the burghers of Buda).[173] However, the walls were never built, leading some scholars to reject the importance of this privilege and to state that Gyöngyös never lost its village status.[174] No doubt, the term *oppidum,* applied to Gyöngyös, prevailed from the 15th century on, but this was undoubtedly the result of the royal privilege.[175]

The date of the foundation of the Franciscan monastery of Our Lady is unknown. Art historians assign it to the 14th–15th centuries, and it may thus have been founded by Tamás Szécsényi.[176] The monastery is situated in the southeastern corner of the town, and the area around it was open until the mid-19th century.[177] The Franciscan church is single-aisled, and bears a close resemblance to the Observant church at Szeged. However, it is smaller than the Szeged church and its sanctuary terminates in three sides of an octagon[178] (Fig. 10). The originally Gothic chapel of the Holy Ghost was situated approximately 100 m to the southwest of this church. In the late 15th century this chapel was attached to the house of the Beginas.[179] The St. Elizabeth Hospital church is situated outside the built-in area of the town, on the southern side of the road leading to Eger, at the point that Bene Street forks into the northern and eastern streets. The exact date when this originally Gothic church was built which today is mostly Baroque in appearance, remains unknown. It has been suggested that the church had been already standing in the early 14th century, even though there is no factual data supporting this date. The first reliable data on the church date from the Late Middle Ages.[180]

It is remarkable that the house of the Beginas, the Franciscan monastery and the hospital were all erected in the southeastern corner of the town — the first two on the fringes of the built-in area, the third outside it. The road from Pest to Eger passed along the fringes of the city and travellers could, if they wished, by-pass the Gyöngyös marketplace. These three churches and the Corpus Christi-St. Orban chapel each delimited to the east, south and west, the built-in area of Gyöngyös in the Middle Ages. The northeastern limits of the town have not been located yet. A Turkish tax census of the year 1550 that lists the male population of the town according to streets offers further starting points for

reconstructing the topography of the town. The census lists 300 houses in the town.[181]

The route taken by the Turkish census-takers can be accurately reconstructed, especially from Tód (or, rather, Tó) Street. From there they proceeded to the islet in

Table 3. Breakdown, by street, of the adult male population of Gyöngyös in 1550

| Street | Priests | Married | Bachelor | Total | Merchants | Craftsmen | Percentage of merchants and craftsmen |
|---|---|---|---|---|---|---|---|
| Nagy St. | – | 156 | 72 | 228 | 4 | 35 | 17.1 |
| Virág St. | – | 55 | 9 | 64 | 1 | 2 | 4.7 |
| other Nagy St. | – | 210 | 107 | 317 | 4 | 52 | 17.7 |
| Tód (!) St. | – | 69 | 27 | 96 | – | 11 | 11.5 |
| Sziget St. | – | 46 | 10 | 56 | 1 | 6 | 12.5 |
| Solymos St. | – | 186 | 86 | 272 | – | 27 | 9.9 |
| Bene St. | 11[182] | 117 | 49 | 177 | – | 23 | 13.0 |
| Total | 11 | 839 | 360 | 1210 | 10 | 156 | 100.0 |

the Nagy stream (Sziget Street) by turning north on the western bank of the stream, returned to the east bank in the north, and headed south along Solymos Street. Turning east at Bertalan church, they wound up their route in Bene Street. The high number of priests recorded to have lived near the beginning of the street indicates that the parsonage employed several assistants and chaplains.[183] The route of the census-takers clearly indicates that the 'other' Nagy (Great) Street can be identified with the marketplace, which indeed was the most populous street in town. The location of Virág Street and the 'first' Nagy Street is still controversial. The latter can probably be identified with the road leading to Eger on the southeastern limits of the town, the former with the road running parallel with the marketplace and leading north from the house of the Beginas. The parcelling out of the lots must definitely have begun by this period, since over 800 households, i.e. over 4000 people were to be found on the building plots (obviously ground plots). It is nonetheless clear that this period saw no considerable alterations in the gridded street system dating back to the turn of the 13th–14th centuries.

The number of the inhabitants in medieval Gyöngyös also indicates that the town had been an important

[173] *CD* VIII/3, 716–718.

[174] Dezséri Bachó (1942) 68–73.

[175] D. Csánki: *Magyarország történelmi földrajza a Hunyadiak korában (A historical geography of Hungary in the age of the Hunyadis).* Budapest (1890) Vol. I, 54; *HMM* III, 13–14.

[176] *HMM* III, 161; Dezséri Bachó (1942) 101-102.

[177] *HMM* III, 23, Map.

[178] *Ibid.,* 161.

[179] *Ibid.,* 200.

[180] *Ibid.,* 30; Dezséri Bachó (1942) 106–107.

[181] L. Fekete: *A hatvani szandzsák 1550. évi adóösszeírása (The 1550 tax register of the Hatvan Sanjak).* Jászberény (1968) 37–42.

[182] Ten priests and one 'scribe', with reference to their marital status.

[183] On the evidence of the location they could not be Franciscans who, apparently, were not included in the census. The Orban (previously Corpus Christi) church was owned by the Protestants (*HMM* III, 44). The church of St. Elizabeth was abandoned in the 16th century, and was restored only later (*ibid.,* 30). There is no explanation for the lack of reference to the Franciscans.

settlement. The monastery of the Mendicant order, the house of the Beginas and the hospital all reflect its urban character. 19 residents matriculated at foreign universities (12 in Vienna, 7 in Cracow) between 1440–1514, i.e. the town ranked 53rd–55th among the Hungarian settlements.[184] The only medieval guild we know of was that of the butchers (1498).[185] Food processing must have been flourishing in the town, obviously on account of the large number of inhabitants. The 1550 register also indicates a specialized, high-level craftsmanship. Of the adult males 13.7 per cent were engaged in handicrafts or trade.[186] This ratio is higher — approximately by 18 per cent—if we consider the paterfamilias. This number corresponds to the average of the Hungarian market towns rather than to that of the towns.[187] However, the number of crafts differs sharply from the average; 32 different crafts are recorded in Gyöngyös, reflecting a highly developed division of labour. As a comparison we can quote the market town of Gyula which, in the period before 1526, could boast a highly differentiated handicraft industry, but which included only 22 crafts.[188] The number of crafts practised in Gyöngyös corresponded to that of Pest, the second largest town of the country.[189]

Table 4. Craftsmen in Gyöngyös in 1550[190]

| Craft | Branch | Percentage | Craftsmen | Percentage |
|---|---|---|---|---|
| metallurgy, manufacture of arms | 7 | 21.8 | 29 | 18.6 |
| weaving trade | 4 | 12.5 | 9 | 5.8 |
| leather industry | 3 | 9.4 | 8 | 5.1 |
| wood industry | 6 | 18.8 | 16 | 10.3 |
| food processing | 4 | 12.5 | 17 | 10.9 |
| clothing trade | 3 | 9.4 | 61 | 39.1 |
| building trade, ceramics | 4 | 12.5 | 13 | 8.3 |
| other | 1 | 3.1 | 3 | 1.9 |
| Total | 32 | 100.0 | 156 | 100.0 |

[184] Kubinyi (1971) 75.

[185] V. Bácskai: *Magyar mezővárosok a XV. században (Market towns in 15th century Hungary)*. Budapest (1965) 52, note 76.

[186] We have listed all adult males; not only the married ones, since some of the bachelors were also engaged in handicrafts. Of the merchants, only the traffickers and the tubbers are named, without reference to major wholesalers.

[187] V. Bácskai: *Magyar mezővárosok a XV. században (Market towns in 15th century Hungary)*. Budapest (1965) 32–50.

[188] *Ibid.*, 34.

[189] A. Kubinyi: Budapest története a későbbi középkorban Buda elestéig (1541-ig) (The late medieval history of Budapest until the fall of Buda in 1541). *Budapest története*. Vol. II. Ed. by L. Gerevich. Budapest (1973) 113.

[190] Fekete: *A hatvani szandzsák 1550. évi adóösszeírása (The 1550 tax register of the Hatvan Sandjak)*. Jászberény (1968) 37–42.

Even though the comparative ratio of the crafts practised in Gyöngyös roughly corresponds to that recorded for the other market towns, the high level of specialization and the presence of luxury crafts, such as goldsmiths (6), raises the town above the average (in spite of the fact that the available evidence comes from a period approximately 25 years after the Battle of Mohács). The annual markets in Gyöngyös reflect the significant role played by this town in the exchange of goods. The date of the first markets is not known, but they definitely took place during the saint's day of the three churches (May 25, St. Urban; Aug. 25, St. Bertalan; Nov. 19, St. Elizabeth). The weekly markets were held on Wednesdays, and markets were also held every day.[191]

The appearance of Gyöngyös must have resembled that of Vác and Szeged in the Late Middle Ages (apart from the huge churches), i.e. the urban buildings were concentrated in the heart of the town. In the house under 11 Main Square (the marketplace in the Middle Ages) a Gothic cross-vaulted hall was found with a medieval cellar under it. This building presumably dates from the Late Middle Ages.[192]

*(3) Nyírbátor*

This was one of the major market towns in the Great Hungarian Plain. The first references to Bátor (today Nyírbátor) are roughly contemporaneous with those to Gyöngyös, whose charter is four years younger than Bátor's. The first reference (1272) relates that the king, after donating the village of Hodász approximately 12 km from Bátor, transferred the royal archers to the area of 'Bathar'.[193] If this toponym indeed designated the town of Bátor, it would imply that the territory was — at least in part — in the possession of the king. In 1279, however, the king donated Bátor and Kisbátord, the possessions of Langeus who died without an heir, to the members of the Gutkeled family of noble rank.[194] In 1289 Bereck of the Gutkeled family obtained a royal permit to hold weekly markets in his village of Bátor.[195] The 1279 charter challenges the dating of the village to those years, since the neighbouring village at 'kis' (small) Bátor (Kisbátord) had already existed at that time (the village was depopulated by the next century). The authority of the Gutkeled family definitely contributed to the flourishing of Bátor, and their obtainal of the permission to hold weekly markets; they also settled

[191] *Dl*, 97324; Dezséri Bachó (1942) 122–123.

[192] *HMM* III, 119–122.

[193] *RegArp* II/1, no. 2224, with reference to the land Batar in Ugocsa County. F. Maksai on the other hand, identifies it with Nyírbátor: *A középkori Szatmár megye* (Szatmár County in the Middle Ages). Budapest (1940) 113. The proximity supports the latter opinion.

[194] *RegArp* II/2-3, nos. 2947, 2952. Cf. also Maksai (1940) 113–114; I. Balogh: *Nyírbátor története (History of Nyírbátor)*. Budapest (1956) 5–17; Entz–Szalontai (1969); Fügedi (1972) 182–183; Mező–Németh (1972) 81; Szalontai (1978/2) 73–94; Németh (1979/3) 41–43.

[195] *RegArp* II/2-3, no. 3159.

126

further population groups in the area. The geographical setting also contributed to the development of the settlement. Bátor is situated in the Nyírség, a region covered with wind-blown sand and birch wood. A vast marshland called Ecsed marsh lay not far to the east. The merchants bypassing the marsh were bound to call at Bátor.[196]

Perceiving the favourable location of the settlement, the Gutkeled family chose Bátor as the centre of their estate. The family who changed their name to Báthori after their estate, soon became one of the most famous feudal dynasties in Hungary's history. The Transylvanian princely dynasty and the Polish king were descendants of this lineage. The formation of the Bátor estate can be assigned to the 14th century. Despite the castle erected in the Ecsed marsh between 1334–1354 (they took possession of the marsh in 1322–1329), Bátor remained their *possessio principalis et capitalis* where another castle was built between 1354–1364. This castle, however, was soon demolished. Ecsed Castle became the permanent residence of the family, and Bátor remained the economic centre of the estate.[197] In 1330 the family managed to obtain a royal patent on their Bátor estate. This patent guaranteed the *hospites* and serfs immunity from the authority of the royal and county judges and exempted them from royal taxation as "burghers and *hospites* of a quasi free town". The rights to hold courts in matters of blood guilt was at the same time granted to the landowners.[198] Since the franchise protected the interests of the landowner, it could not turn the settlement into a real 'free town' (the same applied to the franchise at Gyöngyös). The people of Bátor enjoyed only few of the privileges granted to the burghers of the other free towns. Two years later the Báthoris managed to obtain staple right for their eponymous village. This right was in force on the roads enclosing the Ecsed marshland to the north and south. The outermost points were Kraszna and Kocsord, from where dealers drove their cattle to Bátor, and Szalacs, the departure point of Transylvanian salt to the west. The southwestern limit was Debrecen, Kálló in the west and Nagyfalu (on the river Tisza) in the northwest — these settlements supplied Szatmár with goods. Thus the area where the staple right could be exercised formed a double concentric circle. A circle with a radius of 24–26 km could be drawn between Bátor, and Kálló and Kocsord, and another circle with a radius of 50–60 km between Bátor, and Debrecen and Szalacs (Nagyfalu and Kraszna lay farther). Thus Bátor could keep a check on Transylvania's trade with Buda, Kassa (Košice) and Poland. According to the decree, the halted goods had to be put up for sale at the weekly market in Bátor.[199] This type of staple right was almost unparalleled in the period. The comparable privileges granted to Esztergom, Buda, Győr, Pozsony (Bratislava) and Lőcse (Levoča) until the early 14th century were in many instances not put into practice by these royal towns.[200] Accordingly, Bátor was the only manorial settlement that was granted this privilege — on good grounds, as far as the transport conditions are concerned. Little is known about how the Báthoris had exercised this right, but in all probability they could not claim their due against the burghers of the royal towns. The significance of Bátor in the 14th century is clearly reflected by the fact that in 1313 it had two priests and that in 1334 it paid the second highest papal tenth in Szatmár County.[201]

The Báthoris had repeatedly divided the settlement among themselves. These divisions make the reconstruction of the groundplan of Bátor almost impossible, to the extent that it has even been proposed that the Late Middle Ages saw considerable alterations in the plan. It would appear that the settlement was not fortified[202] and some of the streets, even if not all, can be identified with a fair measure of accuracy.[203] The *possessio* of Bátor was divided first into three parts, in 1354.[204] In this period the village had two streets called *maior* or *corporalis platea* — one of which bore the name of Tótzug (or Tószög, a reference to the nearby marshland). Branching off from this street were two *plateae*: Csebe Street and Bogát Street. Pócsi Street, Vasvári Street, Marheyk Street (called properly Marharth elsewhere[205]), Téglás Street and an unnamed street were collectively called the *vicus*. Nemes Street must have been a small street somewhere in the middle of the village, since it was referred to as *viculus*, *plateuncula* or even *platea*. All three holders received a share of this street. The street ran in a north to south direction, with the parson's seat at one end. The right of presentation over the St. George parish church remained a jointly held privilege. The record on the partition calls the marketplace a *locus fori*, where 18 butcher's stalls were divided. After the death of one of the owners, his share was partitioned again in 1373.[206] The record on this partition also mentions the *locus fori*, and the Vásár (Market) Street. In all probability the two names referred to the same location (*forum*, market or marketplace). A certain Szolga Street is also mentioned in this source.

The two documents reveal that Bátor was an important settlement with a number of streets. It represented a settlement type, fairly common in the trans-Tisza territory, which expanded radially from the nucleus of the village. The streets were named after neighbouring villages, i.e. they bore the name of the village to which

[196] Cf. note 194.

[197] Note 194, and also Fügedi (1972) 182–183; Fügedi (1977) 104–105; 129.

[198] *CD* VIII/3, 404–411.

[199] I. Gál: Szabolcsvármegyei községek iratai (Documents of settlements in Szabolcs County). *LevKözl* 7 (1929) 119; Entz–Szalontai (1969) 7.

[200] S. Domanovszky: *A szepesi városok árumegállító joga* (*The staple right of the towns in Szepes county*). Budapest (1922) 24–29; E. Fügedi: Középkori magyar városprivilégiumok (Privileges of medieval Hungarian towns). *TBM* 14 (1961) 41–42.

[201] Maksai (1940) 113; Németh (1979) 42.

[202] Fügedi (1972) 182–183.

[203] Maksay (1971) 70. Fig. 17.

[204] *AO* VI, 159–161.

[205] Maksai (1940) 114.

[206] *CD* IX/4, 672–681.

127

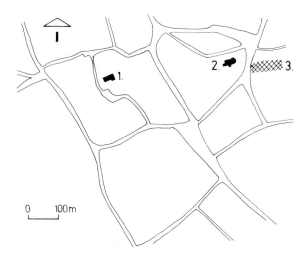

Fig. 11. Groundplan of Nyírbátor. 1. Franciscan (minorite) monastery, 2. St. George's parish church, 3. site of a late medieval castle

they led.[207] Bátor's neighbours were Bogát in the southwest, Pócs in the northwest, Vasvár in the southeast and Téglás farther south.[208] If these settlements are ranked according to the routes of the long-distance trade, we see two intersecting main roads. One of them included Pócsi Street in the northwest and its continuation, Vasvári Street in the southeast. This road bypassed the Ecsed marsh in the south and led through the village of Nagykároly (Carei). The other main road was Bogát Street, coming from Debrecen in the southwest, and its northeastern continuation was either the unnamed street or Marharth Street. This road led to Szatmár (Satu Mare) on the northern side of the marsh. The two *plateae corporales* were relatively easy to identify, since they ran parallel in a north to south direction. The western street can be identified with present-day Bajcsy Street and the eastern one with Kossuth Street and its continuations, Szabadság Square and Árpád Street. The triangular Szabadság Square can probably be identified with the medieval Vásár Street, and thus with a section of one of the *plateae corporales*. According to a charter of 1373 the orientation of this street was east to west, but in reality it had a southeast to northwest direction. Nemes Street can most definitely be identified with present-day Báthori István Street, which connects the square with the parish church and the castle. The western continuation of this street connects the market place with the other *platea corporalis* on the other side of the square (today Zrínyi Ilona Street; Fig. 11).

In short, the centre of Bátor in modern times corresponded roughly to the 14th century perambulations. Nemes Street under the church hill was presumably the core of the village (this is why all three branches of the Báthori family obtained a share of it). The next phase in

the development of the village was the intersection of the two main roads at Vásár Street. The settlement of Tótzug, the second main street, must have taken place during the last phase of development. This street, originally a side-street, was populated by foreign settlers (*Tót*, Slavs-Slovaks; *Zug*, an almost inaccessible corner). By the year 1354, Tótzug became one of the main streets in Bátor. This can obviously be traced to the conscious settlements policy of the landowner.

However, there are other topographical problems too. The two priests mentioned in the sources perhaps indicates that the village had had two churches. However, the record on the partition in 1354 only mentions one. The St. Veronica chapel was definitely standing by the late 15th century in the street named after the chapel, which was later called Szentvér Street (today Rózsa Ferenc Street). This street led to the east from Vásár Street, and was the first side-street to the south on the eastern side of the eastern main street.[209] We have seen that the parish church was dedicated to St. George. The imposing late Gothic single-aisled church (today used by the Reformed church), dates from the late 15th century (it was completed in 1488, but the work continued into the next decade; Fig. 12). In the immediate vicinity of this building a 13th century church consisting of a sanctuary with polygonal termination, an octagonal nave and a rectangular frontal tower was uncovered. This church, however, can probably be identified with the circular Corpus Christi chapel mentioned in 1444,[210] and thus it cannot be identified with the St. George parsonage mentioned in 1354. It would appear that this church functioned as the grave chapel of the parsonage. The original parish church was presumably pulled down prior to the building of the new church.[211] These assumptions obviously require archaeological confirmation. The early importance of St. George's church is shown, among others, by the fact that the annual markets in Bátor were held on St. George's Day, i.e. coincided with the annual festival of the church.[212]

Further questions are raised by the Franciscan church and monastery. Géza Entz considered this single-aisled hall-church to be a uniform structure and rejected all suggestions that a predecessor of this church was already complete in the 14th century. No traces of an earlier building can be identified in the church, although the orientation of the sanctuary differs slightly from that of the nave. The church and the adjoining monastery were built at the turn of the 15th–16th centuries (Fig. 13).[213] The only sign indicating the existence of an earlier church is the different orientation of the two parts of the

[207] Maksay (1971) 71.

[208] Two settlements named Téglás can be considered: one lies near Ömböly, in Szatmár county, the other near Hadház, in Szabolcs county. The location of the streets supports the former. Csánki (1890) Vol. I, 486, 527.

[209] Entz–Szalontai (1969) 8–10.

[210] *Ibid.*, 39–61. For the Corpus Christi chapel cf. *ibid.*, 43.

[211] Cf. also Németh (1979) 42–43.

[212] 1382: A. Fekete Nagy: A Petróczy levéltár középkori oklevelei (The medieval charters in the Petróczy archive). *LevKözl* 9 (1931) 65. A 1466 source also mentions the annual fair without naming its day. *Dl*, 55823.

[213] Entz–Szalontai (1969) 10, 22–25; M. B. Gyürky: *A Báthoryak nyírbátori templomai (The churches of the Báthorys in Nyírbátor)*. Budapest (1943) 10, 13–14. She assigns it to the 14th century.

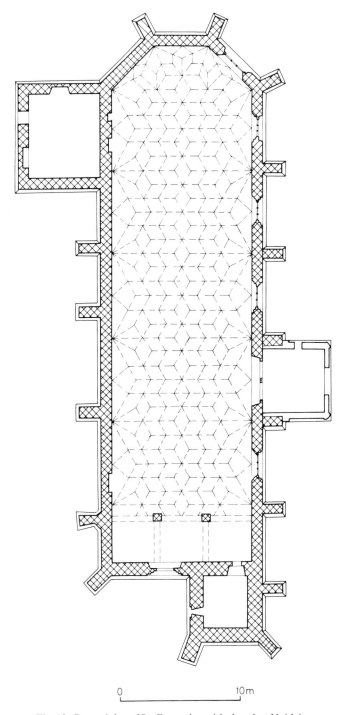

Fig. 12. Groundplan of St. George's parish church at Nyírbátor

church. It would nonetheless have been rather strange if a settlement comparable to Bátor in terms of economic significance would not have had either a monastery of the Mendicant order, or a hospital. The monastery is situated in the block between the two *plateae corporales* near, but not on, the boundary of the town. This suggests an early date for the building. The location of the 14th century castle of Bátor is unknown. The excavations in plots to the east of the parish church have brought to light the remains of a U-shaped palace. On

the evidence of Kálmán Magyar's excavations this building can be assigned to the 15th century only.[214] Finds from the 14th century were very scarce at the site.[215] Considering its location, this palace may be

[214] K. Magyar: *Az ötvöskónyi Báthori várkastély (The fortified castle of the Báthoris at Ötvöskóny)*. Kaposvár (1974) 14–19. Cf. Entz–Szalontai (1969) 61-63.
[215] D. Csallány's report in *RégFüz* I. 13 (1960) 112; Szalontai (1978) 80–81.

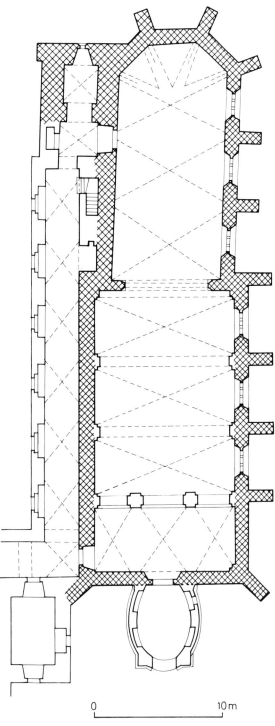

Fig. 13. Groundplan of the Franciscan (Minorite) church at Nyírbátor

identified with the castle, but the archaeological data challenge this assumption. Presumably this palace was built to replace the castle demolished nearly a hundred years earlier.

Bátor is considered a typical market town in the literature. Its urban nature is reflected by the street network and the significant role played by the town in the trade of the area (besides the staple right, the town

was entitled to hold annual and weekly markets, and its inhabitants regularly visited distant markets).[216] The town also had a highly developed handicraft industry. Besides the number of butcher's stalls, the first goldsmith settled in the town as early as the 14th century.[217] Data on the other crafts have also survived.[218] The monastery of the Mendicant order — presumably dating from a later period — and the number of people studying at foreign universities also indicate the significance of the town. However, these latter data rank Bátor below Gyöngyös — at least in the Late Middle Ages. Between 1440 and 1514 nine residents pursued their studies at foreign universities (one in Vienna, eight in Cracow), i.e. in these terms, the town ranked 112nd–125th in the country.[219] Regrettably enough, the paucity of relevant sources does not allow the reconstruction of the phases in the development of Bátor for two hundred years during the late medieval period. The 14th century charters, including the two records on the partition of the town, usually refer to Bátor as *possessio*. By that time this word was used for denoting a village.[220] It was only in the 15th century that the town was generally referred to as *oppidum*.[221] Thus Nyírbátor was still a village in the 14th century despite its urban street network, its markets, its staple right and other privileges. The serfs' efforts toward self-government were blocked by the landowners' authority. The privileges granted to the town in 1330 safeguarded the interests of the landowners rather than those of the serfs. There were only two factors that facilitated Bátor's urbanization: Its geographical position was good for traffic and its status of manorial centre, even though the latter soon became an obstacle to the town's development. Neither were special privileges granted to Bátor, when it was already an *oppidum*, in the 15th century. A charter of the Bátor magistracy, dating from 1522, is instructive in this respect. It was issued by three judges and the "other jurymen" instead of the usual signatories of one judge and 12 (or 6) jurymen. In the *corroboratio*, the seal is referred to as *signum* (sign) instead of *sigillum* (seal) — and it was indeed only a signet.[222] The attitude of Bátor's burghers towards the peasant uprising in 1514 can also be considered characteristic. Despite the well-known role played by the burghers of the market towns in the Great Hungarian Plain in this uprising, the actions of the population of Bátor were rather ambiguous. The arrival of a peasant army to the town prompted a part of the population to take shelter in the Franciscan monastery, and only later did they join the insurgents but, so it would appear, not of their own free will. This is also reflected by the

[216] E.g. at Mezőtúr: Kubinyi (1980) 443.

[217] Entz–Szalontai (1969) 8.

[218] Maksai (1940) 114.

[219] Kubinyi (1971) 76.

[220] I. Szabó: *A falurendszer kialakulása Magyarországon (X–XV. század) (The evolution of the village system in Hungary in the 10th–15th centuries)*. Budapest (1966) 52–53. Earlier sources also refer to Bátor as *villa* meaning 'village': Mező–Németh (1972) 81.

[221] Csánki (1890) Vol. I, 506.

[222] *Dl,* 56431.

amount of restitution imposed on Bátor following the suppression of the revolt that was less than that on neighbouring villages.[223]

## (4) Miskolc

Miskolc, the second largest town in modern Hungary, did not in the Middle Ages belong to the free royal towns. Its plan in modern times bears a close resemblance to that of Gyöngyös. It also had a gridded street system: east to west, present-day Széchenyi Street and its continuation, Hunyadi Street, and north to south, present-day Kazinczy Street and its continuation, Szemere Street. The town was protected by a curved rampart and ditch system, and the town gates stood at the ends of the intersecting streets. The roads leading through them still bear the names of these gates (Zsolcai gate in the east, Csabai gate in the south, Győri gate in the west and Szentpéteri gate in the north.) Each gate was named after the direction that the road passing through it had led to. There had been a fifth gate in the town (Fábián gate in the north), but the road passing through it did not lead to the main intersecting street. The first reference to the gates dates from 1562. This source mentions the Diósgyőri gate (today Győri for short) and the gate of the Blessed Virgin (later Szentpéteri gate). The Zsolcai gate is mentioned in later sources only, in the 18th century, which marks the probable date of this gate's construction (in the preceding centuries a marshland area lay in that direction).[224] Therefore, the grid street system is likewise not original in Miskolc, neither can it be assigned to the Middle Ages, at least not in this form. The building of the defensive rampart and ditch can most probably be linked to the Turkish raids in the 16th century. The town had never had stone walls.

On the strength of the archaeological evidence and written sources, the history of Miskolc can be traced back to very early periods. The area of the town had already been settled in prehistory, and was resettled at the time of the Magyar conquest.[225] A cemetery dating from the Conquest period was uncovered 5 km north of the town centre.[226] Anonymous, the Hungarian chronicler also mentions the town. In his account, Árpád, the leader of the Magyar tribes, donated Bunger, father of Bors, a vast stretch of land between the rivers Tapolca and Sajó called "Miskoucy", and also the castle of Geuru (Győr). These possessions, together with Bors' own castle called Borsod, were later united by Bors into

a county.[227] Until the early 14th century, Miskolc had been in the possesion of the Miskolc clan of noble rank, who often called themselves Bors. Thus the person called Bors in the chronicle could have been the ancestor of the Miskolc clan.[228] The family chose the Benedictine St. Peter's monastery at Tapolca, approximately 2.5–3 km southwest of Miskolc, as their burial place. The monastery, lying in the vicinity of a thermal spring and, possibly, a pagan cult centre, is thought to have been founded by the family as a clan monastery sometime before the mid-12th century.[229] The centre of the family's estate is not known, it had perhaps lain in the settlement of Miskolc.[230] A source from 1219 carries the following datum. The Ishmaelites of Nyír (the Moslem merchants of a northeastern Hungarian area, the Nyírség) accused the people of Sajóvámos of theft. These people also included the serfs of the Tapolca monastery of the Miskolc family.[231] The place-name Vámos refers to the right of the settlement to exact toll, and indeed, Sajóvámos lies at the intersection of two main roads. One of them leads from the Sajó basin to the Boldva basin in the north, the other connects Miskolc (and Tapolca) with Szikszó (and eventually with Kassa (Košice) and Poland).[232] Vámos lies some 12 km northeast of Miskolc, indicating that the environs of Miskolc had been visited by the long-distance merchants well before the Mongol invasion (1241).

For alleged breach of faith, King Charles Robert confiscated the possessions of the Miskolc family in 1312 and donated them to the sons of Miklós Szécsi. They also received the estates of Miskolc, Csaba and Mályi in 1230.[233] For more than a decade the Miskolc family sued for their rights, but finally the Szécsis managed to strengthen their hold over these estates. By this time Miskolc ranked as an important settlement — in 1327 fifty noblemen were held captive in the town.[234] When King Louis the Great confirmed the Szécsis in their possessory right in 1360, he called Miskolc a *villa maior* and mentioned its market customs. In other words, Miskolc steadily gained in importance and was by that time a village authorized to hold markets.[235] The Szécsis held Miskolc (and the patronage of the Tapolca monas-

[223] A. Fekete Nagy–V. Kenéz–L. Solymosi–G. Érszegi: *Monumenta rusticorum in Hungaria rebellium anno MDXIV.* Budapest (1979) 380, 475–483.

[224] D. Nyiry: Miskolc város "sántza vagy árka" (The "mound or ditch" at Miskolc). *Történelmi és Régészeti Közlemények (Miskolc thj. város Hivatalos Értesítőjének melléklete)* 1 (1926) 3–6.

[225] Cf. Komáromy (1960) 3–4; Komáromy (1966) 389–401; Horváth–Marjalaki Kiss–Valentiny (1962) 18–22.

[226] G. Megay: Honfoglaláskori temető Miskolc észak-keleti határán (Conquest period cemetery on the northeastern outskirts of Miskolc). *ArchÉrt* 88 (1961) 100–108.

[227] *SRH* I, 72.

[228] Györffy (1963) 789.

[229] J. Major: Miskolctapolca fejlődése a terület funkcionális változásainak tükrében (The development of Miskolctapolca as reflected by functional changes in the area). *Településtudományi Közlemények* 27 (1978) 20–28.

[230] Komáromy (1960) 6–7; Horváth–Marjalaki Kiss–Valentiny (1962) 26.

[231] J. Karácsonyi–S. Borovszky: *Az időrendbe szedett váradi tüzesvaspróba-lajstrom (Chronological list of the fire-ordeals in Várad).* Budapest (1903) 229.

[232] J. Major: Miskolctapolca fejlődése a terület funkcionális változásainak tükrében (The development of Miskolctapolca as reflected by functional changes in the area). *Településtudományi Közlemények* 27 (1978) 24–26.

[233] E. Leveles: Miskolc város megváltása (The redemption of Miskolc). *Történelmi és Régészeti Közlemények Miskolc város és Borsod megye múltjából* 2 (1927) 176–178.

[234] Györffy (1963) 789–790.

[235] E. Leveles: Miskolc város megváltása (The redemption of Miskolc). *Történelmi és Régészeti Közlemények Miskolc*

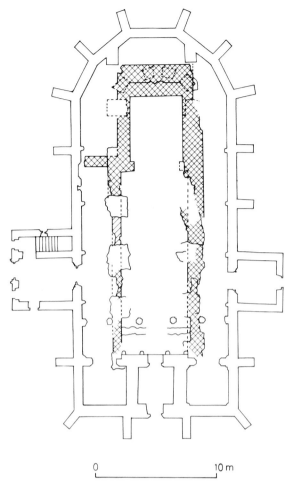

Fig. 14. Groundplan of St. Stephen's parish church at Miskolc, with the remains of the earlier Árpádian Age building

from the site was assigned to the 8th–9th centuries by the excavator. Bipartite wattle-and-daub structures, dated to the 10th–11th and 12th–13th centuries, were built in the period between the Magyar conquest and the Mongol invasion. The 12th–13th century building was destroyed by fire, probably during the Mongol invasion. The copper coins of King Béla III (1173–1196) and the pottery sherds recovered at the site offered a firm basis for dating the building, which had approximately 50 cm thick walls supported by posts over 22 cm in diameter. The western room of the building housed a large-sized oven. The excavator attempted the reconstruction of the building itself. The two large-sized post-holes found north of the building were thought to have been the posts supporting the gutter. In his opinion the building functioned as a tavern or a stall, on account of its proximity to the Szinva ferry. The sheep, pig and cattle bones found north of the building, scattered over a 8 m² large area apparently supported the tavern theory. After the Mongol invasion this area remained unoccupied for a longer time. The 15th century saw the construction of a wattle-and-daub house reinforced with posts. In the 16th century this structure was replaced by a stone building. The remains of a bipartite wattle-and-daub house were uncovered in the trench east of this plot. This structure can be assigned to the second half of the 13th century, i.e. to the years after the Mongol invasion. One of the rooms contained the remains of a large-sized oven, the other a storage pit with corner vaults and a wooden staircase leading down from the floor level. This house was replaced by a stone building — sometime in the 14th century or in the early 15th century — whose plan could not be reconstructed (Fig. 15).[237]

József Komáromy, the leader of the excavations, realized that the types of plots common in the area had nothing in common with the original strip-holdings in Miskolc.[238] In his opinion this area, extending from the Szinva ferry to the ancient east to west cart-road, served as the early marketplace of the village. After the Mongol invasion the market was transferred to the vacant plots, which were built in only later, when the cart-road began to be used as a street market.[239] The first reference to the market dates from the second half of the 14th century, but this by no means implies that there was no marketplace earlier. This assumption is supported by the above-quoted reference to Sajóvámos, dating from 1219. Thus there are grounds for assuming that the former centre of the settlement lay in this area, near the Sötét gate.

To set the facts in their proper perspective, we also have to consider the ecclesiastical conditions of the period. The parish church of Miskolc, erected on the Avas hill south of the river Szinva, today exhibits Gothic

tery) until 1364, when the king annexed Miskolc and a number of other estates in Borsod County to the castle of Diósgyőr, which was already possessed by the king.[236] Thus Miskolc became subordinated to Diósgyőr castle, lying some 3 km west of it, and this remained unchanged for centuries.

The written records and the archaeological evidence both reflect that the royal possession opened a new chapter in the history of the town. The excavations conducted in the area of the so-called Sötét (Dark) gate were especially fruitful. The gate was a very significant topographic centre, since it was the meeting-point of the road crossing the river Szinva from the southeast and the more or less east to west oriented road which later became the main street of Miskolc (present-day Széchenyi Street). The excavations have revealed that the area was settled since prehistory and the presence of structures immediately preceding the Magyar conquest is reflected by the burnt fragments of wattle-and-daub, the fireplaces and the postholes. The pottery recovered

*város és Borsod megye múltjából* 3 (1928) 208–209. We reject the distinction based on the terms *villa* and *possessio* in the earlier literature.
    [236] Szendrei (1890) 53–58.

    [237] J. Komáromy: A miskolci sötétkapu melletti ásatások jobbágyházai (The peasant houses uncovered near the Sötét gate in Miskolc). *HOMKözl* (1955) 18–21; Komáromy (1957) 70–101.
    [238] Komáromy (1966) 400, note 6.
    [239] Komáromy (1957) 83; Komáromy (1960) 8–10; Komáromy (1962) 6; etc.

features. However, the excavations in 1941 revealed that the predecessor of the church was built in the Árpádian Age (the ancient foundation walls were found inside the church; Fig. 14). The 8.1 m long sanctuary of the present church had a square termination, the nave was 19.4 m long and was 7.43 m wide inside. The tower in front of the church presumably dated from the 14th century.[240] The church was dedicated to King St. Stephen. For a long time this was the only parish church in the town. This is indicated by King Sigismund's decree of 1411, which granted Miskolc the right to elect its own parish priest — and this right applied to St. Stephen's church and both towns (civitates), Old and New Miskolc.[241] The contemporary seal of the town, depicting a crowned head, also points to the importance of the settlement. The seal first appears on the oldest surviving document (1389), and it is well discernible in the sealing with the inscription + SIGILLVM + CIVITATIS MISKOLZ that dates from 1433. Since in this sealing the head of the king is depicted with a beard parted in the centre, there is a consensus that it portrays King Sigismund. However, we are of the opinion that the king shown in the seal is St. Stephen, whose depiction was based on the iconography of Sigismund, the then ruler. This possibility is supported by the fact that later seals, dating from the period when the town was already Protestant, indisputably depict the head of St. Stephen.[242]

The 1941 excavations provided no clues for the exact dating of the early-period church. Only a general date within the Árpádian Age could be established, most probably the 13th century, but the church could well have had antecedents. Since the church lies on the southern bank of the river Szinva, the original settlement of Miskolc must also have been located near the river. It has been proposed that the original nucleus of the settlement lay south of the river, in an area above its floodplain, and that the only road in the settlement leading to Diósgyőr passed through this area as the continuation of the later Felső Papszer Street.[243] In his monograph of the town János Szendrei also located the old town (Old Miskolc, mentioned in 1411) to the right, i. e. the southern bank of the river Szinva, and the new town to the left bank.[244] It is beyond doubt that the area north of the Szinva had already been inhabited prior to the Mongol invasion. This, however, does not exclude the possibility that the original nucleus of the settlement also extended to the southern bank of the river, to the later Papszer quarter. Komáromy located the centre of

the estate of the Miskolc family to the area east of the church, and in his opinion the predecessor of Rákóczi Street passed through this land, leading to the north by crossing the Szinva (the section of Rákóczi Street north of the river was the site where the Sötét gate was excavated). Komáromy located the serfs' village, apparently an agglomerated settlement, to the area north of the river, and the manorial centre and the church to its south.[245] This suggestion remains to be proven but it would nonetheless appear that the early significance of Rákóczi Street is indisputable. The main road of the settlement which connected the monastery of the Miskolc family in Tapolca with the leader Bors' castle in Diósgyőr in the Árpádian Age, apparently ran along the route of present-day Rákóczi Street. As we have already seen, the road turned west after crossing the Sötét gate and led into the later market street (Fig. 16). However, the south to north road did not terminate in its intersection with the east to west road. Its continuation to the north gradually gained in importance, since this was the main trade route connecting Buda with Kassa (Košice) and Poland via Gyöngyös (and Eger with a short detour).[246]

The major change in the development of Miskolc which, on the evidence of the marketplace had undergone initial urbanization, had been brought about by its coming under royal seigniory. The present-day structure of the centre of the town can practically be traced to this period. Lajos Marjalaki Kiss, the enthusiastic historian of the region, spared no effort in collating the data on plots in old land registers and maps, and in many cases he was able to trace back the plot owners to the Middle Ages, thus verifying the medieval origins of the distribution of plots. During the period of the royal seigniory the east–west road leading to Diósgyőr became the new main street and, simultaneously, the market street of Miskolc. By repartitioning the land, a new plot system was created with 12–14 m wide plots, each having an area of one 'small' hold (1,100 square fathoms = 0.39556 ha). This division differed from that of the preceding agglomerated settlement, thus the introduction of new holdings probably involved a new areal organisation (which, however, cannot be linked to the law of 1351, as had been assumed by Marjalaki Kiss). The settlement built along the east to west street (today Széchenyi Street) became the Old Town of Miskolc, while in the area south of the Szinva, cotters' holdings were established.[247] The formation of New Miskolc, i.e. the New Town of Miskolc, can also be assigned to the early phase of the royal seigniory. According to the first reference to the town dating from 1376, one of the members of the town council was called Újvárosi (de Noua Ciuitate).[248] The above cited charter of 1411 also draws a distinction

[240] G. Megay: A miskolci avasi templom 1941. évi ásatásának eredményei (Results of the 1941 excavations of the Avas church at Miskolc). HOMÉ 9 (1970) 137. A circular-ended sanctuary is reconstructed by Horváth–Marjalaki Kiss–Valentiny (1962) 186–192. Megay's findings apparently contradict this theory.

[241] Szendrei (1890) Vol. III, 494.

[242] Szendrei (1886) Vol. I, 135–142.

[243] G. Zsadányi: Az utak szerepe a mai Miskolc kialakulásában (The role of roads in the development of present-day Miskolc). HOMKözl (1955) 28.

[244] Szendrei (1904) Vol. II, 64.

[245] Komáromy (1960) 6.

[246] Györffy (1963) Vol. I. Map of Borsod.

[247] L. Marjalaki Kiss: A miskolci Kötel Könyv 1702-ből. Miskolc ősi telepítésű jobbágy és zsellér házhelyei (The 1702 Kötel book of Miskolc. The ancient serfs' and cotters' plots in Miskolc). HOMKözl (1956) 39–48; Marjalaki Kiss (1957) 102–127; Marjalaki Kiss (1958) 133–153.

[248] Szendrei (1890) Vol. III, 63–64.

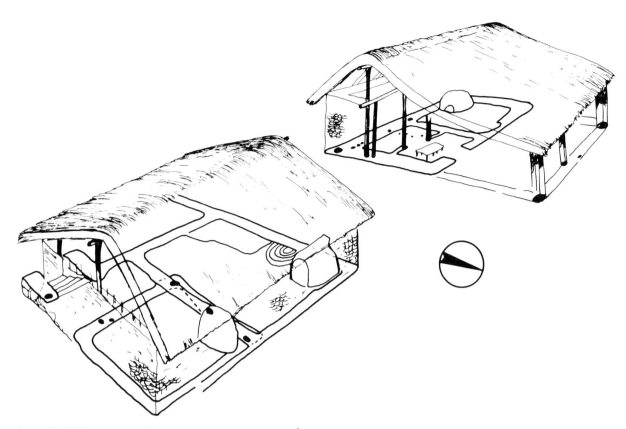

Fig. 15. Reconstructed groundplan and structure of the Árpádian Age houses uncovered near the Dark Gate of Miskolc

between the Old and New Town of Miskolc.[249] A number of charters from 1433 were made out by the council of the Old Town of Miskolc.[250] Comparable charters issued by the New Town council are also known.[251] All these sources contrast the Old and New Towns of Miskolc. However, a document of 1445 makes mention of St. Stephen's parsonage in *Antiquamiskolcz,* and the parsonage of the Blessed Virgin in *Nouamiskolcz,* i.e. it differentiates between Old and New Miskolc.[252]

It is still not clear whether Old Miskolc can be identified with the Old Town, and New Miskolc with the New Town, and neither is their precise location known. According to Marjalaki Kiss, the 13th century town

part, Old Miskolc, lay on the southern side of Széchenyi Street (the medieval market street), while New Miskolc to the north of this street only evolved in the 14th century. He dated the New Town of Miskolc to the end of the 15th century and located it further north, somewhere on the banks of a stream called Pece.[253] This is challenged by an abundance of sources which speak of a New Town instead of New Miskolc beginning with 1376. The church of the Blessed Virgin, the parish church of New Miskolc in 1445, was situated in New Town Street,[254] supporting thus the identification of New Miskolc with the New Town of Miskolc. It has been pointed out above that Szendrei considered the river Szinva to have been the boundary between the Old and New Town.[255] This is probably erroneous since the area south of the river was dotted with independent cotters' settlements (cf. below); Marjalaki was also wrong in identifying the market street with the boundary line. A 1433 clause by the council of the Old Town mentions a garden north of the street, i.e. in the town part which Marjalaki Kiss identified with New Miskolc.[256] While the Old Town council regularly authorized the sale of houses in the market,[257] the New Town council did not.

[249] Cf. note 244.

[250] 1433: *antiqua civitas de Myskolcz. Dl,* 83665; 1453: *veteris civitatis Miskolcz.* Szendrei (1890) Vol. III, 88; and similarly 1458: Szendrei (1890) Vol. III, 89; 1469: *Dl,* 83780; 1506: *Dl,* 88946. The *intitulatio* of a 1499 charter mentions *vetus civitas oppidi Myskolcz. Dl,* 102286. In 1523 a charter was issued by *vetus opidum Myskowlcz. Dl,* 65652. A charter of 1503 differentiates between the judges and jurors of the *vetus* and the *novum oppidum de Myscolcz.* Szendrei (1890) Vol. III, 132–136, 138–139.

[251] 1521: *nova civitas Myskolcz. Dl.* 65651. One of the sides, however, is referred to as *inhabitator veteris oppidi Myskolcz.* Cf. also note 250. A 1461 source also differentiates between the judges and jurors of the *antiquum* and the *novum oppidum Myskolcz.* Szendrei (1890) Vol. III, 98.

[252] Lukcsics (1938) Vol. II, nos 827, 829.

[253] Marjalaki Kiss (1957) 104–107.
[254] Szendrei (1904) Vol. II, 139, 300, etc.
[255] Cf. note 244.
[256] *Dl,* 83665.
[257] E.g. *Dl,* 102286.

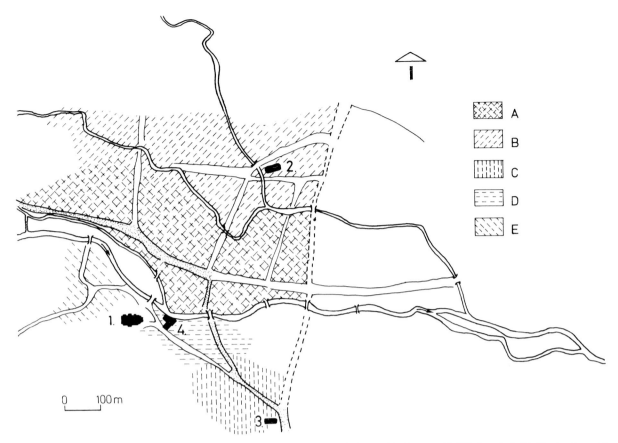

Fig. 16. Miskolc in the Middle Ages. A. Old Town, B. New Town, C. Mindszent, D. Papszer, E. Tót Street. 1. St. Stephen's parish church, 2. parish church of the Blessed Virgin, 3. Mindszent hospital church, 4. Gothic school building. The dotted line marks the direction of the road entering the town in the south and leading towards Diósgyőr to the west

Accordingly, the area between the southern branch of the Pece and the Szinva can be identified with the territory of Old Miskolc, or the Old Town of Miskolc, the area south of the Szinva with the plots distributed among the cotters, and the New Town, or New Miskolc, can be located in the area north of the Pece stream.

As mentioned above, the road leading to Diósgyőr, the centre of the estate, became the axis of the Old Town. This road — the only road in town if we disregard the few small lanes branching off from it — was called *theatrum*, or market, and the strip holdings were located on both sides of it.[258] On the evidence of the charters, the houses in the market were east–west orientated.[259] A 1504 charter mentions a stone building in the area.[260] Archaeological excavations have brought to light remains of a 14th century stone structure in Miskolc,[261] although wattle-and-daub houses erected around a

framework of wooden posts were still built as late as the 15th century.[262] The northern row of houses in the market also included stone buildings. From under a 15th–17th century 'nobleman's mansion' the remains of a 15th century 'serf's house' — burnt daub fragments and parts of an oven — have come to light. The structure considered to have been a 'nobleman's mansion' was obviously built of stone. Next to this building was a 15th century stone house with Gothic door and window frames.[263] This site has also yielded pottery sherds, dating primarily to the 14th century or later, although 13th century fragments have also come to light.[264] These finds contradict the theory still advocated by some scholars that the northern side of the market street was settled in the 15th century, while the area surrounding the present-day theatre building, where the excavations were conducted, became populated only in the late 15th century.[265] The few objects brought to light by the

[258] Marjalaki Kiss (1957) 104. He and Komáromy (1962) 6–8, have suggested that the southern part of the market street—the former marketplace—had been left open for a certain period of time. This theory was contradicted by Komáromy's excavations.

[259] 1478: *Dl*, 83828; 1499: *Dl*, 102286; 1504: Szendrei (1890) Vol. III, 142.

[260] Szendrei (1890) Vol. III, 142.

[261] Komáromy (1957) 88.

[262] *Ibid.*, 85.

[263] Cf. Komáromy's report in *RégFüz* I. 10 (1957) 60; Komáromy (1960a) 6–7.

[264] J. Komáromy: Jelentés a Miskolci Nemzeti Színháznál végzett leletmentésről (Report on the rescue excavations at the national theatre in Miskolc). *HOMÉ* 2 (1958) 156–160.

[265] Horváth–Marjalaki Kiss–Valentiny (1962) 30-31.

excavations and the evidence furnished by the charters indicates that in the Middle Ages primarily terre pisé, or wattle-and-daub houses were constructed in the market, and that the number of the stone structures increased considerably only during early modern times. It can by no means be considered accidental that the charters on the sale and purchase of houses hardly ever mention stone structures.

The northern end of the market street widened into a triangle. The street leading north from one corner of the triangle—Fábián Street—was mentioned in the earliest charter of the town (1376).[266] In the second half of the 16th century the southern section of the street near the market was named Mészár Street after the butcher's stalls set up there. In the 17th century the street terminated at the Fábián gate in the north.[267] The earliest reference to the butcher's stalls, a 1489 charter, states that they stood near the market, with the last stall standing in line with it.[268] The western continuation of the marketplace, from Fábián Street, was called Hunyad Street in the 16th century (today Hunyadi Street).[269] The source also mentions a certain Malom (Mill) Street in the Old Town which led to the mill of the parson.[270] Since this mill was active in Malom dike on the northern branch of the Szinva,[271] Malom Street was in all probability a southern branch of the market between Fábián Street and the line of the Dark gate. In short, these streets were presumably projections of the marketplace.

Present-day Palóczy, Batthyány and Horváth Lajos Streets were called Újváros (New Town) Street in modern times.[272] Palóczy Street, and its continuation, Horváth Lajos Street, run parallel with the market street to its north, between the branches of the Pece stream. In our opinion the section called Horváth Lajos Street had not existed in the Middle Ages. Batthyány Street branches off from Palóczy Street to the northeast and forms a triangular square (Deák Ferenc Square). This square had been the centre of the New Town — as suggested by the wall remains and the ribbed vault fragments dating from the 14th century at the latest, from the Gothic parish church of the Blessed Virgin, brought to light in present-day Deák Square, west of the modern Minorite monastery.[273] The dating of the church to the last two decades of the 15th century[274] is undoubtedly erroneous since the building had already been standing in 1445 and served as a parsonage.[275] Regrettably enough, we hardly know more about the medieval topography of the New Town. A source of 1521 mentions a street named Kis Kassa.[276] This street, also referred to in modern sources, has not been located yet. In the mid-16th century the street was the property of the Sajószentpéter parsonage (a market town 16 km north of Miskolc) and was demolished in 1554. In the light of these data, several studies attempted to identify it with the farmsteads lying outside the later Szentpéteri gate.[277] The above-cited source of 1521 apparently supports this assumption: the object put up for sale was not a house, but farmland: predium... vulgo Thelekh. Accordingly, Kis Kassa may have lain on the outskirts of the New Town, to the north or east (hills planted with vines stretched west and northwest of the town). Matters are further complicated by the problems of the manorial right of the Sajószentpéter parsonage since in 1521 the street came under the authority of the New Town council. It could be that only part of the street belonged to the Sajószentpéter parsonage, while the other part, the section nearer to the town, was under the jurisdiction of the New Town. However, 16th century sources mention houses in Kis Kassa Street, and thus the name of the street can be interpreted either as a reference to its direction towards Kassa (Košice) — if so the street lay in the north —, or to the burghers from Kassa who had settled in Miskolc.

A register of 1563 offers a basis for reconstructing the late medieval groundplan of the settlement.[278] Surprisingly enough, the area of the New Town practically matched that of the Old Town, i. e. the town proper. Even more significant is the fact that the town's population included only landowning serfs. There was a separate cotters' quarter that included four streets.

Mindszent Street was named after the All Saints Hospital, first mentioned in a 1489 charter. The possessions of the hospital included a mill, meadow-land and a forest in the village of Csaba, south of Miskolc. It was the duty of the parson of St. Stephen's church and the burghers to nominate two males to govern these holdings.[279] The hospital lay in the southern outskirts of the town, near the point where the road coming from the south turned northwest. The cotters' holdings at the start of this road belonged to the church of Mindszent, and thus their street was called Mindszent Street. After the Reformation, Miskolc turned Calvinist and the revenues of the Mindszent church were used for the maintenance of Tapolca abbey which was demolished by the Turks.[280] Mindszent Street, the property of the Catholic abbey, was no longer under the jurisdiction of the Reformed town and remained an independent village until 1880 — even though it had no holdings or grazing lands beyond its boundaries, and was practically enclosed by the boundaries of Miskolc.[281]

Papszer and Tót Street (later Toronyallja Street)

[266] Szendrei (1890) Vol. III, 63–64.
[267] Marjalaki Kiss (1958) 136–137.
[268] Dl, 83949.
[269] 1582: Szendrei (1890) Vol. III, 255–260; Marjalaki Kiss (1958) 135.
[270] 1506: Dl, 88946.
[271] Horváth–Marjalaki Kiss–Valentiny (1962) 93, Fig. 30.
[272] Marjalaki Kiss (1958) 138–139.
[273] For a brief survey see Horváth–Marjalaki Kiss–Valentiny (1962) 32; and RégFüz I. 20 (1967) 92.
[274] As stated in Horváth–Marjalaki Kiss–Valentiny (1962) 32.
[275] Cf. note 252.

[276] Dl. 65651.
[277] Szendrei (1904) Vol. II, 174–175.
[278] Ibid., Vol. III, 232–234.
[279] Ibid., Vol. III, 121; Z. Somogyi: A középkori Magyarország szegényügye (Poor relief in medieval Hungary). Budapest (1941) 103.
[280] Szendrei (1904) Vol. II, 231–233.
[281] Ibid., Vol. IV, 160, 287.

Table 5. The quarters of Miskolc in 1563

| Quarters | Plots | Desert plots | Town houses | Noblemen's houses | Cotters' houses | Total |
|---|---|---|---|---|---|---|
| *oppidum* Miskolc | 136 | 2 | 5 | 17 | – | 160 |
| New Town | 108 | 19 | – | 4 | – | 131 |
| Mindszent Street | – | – | – | – | 19 | 19 |
| Papszer, Tót and Pecze Streets | – | – | – | – | 53 | 53 |
| Total | 244 | 21 | 5 | 21 | 72 | 363 |

were the continuations of Mindszent Street on the southern bank of the Szinva, near the Avas hill and the church of St. Stephen. The cotters living in this area were subjected to the parsonages,[282] since the town had retained the parsonage's right of presentation. The school of the town (the present-day museum building), the only secular building still standing in Miskolc that preserves Gothic elements, stood in Papszer Street (Fig. 17). The building dates to the 15th century.[283] On the evidence of its name, Papszer, the third cotters' street, probably extended along one of the branches of the stream in the southeastern corner of the New Town.[284]

The late medieval topography of the town, which has remained practically unaltered, was obviously preceded by a settlement of different type. The transformation can be assigned to the second half of the 14th century, i. e. to the beginning of the royal seigniory. Besides founding the New Town with its triangular square, the king also replanned the Old Town, e.g. the market street became the axis of the settlement. Some sort of central planning is reflected by the division of the two towns into roughly equal plots, and also the parcelling

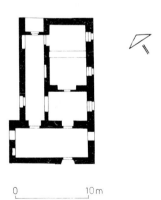

0 _____ 10 m

Fig. 17. The Gothic school building at Miskolc

out of cotters' holdings in separate areas on the outskirts of both towns. However, these features still fail to answer our basic question of whether Miskolc was a town *sensu stricto*.

We have already singled out various factors conducive to the urbanization of Miskolc, such as its geographical position and communications potential which led to the emergence of the marketplace. The groundplan of the town — the market street and the triangular square — does not contradict the urban nature of the town.[285] It is nonetheless conspicuous that in the 15th–16th centuries Miskolc had practically only two main streets: the market street in the Old Town and the triangle-shaped square in the New Town. All the other 'streets' were only side roads or passage-ways linking the nuclei of the Old and New Town. The decisive factor is that there were no parallel streets in the settlement — except for the more or less independent cotters' streets. Accordingly, the criterion distinguishing the Austrian 'Markt's from the towns proper can also be applied to the settlements in Miskolc: in both cases the settlements had a marketplace, but no side-streets.[286] A comparison of this type of settlement with the episcopal towns which consisted of a number of streets, or with the groundplan of Nyírbátor, clearly shows that in the case of Miskolc the king basically founded a settlement whose legal status ranked lower than a town, i. e. a 'Minderstadt'.[287] This is supported by the otherwise unintelligible phenomenon that, simultaneously with the complete reorganization of the Old Town, a separate settlement was founded in its vicinity (the New Town which soon also gained legal independence), the cotters' streets were subordinated to the competent town council only to a certain extent. It appears that the primary aim of the royal landowner was the formation of self-governing market towns rather than unified towns. The landowner apparently agreed with the principle of *divide et impera*. At the same time it is rather conspicuous that while stone buildings were rare in the medieval towns of central eastern Hungary the erection of stone structures in Miskolc appears to have begun well before the year 1526 on the evidence of the archaeological excavations.

The topography and architecture of Miskolc suggests that the town ranked somewhere between town and village, even though its steady urbanization is indisputable (as shown by the developments in the economic, legal and other spheres). The town definitely had the privilege to hold annual markets, proof of which comes from a charter of 1521, although the date and number of these markets are not known.[288] In the 17th century two annual markets were held: one on Ascension Day, the other on St. Lucas' Day. Both markets presumably had their origins in the Middle Ages (Miskolc turned Protes-

[282] Marjalaki Kiss (1958) 139–141.

[283] B. Horváth Jr.: Miskolc legrégibb középülete, a Múzeum (The Museum—The oldest public building in Miskolc). *HOM Közl* (1955) 1–6; Komáromy (1960a) 3, 8–9, 15.

[284] Marjalaki Kiss (1958) 134.

[285] Cf. note 156, and also Katzinger (1978) 87–99; R. E. Dickinson: *The West European City: A Geographical Interpretation.* London (1962) 323–325.

[286] Katzinger (1978) 99.

[287] H. Stoob: Minderstädte. Formen der Stadtentstehung im Spätmittelalter. *Vierteljahrschrift für Sozial- und Wirtschaftsgeschichte* 46 (1958) 1–28.

[288] Szendrei (1890) Vol. III, 167.

tant after the Reformation).[289] The weekly markets were held on Wednesdays (presumably since the Árpádian Age).[290] The right to hold weekly and annual markets was undeniably one of the main prerequisites to urbanization,[291] even though it does not automatically turn a settlement into a town. Miskolc had at least two guilds in the Middle Ages — the patent of the butchers' guild dates to 1508, that of the cobblers' to 1521. The latter endowed the Miskolc guild with the privileges of the cobblers in Pest.[292] The importance of the Miskolc craftsmen in the Late Middle Ages is reflected by the fact that in the early 16th century the bishopric of Eger bought rifles from the local gunsmiths.[293] A tax roll dating to 1548 offers the following information.[294]

As shown in the table, 40 of the 235 patres familias were engaged in handicrafts (17 per cent). This ratio is 20 per cent if the 7 merchants are included. This percentage is comparable to the one calculated for Gyöngyös (see Table 4), and also with the average for the market towns (apart from the higher-than-average ratio of metallurgy in Miskolc), and it is lower than that in the towns proper. The crafts practised in Miskolc numbered half as less as in Gyöngyös, but it should be recalled that the latter town had about four times as many inhabitants as Miskolc. Neither should it be forgotten that from the 14th century on, Miskolc and its environs, and also Gyöngyös, became more and more the centres of viticulture.[295] This obviously speeded up the social division of labour in these areas. In short, the economy of Miskolc also proves that it ranked between town and village.

The legal status of the town is a far more complicated issue. According to the legend of the seal of the above-cited 1433 charter, the settlement called itself civitas (town) which, of course, should not be taken to indicate that Miskolc was a free royal town (as proposed by a number of local historians).[296] The charters issued in connection with the exchange of property between the king and the Szécsi family invariably refer to the settlement as possessio, i.e. village (the latest charter

Table 6. Craftsmen in Miskolc in 1548

| Craft | branch | percentage | craftsmen | percentage |
|---|---|---|---|---|
| metallurgy, manufacture of arms | 4 | 25 | 11 | 27.5 |
| weaving | 1 | 6.2 | 2 | 5 |
| leather industry | 1 | 6.2 | 2 | 5 |
| wood industry | 2 | 12.5 | 2 | 5 |
| food processing | 2 | 12.5 | 5 | 12.5 |
| clothing trade | 3 | 18.9 | 14 | 35 |
| building trade, ceramics | 1 | 6.2 | 2 | 5 |
| other | 2 | 12.5 | 2 | 5 |
| Total | 16 | 100.0 | 40 | 100.0 |

dates from 1366).[297] The earliest still extant charter of the town (1376), which mentions a burgher of the New Town (de Noua Ciutate) among the members of the jurymen, speaks of the territorium of the town (civitas) and bears the seal of the civitas.[298] However, King Sigismund's charter of 1395, the first known charter of Miskolc which granted the town the ius gladii, i.e. criminal jurisdiction, refers to the settlement as a market town (oppidum).[299] This term is used in the charters issued by later rulers, e.g. in King Albert's 1439 charter, although Sigismund in 1411 used the term civitas.[300] In ratifying its own charters, the town council usually referred to the seal of the civitas (as in the years 1416, 1433, 1453, 1458). All but the first were issued by the council of the Old Town (antiqua civitas). The 1416 charter carries no reference to that part of the town.[301] In 1461, however, the council referred to itself as being the judge and jurors of Miskolc oppidum, and it used the same term in the charter itself.[302] From that time the charters of the Old Town used the terms vetus civitas and oppidum alternately in their intitulationes.[303] In the texts, the town is called either civitas[304] or oppidum.[305] This would clearly suggest that, at least from the late 14th century, the landowner considered his property an oppidum, even though the council had—ever since the town became a royal possession and even before that,

[289] Ibid., Vol. II, 304. The market held on St. Lucas' Day may have been the legal successor of the market held in the market town of Muhi between 1500 and the town's perdition. G. Wenzel: Diósgyőr egykori történelmi jelentősége (The former historical significance of Diósgyőr). Pest (1872) 76, no. 180. Remarkably, a 1580 permission named the Wednesday before New Year's Day and the Wednesday before Easter as market days in Miskolc, and the Thursday before New Year's Day in Muhi. By this time Muhi was only a village (possessio). Szendrei (1890) Vol. III, 251.

[290] ZsO II/1, no. 3276.

[291] B. Schwineköper: Die Problematik von Begriffe wie Stauferstädte, Zähringerstädte und ähnlichen Bezeichnungen. Südwestdeutsche Städte im Zeitalter der Staufer. Ed. by E. Maschke–J. Sydow. Sigmaringen (1980) 134–135.

[292] 1508: Szendrei (1890) Vol. III, 150–152; 1521: ibid., 165–170.

[293] Ibid., Vol. II, 160–161.

[294] Ibid., Vol. III, 195–202.

[295] J. Major: Miskolctapolca fejlődése a terület funkcionális változásainak tükrében (The development of Miskolctapolca as reflected by functional changes in the area). Település-tudományi Közlemények 27 (1978) 30–31.

[296] Cf. note 242.

[297] Szendrei (1890) Vol. III, 61; cf. I. Szabó: A falurendszer kialakulása Magyarországon (X–XV. század) (The evolution of the village system in Hungary in the 10–15th century). Budapest (1966) 51–54.

[298] Szendrei (1890) Vol. III, 63.

[299] Ibid., 71.

[300] Ibid., 87 (1439) and 493 (1411).

[301] Ibid., 80–82; Dl, 83665; Szendrei (1890) Vol. III, 88–89, 89–91.

[302] Ibid., 93–94.

[303] Cf. note 250.

[304] 1469: Dl, 83780; 1494: Dl, 86715; 1497: Szendrei (1890) Vol. III, 128–129; 1506: Dl, 88946.

[305] 1478: Dl, 83828; 1499: Dl, 102286; 1501: Szendrei (1890) Vol. III, 131; 1521: the charter of the Nova civitas concerning one of the inhabitants of the vetus oppidum. Dl, 65651; 1522: Dl, 65652.

from the moment of its foundation—consistently used and rather obstinately clung to the term *civitas*. From the 1460s on, the burghers of Miskolc were repeatedly compelled to use the term *oppidum* when referring to their town. In order to understand this we have to add that in the 14th century the towns and the town-like settlements were usually referred to as *civitates*. The differentiation within this category occurred sometime in the late 14th century: from this time on only the more urbanized settlements which ranked higher in the legal hierarchy were termed *civitates*, while those not meeting these specifications were called *oppida*.[306] No matter how obstinately the burghers of Miskolc clung to their former title, they eventually had to adopt the term *oppidum*.

The *intitulationes* of the town charters also shed light on the composition of the public authorities. With the exception of the first charter (1376), which mentions one judge and four jurors, all later charters (irrespective of the place of their issue) mention two jurors only beside the judge, and the burghers and *hospites* are referred to only in general terms.[307] The councils in the Hungarian towns, including most of the market towns, generally consisted of 12 jurors. In other market towns this number was smaller: six, four or occasionally two as, for example, in Sátoraljaújhely, also in northeastern Hungary, although the two jurors there were assisted by 12 'old men'.[308] To all appearances, a similar set-up can be assumed for Miskolc. Two of the town charters refer to the two jurors assisting the judge as *iurati censum exigentes*, i.e. tax-collecting jurors.[309] The second half of the 16th century apparently brought changes in this respect. The keeping of the 1569 *protocollum* of Miskolc was attended by the chief justice, four jurymen (specified by name) and the senators.[310] A charter of 1570 was issued by the authority of a judge, four royal tax-collecting jurors and the other jurors.[311] According to a minute book of 1585, the council included the chief justice, ten other persons specified by name, four 'jurymen' and the representatives of the local nobility.[312] In the 17th century the market town of Tokaj, to the east of Miskolc, was governed by the chief justice, two assistant justices and a number of jurors who were members of the council.[313] The composition of the councils in the northeastern towns of Hungary differed from that of towns in other parts of the country: instead

of the usual one judge plus 4–6–12 jurors, these towns had a judge, two jurors and a number of other people who acted as members of the council. The two jurors assisted the judge in collecting taxes and in a number of other matters (cf. Tokaj). This system does not necessarily indicate the backwardness of urban autonomy—it was rather the result of other urban privileges, about which little is known. In 1376, and again in the second half of the 16th century, Miskolc had four jurors assisting the judge. In all probability they represented the two town parts. In the 14th century the Old and New Town of Miskolc presumably had one judge in common, and in the second half of the 16th century the two town parts were at last united.

Lack of space prevents us from surveying all the privileges granted to Miskolc in the Middle Ages. The crux of the matter is that these never quite equalled the privileges of the free royal towns. For example, Miskolc obtained the right to use green sealing-wax in 1512,[314] when all the major towns already strived for the procurement of the red wax.[315] The main obstacle to the development of Miskolc in the Middle Ages was that it was not unified. This was apparent not only in the difference between the Old and New Town, but also in the special privileges of the cotters. In 1471 King Matthias exempted the cotters of Miskolc from taxation. At the request of "all the cotters of Miskolc *oppidum*" King Ulászló II endorsed this privilege in 1495 with the provision that in return the cotters were obliged to send 12 workers each day for service in the Diósgyőr castle. In answer to a request of two representatives of the cotters of Miskolc, Queen Anne in 1503 prolonged this privilege without alterations. It was again approved in 1516 by King Louis II.[316] In short, the detached settlement of the cotters enjoyed a number of specific privileges, and it was obviously more dependent on the Diósgyőr estate than the town council itself. The term 'the poor men', unusually stressed in the *intitulatio* of a 1489 town charter, probably refers to the cotters' community. The charter, a bequest for ecclesiastic purposes,[317] was issued by the Miskolc council and the "community of the rich and poor burghers and *hospites* of Miskolc".

The prosperity of Miskolc is indicated, among others, by the extension or rebuilding of St. Stephen's parish church (which at first was the only church in town, and later became one of the churches in the Old Town). Following gradual extensions up to the early 15th century, it was then rebuilt into a three-aisled Gothic church between 1470–1489. The new church was practically erected around the old one. (It was 19 m wide and 42.5 m long.[318]) The grave chapel of St. Michael stood in

[306] Ladányi: Libera villa, civitas, oppidum. Terminologische Fragen in der ungarischen Städteentwicklung. *AnnUnivBud* 18 (1977) 20–29.

[307] Cf. the charters cited in the notes above, *passim*.

[308] Mályusz: A mezővárosi fejlődés (The development of market towns). *Tanulmányok a parasztság történetéhez Magyarországon a 14. században*. Ed. by Gy. Székely. Budapest (1953) 140–142.

[309] Szendrei (1890) Vol. III, 246.

[310] A. Kubinyi: Szolgabíró (Assitant justice). *Magyar Nyelv* 53 (1957) 207.

[311] Szendrei (1890) Vol. III, 246 (1570). The singular form of *exactor* is obviously a misprint.

[312] *Ibid.*, Vol. III, 507.

[313] Kubinyi: Szolgabíró (Assistant justice). *Magyar Nyelv* 53 (1957) 207.

[314] Szendrei (1890) Vol. III, 155–156.

[315] I. Szentpétery Jr.: A vörös viaszpecsét bizonyító ereje a középkorban (The probative value of red sealing wax in the Middle Ages). *Szentpétery Emlékkönyv*. Budapest (1938) 444.

[316] 1471: Szendrei (1890) 107–108; 1495: *ibid.*, 127–128; 1503: *ibid.*, 139–141; 1516: *ibid.*, 160–162.

[317] *universitas civium et hospitum divitum et pauperum de Myskolcz. Dl.* 83949.

[318] Horváth–Marjalaki Kiss–Valentiny (1962) 186–192; G. Megay: A miskolci avasi templom 1941. évi ásatásának ered-

its immediate vicinity. The St. George chapel on Avas hill was demonstrably erected as early as 1376.[319] These churches, together with the parsonage of the Blessed Virgin and the All Saints Hospital, represented the ecclesiastical institutions of Miskolc. The town had no monastery of the Mendicant order.

A number of other factors also contributed to the development of Miskolc. Even though Miskolc was the wealthiest market town in the Diósgyőr estate it was by no means the only one, and could not enjoy the advantages of being in a central position. This position was 'usurped' by the market town of Diósgyőr, which lay in the castle's immediate vicinity and, in fact, had a more unfavourable position. The market towns of Keresztes, Kövesd and Muhi also belonged to the estate.[320] Even though Miskolc never became a central place in the estate — in spite of its presumably being the most significant market —, it did become a political centre by the second half of the 15th century. The general assemblies and tribunals of Borsod County, previously held in the market town of Sajószentpéter, north of Miskolc, were gradually transferred to Miskolc after the 1450s.[321] The weekly tribunals were originally held on Thursdays,[322] but from the last years of the century they took place on Wednesdays.[323] This event thus coincided with the weekly markets in Miskolc,[324] and thus the nobility attending to their affairs in the town obviously also visited the market, which undoubtedly enhanced the central place nature of the town.

The burghers of Miskolc also attended foreign universities. 15 people matriculated at such institutions (2 at Vienna, 13 at Cracow) between 1440–1514. Miskolc thus ranked 67th–70th among the other towns in the country, outstripping Eger, the episcopal see, which was 71st–73rd with 14 university students. In this respect Miskolc preceded Nyírbátor, but was in turn preceded by Gyöngyös.[325]

### (5) Ráckeve

Kevi or Kis-Kevi, the last-founded medieval town in Hungary, now called Ráckeve, is unparalleled in many respects among the other towns. Ráckeve lies south of the capital, Buda, near the southern tip of Csepel Island, one of the largest islands in the Danube, on the left bank of the so-called Ráckeve branch of the river. Throughout the Middle Ages the island had, apart from

a few part-holdings, been owned by the kings, and was used primarily as a hunting-ground. The royal seigniory, the proximity of Buda and its sister town, Pest, and also the nearby ferries were all conducive to the prosperity of the local serfs. It was thus by no means accidental that the Late Middle Ages saw four market towns on the island (Csepel, Tököl, Szentmárton, Kevi), most of which lay near the ferries. From the 15th century the kings considered the island as part of the crown lands of their queens. The first phase of the island's economic development was marked by hunting and a flourishing stock-breeding, that were later replaced by corn and vegetable cultivation, as well as viticulture.[326]

The oldest and, at the same time, most important ferry on the main, right-side branch of the Danube was Lórév near the southern tip of the island.[327] Remarkably enough, no comparable ferry is known to have been established on this branch for quite a long period. The settlement of Ráckeve was particularly suited to this purpose—the present-day road leading to Lórév (approximately 9 km southwest of Ráckeve) branches off from the Ráckeve Danube bridge. In short, Ráckeve was predestined for a rapid development. However, the original settlement lay some 3 km north of the present-day town. Its core was St. Abraham's monastery, first mentioned in a 1211 charter. It was presumably demolished by the Mongols — its two towers were still remembered in the early 19th century. This building cannot be identified with the circular-ended, rectangular church uncovered in 1862, the vicinity of which also yielded Roman artefacts. It can more plausibly be identified with a grave chapel or with the church of the village near the monastery. Recent excavations in the area have brought to light a cemetery and a number of 13th–14th century artefacts. To all appearances these finds marked the spot where the short-lived St. Abraham's monastery and the settlement of Szentábrahámtelke had stood.[328]

The interesting point is that King Ulászló I granted the Serbs, fleeing the Turks from the *oppidum* of Kevi and the associated villages of Bálványos and Skronovecz, permission to settle in the wasteland (allegedly the site of an earlier settlement) near St. Abraham's church on royal Csepel Island and reinforced their earlier freedoms.[329] In other words, this was the deed of the foundation of Ráckeve. The above-mentioned archaeological finds date the destruction of the original settlement to the 14th century at the latest, in

ményei (Results of the 1941 excavations of the Avas church at Miskolc). *HOMÉ* 9 (1970) 129–170.

[319] Horváth–Marjalaki Kiss–Valentiny (1962) 32.

[320] Csánki (1890) Vol. I, 165–166.

[321] 1398: *ZsO* I, no. 5480; 1401: *ibid.*, II/1, nos 1200, 1220; 1402: *ibid.*, no. 1648, etc.

[322] Cf. 1465: *Dl,* 90060; 1466: *Dl,* 90066; 1476: *Dl,* 90166; 1496: *Dl.* 90233.

[323] 1498: *Dl,* 75950, 88827; 1499: I. Kellemesi Melczer: *Okmányok a Kellemesi Melczer család levéltárából (Documents from the archives of the Kellemesi Melczer family).* Budapest (1890) 131–132; 1501: *Dl,* 75955, etc.

[324] Cf. note 290.

[325] Kubinyi (1971) 75.

[326] A. Kubinyi: Csepel története a Vasgyár alapításáig (History of Csepel until the founding of the iron mill). *Csepel története.* Budapest (1965) 8–15.

[327] *Ibid.,* 9.

[328] L. Makkai: Pest megye története (History of Pest county). *Pest megye műemlékei I.* Ed. by D. Dercsényi. Budapest (1958) 69–76; D. Dercsényi: Művészettörténeti áttekintés (Art historical survey). *ibid.,* 172; see also *Pest megye műemlékei II.* Ed. by D. Dercsényi. Budapest (1958) 38; S. Tettamanti's excavation report in *RégFüz* I. 29 (1976) 84.

[329] M. Hajdu: Helynevek vándorlása a XV. században (Itinerant toponyms in the 15th century). *Névtani Értesítő* 1 (1979) 21–26. Prof. István Tálasi drew my attention to this study; Magdics (1888) 23–24.

other words, the mention of its privilege in the royal charter is by all means relevant, except for one tiny contradiction: The new settlement was located far from the original one, even though the data indicate a full identity. In 1455 King László V confirmed the Serbs living in the royal village of Szentábrahámtelke or Kiskevi in their *civitas* rights that had been granted to them in their former hometown of Kövin in the Lower Danube area.[330] The name of the new settlement (Szentábrahámtelke or Kiskevi) often occurs in later documents, indicating that the original name of Kiskevi was used primarily for distinguishing it from the former settlement called Kevi.[331] To complicate matters further, Ráckeve was one of the few Hungarian towns which had their history compiled as early as the 16th century. Máté Skaricza, the then reformed preacher of the town, wrote his versified history of Ráckeve in Hungarian in 1581. According to his account, the settlement was first called Szentábrahám after the 'cherry' church of St. Abraham and the trees surrounding it, and later Rácz-Kevi after the Serbs (Rác in Hungarian) who had settled there.[332] His history also relates that the settlement had a chapel dedicated to the Blessed Virgin, and that King Sigismund granted the chapel permission to hold annual markets coinciding with the Festival of the Visitation. After relating the events of the settlement, Skaricza describes how the Serbs built a larger arch to the small St. Abraham church and then agreed with the Hungarians that they would use the church of the Blessed Virgin, while the Hungarians that of St. Abraham. However, it is later mentioned that the Serbs erected the church of the Blessed Virgin in 1487, and they also built a church dedicated to the Holy Cross around the year 1517.[333] Ráckeve indeed had three churches in the Middle Ages, although the third cannot be identified with the Romanesque Benedictine abbey built in 1211. The location of the village of Szentábrahámtelke and the St. Abraham church to an area north to Ráckeve is supported by the 18th–19th century maps and the archaeological evidence. This was then the settlement received by the Serbs of Kevi from King Ulászló I. The change of name can be linked to another franchise of the king, issued simultaneously with the right of settlement. This franchise reiterates the endowment of the Serbs with the site of the former village near the church of St. Ábrahám puszta, adding that the settlers were free to set up a ferry near their new home and to keep boats there.[334] This ferry lay near the site of the later town of Ráckeve and not by the destroyed village of Szentábrahámtelke, the alleged first settlement of the Serbs. It would appear that the refugee Serbs, most of whom were merchants, settled in the area of the ferry rather than in the barren village of Szentábrahámtelke. The area of the ferry had all the potentials for turning into an urban settlement. Instead of taking over the *puszta*

('deserted') St. Abraham church, they erected their own chapel as its legal successor, which they subsequently handed over to the Hungarians.

This assumption explains why no archaeological traces of the 15th century settlement have come to light in the area of St. Abraham's church, and also why Skaricza mentions a church of the same name in the town (after a period of one and a half centuries he could not have been aware of the change of name owing to legal reasons). There is, however, yet another problem, namely the alleged right of Ábrahámtelke to hold annual markets under King Sigismund. The answer calls for a brief survey of the history of Keve, the primary settlement of the Serbs. Keve, or Kovin, lies in Yugoslavia, north of Belgrade on the left, or northern bank of the Lower Danube, almost opposite the mouth of the river Morava. Owing to its strategic and commercial significance, the settlement had enjoyed special royal privileges over the centuries. The first surviving patent was issued by King Sigismund in 1405. In this, the king granted the burghers and *hospites* of Kevi *civitas* the right to hold annual markets at the parish church of the Blessed Virgin on July 2, coinciding with the Festival of the Visitation.[335] Since the burghers of Ráckeve were entitled to the same privileges which they had enjoyed in their former settlement, the fact that the Ráckeve markets were also held on July 2 can confidently be traced to the very same patent. All Skaricza knew was that the patent had been issued by Sigismund. But since the area of the later town had formerly belonged to Szentábrahámtelke, he thought that the privilege had been granted to this settlement (the church of the Blessed Virgin was already standing). In short, the chronicler was wrong on this point. The most important privilege of Kevi *civitas* on the Lower Danube was granted by Sigismund in 1428. This exempted the town from taxation, obliging it to deliver only 100 kg of wax, but in return the town had to guard the royal port (to fend off the advancing Turks from this strategic point). The patent also donated the royal villages of Bálványos and Zkronova to Keve. The burghers were exempted from duty all over the country, and the privilege prohibited the arrest of the town's merchants and their goods. The patent ruled that foreign merchants could sell felt only during the annual markets, and even then only in small amounts, and the same applied to imported wines. It also permitted the town to hold weekly markets (on Tuesdays) and guaranteed the free election of the parish priest.[336] These were the most important clauses in the patent, and at the same time they represent a sample of the main privileges enjoyed by other Hungarian towns. The clause guaranteeing the free election of the judge is missing from the patent, presumably because the town had received this right at an earlier date (the clauses were issued at the request of judge Péter). It was this patent of 1428 that made Keve a town proper. These privileges were augmented by the 1435 charter of Sigismund. It exempted the town from the royal customs duty — the thirtieth — and granted

[330] *Ibid.*, 32–34.
[331] E. g. 1458: *ibid.*, 36, 38; 1464: *ibid.*, 40, 42; 1465: *ibid.*, 43; 1475: *ibid.*, 48; 1481: *ibid.*, 49; 1501: *ibid.*, 60; etc.
[332] *Ibid.*, 83.
[333] *Ibid.*, 88, 90–91.
[334] *Ibid.*, 24-25.

[335] *Ibid.*, 1–2.
[336] *Ibid.*, 4–9.

staple right to Keve *civitas* over the trade between Hungary and Serbia.[337] Disregarding now the minor privileges, Albert's patent of February 24, 1438, must also be mentioned which confirmed the burghers and *hospites* of Keve, Skronovecz and Bálványos in their right to free trade and to take justice into their own hands.[338]

These privileges suggest that the inhabitants of Keve, and the annexed two villages, were primarily engaged in trade with the Balkans, and also that the Hungarian kings supported these strategically important settlements. But the Turkish raids interrupted the peaceful development. In his charter of August 20, 1440, King Ulászló I retained the right to exercise jurisdiction over the burghers of Keve who by that time had fled the town and dispersed in the country.[339] The king signed the above-cited privileges concerning the new settlement of the Serbs on October 10, 1440. These bear out Skaricza's account that the fleeing Serbs first settled on Váci (today Szentendre) Island north of Buda, opposite the royal castle at Visegrád, and moved to Csepel Island only at a later date.[340] This is supported by King Sigismund's patent of 1428, which also settled Bulgarian refugees, also Orthodox Christians, on Szentendre Island. This patent is contemporary with that granted to the town of Keve on the Lower Danube.[341] Consequently, the first wave of the Serbs had reached Szentendre Island in 1440, and they moved to Csepel Island by the end of that year.

It is possible that relations between the former town of Keve and the new settlement of Kiskeve had been maintained for a while. Answering a request by the judge of Keve *civitas*, King Ladislaus V confirmed the town in its privileges in 1453, reserving the right to implement the exemption from duty to Serbian despot George Branković.[342] Two years later, in 1455, he confirmed the privileges of the Serbs in Szentábrahámtelke or Kiskevi, a royal village *(villa)* on Csepel Island, and charged the royal bailiffs in the island with their commission. The patent gave the Serbs permission to return to Kövin *civitas*, which they had left through fear of the Turks. He also mentions the Danube ferry opposite the village.[343] Meanwhile, on the very same day, the king issued a charter confirming the exemption from duty of the town of Kövin at the request of judge Márton and the burghers György and Barrabás. Sigismund's former lord chancellor and George the Serbian despot testified the privileges. This charter also provided guidelines in case of emergencies, such as the inhabitants' fleeing from the Turks or their return to the settlement.[344] The role of the Serbian despot, the refer-

ences to the judge as the governor of the town of Kövin on the Lower Danube and to the possible departures and returns to the town suggest that the settlement at Szentábrahámtelke was not considered final and that part of the population had remained in the original home town. Kövin was still one of the main bases of the Hungarian troops fighting the invading Turks. Captain General János Hunyadi dated several of his charters from this town.[345] King Matthias, who ascended the throne in 1458, confirmed the privileges of the new settlement at the request of judge Márton and the Serbian jurors Barnabás and Márton (in the 1455 document the judge was still referred to as a burgher of Kövin). One of the king's charters describes the suitors as governors in the village of Szentábrahámtelke or Kiskövi on Csepel Island, the other as principals of the possession *(villa or possessio)*.[346] We shall not list all the privileges and their confirmations granted to the town. For particulars the reader is referred to Magdics's edition compiled from the records of the Municipal Archives.[347]

The name of the town is even more intriguing. Originally Keve on the Lower Danube had been called a *civitas* or town, and the new settlement at Ábrahámtelke, 'Kis' (small) Kevi, as village or possession *(possessio)* used in the same sense. The charters issued by King Matthias in 1464 and 1465 still used the latter terms.[348] The royal charter of 1473, however, granted privileges to the *oppidum* of Keve.[349] This term was soon adopted in the other charters, although the term *possessio* also occurs in some.[350] The first reference to a burgher of Ráckeve as an inhabitant of Kevi *oppidum* occurs in a 1464 royal charter.[351] This would imply that the Serbians who in 1440 moved from Keve *civitas* on the Lower Danube to near Ábrahámtelke did not manage to get their new settlement recognized as a town or *civitas*, even though they did enjoy, and even augment, their ancient privileges. In spite of all its privileges, 'Kis' Kevi remained a village until the 1460s, when it was first referred to as *oppidum* or market town. What is odd, however, is that the privileges of Kis-Kevi, referred to as *villa*, *possessio* and finally *oppidum*, did not differ from those of Kevi *civitas* on the Lower Danube. The difference in terminology can be explained in two different ways. One is that the mother town had probably been an early *civitas*, but the title itself — that was inherited later — no longer corresponded to the requirements of the new *civitas* which was why it could not be used.[352] The plausibility of the second explanation de-

[337] *Ibid.*, 11–13, 13–15.
[338] *Ibid.*, 19-21.
[339] *Ibid.*, 21-23.
[340] *Ibid.*, 89.
[341] E. Mályusz: Une colonie bulgare à proximité de Buda au moyen âge. *Studia Slavica Academiae Scientiarum Hungaricae* 13 (1967) 413–425.
[342] Magdics (1888) 25–32.
[343] *Ibid.*, 32–34.
[344] *Ibid.*, 34–36.

[345] On several occasions between 1448–1456, first in his capacity as regent. B. Sebestyén: *A magyar királyok tartózkodási helyei (The residences of the Hungarian kings)*. Budapest (n.d.) 81–83. The data can only be associated with Keve on the Lower Danube owing to the contents of the charters.
[346] Magdics (1888) 36–40.
[347] *Ibid.*, 41–71. (1464–1536).
[348] *Ibid.*, 40–43.
[349] *Ibid.*, 45–46.
[350] 1475: *ibid.*, 48; 1481: *ibid.*, 49; 1501: *ibid.*, 60.
[351] *Dl.* 16034.
[352] Cf. Ladányi: Libera villa, civitas, oppidum. Ter-

pends on whether the town of Kevi on the Lower Danube had been fortified with a wall. In view of its strategic significance, it had probably been a fortified settlement. The town of Kevi on Csepel Island was definitely not fortified, and thus it could not have been a *civitas*. In any case, the answer is definite in the case of the 'later' Kevi. The terminology depended on the outward appearance of the settlement, and not on its privileges. During the first decades of its existence the settlement was called a village — in spite of its privileges —, because of the village-like appearance of the temporary houses of the Serbs. Later the settlement was called an *oppidum* or market town, since it had no defences. This coincided with King Matthias' 1489 decree which confirmed the privileges of Kevi, the queen's *oppidum*, and acknowledged the authority of the municipal judge and jurors over the legal affairs of the town, with the provision that appeals could only be lodged to the lord chief treasurer and then to the king. By releasing the burghers of Kevi *expressis verbis* from the authority of the bailiff of Csepel Island[353] — a practice common in the free royal towns —, Kevi became directly subjected to the king. This in fact was one of the main criteria of urbanization.[354] In this case the king and the queen, whose properties included Csepel Island, must have acted as legal equals. We know that a few years before the patent was issued Queen Beatrix herself, aided by a number of barons and noblemen, the prothonotary and the doctors, administered justice in one of the legal proceedings in the town.[355] The prothonotaries were professional judges on the feudal Court of Appeal, i. e. the queen exercised jurisdiction in agreement with the judges on the Royal Court.

There is no proof whatsoever that Ráckeve had been considered a town in a feudal sense.[356] It was called *város* (town) in Hungarian, as shown by Skaricza's versified chronicle and the surviving 17th century municipal records.[357] This would suggest that the term *oppidum* was translated as *város* (town or *civitas*) instead of *mezőváros* (market town). Since the legal and terminological contradictions can hardly be resolved, special attention must be accorded to the presumed outward appearance of the town. This involves yet newer problems. The present-day town is described as an agglomeration of loosely connected structures — this, of course, applies to the whole of Ráckeve. The town has a main street which runs parallel with the Danube, two other parallel streets and a number of streets leading out of the town radially.[358] Since the town was abandoned after the clashes at the turn of the 16th–17th centuries, the first municipal register dates to 1605, i. e. from the year following the second occupation and

settlement of the town.[359] Since the town has repeatedly been destroyed by fire,[360] the medieval groundplan cannot really be reconstructed from the modern layout. Neither can Skaricza's description of the town be identified with present-day conditions. This description nevertheless offers an authentic picture of the state of urbanization in late 16th century Ráckeve. Skaricza mentions seven marketplaces, one of which, called Tágas Piac (Large Market), must have been the largest. There was a separate haymarket and timber-market, in other words the markets were differentiated according to goods. The area in front of the Serbian church can most probably be identified with the Rácz (Serbian) Market. Skaricza lists the streets in two groups: first the 'up'-streets, then the 'down'-streets, probably the streets leading 'upwards' and 'downwards' from the town centre. Each group includes five streets. Skaricza mentions a 'main up-street' and a 'main down-street', which can be considered to have been part of the same street, and which can plausibly be identified with present-day Kossuth Lajos Street and its continuation Vörösmarty Street (or perhaps Molnár Street) which run parallel with the Danube. (The 'upwards' streets were presumably those leading north from the centre). The list of the alleys in Skaricza's account is admittedly incomplete. The streets of his description can probably be identified with the longer streets running parallel with the Danube, whilst the alleys with the shorter ones connecting the former and running at right angles to the Danube. This arrangement is comparable with the present-day street network. The majority of the streets and alleys, as well as the markets, were named after the craftsmen living in them (e.g. *Olajverő*, 'oil-presser' Street).[361]

Skaricza's description clearly proves that in the 16th century Ráckeve was not a market town-type settlement, since it had more than one market. The markets, streets and alleys rather reflect an urbanized settlement. This is supported by other facts too. Skaricza describes how the refugees began to build new houses shortly after their settlement, and goes on to say that "And soon they acquired stone houses / For they revelled in their prosperity".[362] We have seen that the first stone houses were only built in the late 15th century in the wealthy market towns and in prospering towns like Szeged, Vác, Gyöngyös and Miskolc. In Skaricza's time the town was thus characterised by stone structures. His description is supported by the results of archaeological and architectural investigations. Half a dozen Gothic stone houses are still standing in Kossuth Lajos Street, the main street running parallel with the Danube.[363] The house uncovered during the excavations in István Square, south of Kossuth Lajos Street, differed from those in the main street inasmuch as it was built of mud bricks. On the

minologische Fragen in der ungarischen Städteentwicklung. *AnnUnivBud* 18 (1977) 3–43.

[353] Magdics (1888) 53–55.

[354] Kubinyi (1980) 219, 223–235.

[355] *Dl.* 100989.

[356] Cf. Kubinyi (1980) 215–246.

[357] Magdics (1888) 83–102.

[358] *Pest megye műemlékei II.* Ed. by D. Dercsényi. Budapest (1958) 9.

[359] Magdics (1888) 94.

[360] Cf. note 358.

[361] Magdics (1888) 91–92.

[362] *Ibid.*, 89.

[363] *Pest megye műemlékei II.* Ed. by D. Dercsényi. Budapest (1958) 37; A. Gergelyffy: Középkori lakóházak Ráckevén (Medieval dwelling houses in Ráckeve). *Építés- és Építészettudomány* 5 (1973) 405–411.

evidence of the surviving walls, the 40×20×15 cm mud bricks were tempered with straw and chaff. The house was later destroyed by fire, probably during the Turkish raids. The coin finds date the conflagration to the years after 1528.[364] The medieval stone structures represent two architectural periods. The first group of houses was built in the second half of the 15th century in late Gothic style, the second group in the early 16th century with traces of the Renaissance visible. Each house had a cellar: these barrel-vaulted rooms all faced onto the street and were built at right angles to it.[365]

To all appearances, the stone houses were the residences of the merchants. Regrettably enough, the artefacts unearthed in 1 Kossuth Lajos Street — the site of a merchant's house — are still unpublished. All we know is that the site yielded some stone tiles.[366] The finds from the mud-brick house in István Square have already been published. Since the ruins were covered with an 8–10 cm thick, even layer of charred grain, the excavator suggested that it had fallen onto the ruins when the roof collapsed. In his opinion the merchant owing the house had stored the stockpiled grain in the loft only temporarily, since this practice was not common in the period.[367] This would suggest that the owner of the house was a corn-merchant. Even though this possibility cannot be dismissed, it must be noted that the other finds from the site allow another interpretation. The ploughshare, a wrought-iron chain terminating in a hook, a fish-spear, nails, a hatchet and a horse-shoe,[368] suggest that the owner of the house had been engaged in some kind of agricultural activity — part-time or full-time —, including fishing. Consequently, the house may have belonged to a corn-merchant who was also engaged in agriculture or to a peasant who also traded his corn.

The inhabitants of Ráckeve were engaged primarily in commerce. Besides the above-cited commercial privileges, the surviving medieval charters all point to a relatively early trade in the town. A Serb from the market town of Kevi, who in 1464 transported some sort of goods to Buda, had his wares weighed on the municipal balance.[369] In 1476 Ráckeve entered into litigation over a duty conflict in Nagyvárad on the side of the leading free royal merchant towns of the country (Buda, Pest, Székesfehérvár, Kassa (Košice), Pozsony (Bratislava), Eperjes (Prešov), Bártfa (Bardejov), Lőcse (Levoča) and the towns in Transylvania).[370] Since

Nagyvárad (Oradea) was one of the major market towns on the road leading to Transylvania this proves trade contacts with Transylvania. In 1481 following a legal strife, the owner of the tollhouse at Bolcs, near Várad, made a promise to the judge of Ráckeve that he would not exact toll from the burghers of Keve unless their cartload contained foreign goods.[371] Another piece of evidence for Ráckeve's trade with Transylvania dates from the same year: two merchants, a certain Nicholas called the Greek from Tergovişte (Wallachia) and another one from Szeben (Sibiu) struck up a conversation in Kolozsvár with a Serb from Keve named Keresztes on the affairs of another Szeben merchant. As it turned out, Keresztes had been sent to the Szeben merchant in question by Haller, a merchant in Buda (a burgher of Nuremberg by birth).[372] It would appear that Keresztes of Ráckeve was in some way subordinated to Haller. The man from Tergovişte was Orthodox by religion, similarly to Keresztes. In 1482–1483 the interest of the merchants in Keve was directed towards a completely different region. They were engaged in litigation with Miklós Szécsi, the owner of the tollhouse at Muraszombat on the southwestern boundary of the country. According to the tariffs, the Keve merchants passed the customs at Muraszombat with heaped or 'baled' carts, with horses, oxen and sheep.[373] This means that they drove livestock out of the country in exchange for felt.[374] These facts and the known privileges clearly indicate that soon after its foundation Ráckeve became one of the most significant merchant towns in the country. Its commerce raised the town above the average market town, since it had commercial contacts throughout the country and even abroad (including the towns in the northern Balkans). Contacts with the south and east were facilitated by the fact that the burghers of Keve were Orthodox by religion, and this probably eased the setting up of business contacts with the Romanian, Serbian or Greek merchants of the same faith. The town's location on the fringes of the Great Hungarian Plain proved ideal for taking a share in the country's cattle export, which in this period brought prosperity to a number of the towns in the region (Pest, Szeged, etc).[375] The town of Keve also shared their

[364] J. Fegyó: Késő középkori lakóház leletmentése Ráckevén (Rescue excavation of a late medieval dwelling house in Ráckeve). StudCom 2 (1973) 93–105.

[365] A. Gergelyffy: Középkori lakóházak Ráckevén (Medieval dwelling houses in Ráckeve). Építés- és Építészettudomány 5 (1973) 405–411.

[366] J. Fegyó: Késő középkori lakóház leletmentése Ráckevén (Rescue excavation of a late medieval dwelling house in Ráckeve). StudCom 2 (1973) 93.

[367] Ibid., 104.

[368] Ibid., 101–102, 104.

[369] Dl, 16034.

[370] A. Kubinyi: A városi rend kialakulásának gazdasági feltételei és a főváros kereskedelme a XV. század végén (Economic conditions of urban development and commerce in

the capital in the late 15th century). TBM 15 (1963) 191. As early as 1472 the king had the oppidum of Régen in Transylvania, owned by the Bánfi family of Losonc, confiscated by the Transylvanian voivod "on account of the royal Serbs of Kevi in Csepel Island". Accordingly, the Serbs of Kevi doing business in Transylvania must have experienced insults from the Bánfis. Dl, 97345.

[371] Dl, 26643.

[372] A. Kubinyi: Die Nürnberger Haller in Ofen. Mitteilungen des Vereins für Geschichte der Stadt Nürnberg 52 (1963–64) 114.

[373] Dl, 100989.

[374] Cf. O. Pickl: Die Auswirkungen der Türkenkriege auf den Handel zwischen Ungarn und Italien im 16. Jahrhundert. Die wirtschaftliche Auswirkung der Türkenkriege. Ed. by O. Pickl. Grazer Forschungen zur Wirtschafts- und Sozialgeschichte 1. Graz (1971) 125.

[375] A. Kubinyi: Die Städte Ofen und Pest und der Fernhandel am Ende des 15. und am Anfang des 16. Jahrhunderts. Der

prosperity. Felt was probably acquired as a countervalue to the cattle export.

Handicrafts also played an important role in the early development of Keve. A surviving decision of an arbitration court, convened in the 1470s by King Matthias, throws light on the state of the municipal butcher's stalls and the butcher's trade in general. The decision ruled that the stalls set up on 'common land', i. e. on public domain, could be sold only to the judges or to the community of the *oppidum*, but not to foreigners. Foreign butchers were allowed to sell meat in the town only on Saturdays, on the day of the weekly markets.[376] This would suggest that, similarly to several other Hungarian towns, the ownership of the stalls was separate from the practice of the trade,[377] and was subject to free sale and purchase. The council's aim was to pass the stalls into the town's proprietorship, and to guarantee the supply of meat by permitting foreign butchers to sell their meat on Saturdays.

The specialization of the handicrafts again highlights the urban nature of the settlement, even though these data reflect conditions in 1546, in the first years of the Turkish occupation.[378]

Of the 664 adult males, 23 per cent were engaged in handicrafts. This ratio is 28.9 per cent if we include the 530 patres familias. The breakdown by trades was 56 tailors, 18 cobblers, 10 butchers, 8 fishermen, 8 barbers, 8 carpenters, 7 furriers, 6 blacksmiths and 5 goldsmiths. The other branches were represented by less than five craftsmen. The merchants, who obviously had the greatest share in the economic prosperity of the town, must have been present in great number. Their exact number could not be established. All we know is that there were nine shopkeepers and one inn-keeper, as is indicated in a Turkish register.

The importance of Ráckeve in the Middle Ages is also reflected by the fact that the period saw the building of three churches. Two of these are known only from modern depictions of the town since they were demolished in the late 18th and early 20th centuries. The church of the Holy Cross, built around 1517 in the southern part of the town, became Catholic in modern times. An 18th century depiction shows a late Gothic church with a brickset tower and with a buttressed sanctuary with polygonal termination. The width of the latter equalled that of the nave.[379] The medieval *patrocinium* of the other church, which turned Reformed in modern times,

Table 7. Craftsmen in Ráckeve in 1546

| Craft | branch | percentage | craftsmen | percentage |
|---|---|---|---|---|
| metallurgy, manufacture of arms | 6 | 24 | 17 | 11.1 |
| weaving | 2 | 8 | 4 | 2.6 |
| leather industry | 3 | 12 | 7 | 4.6 |
| wood industry | 3 | 12 | 3 | 2.0 |
| food processing | 5 | 20 | 26 | 17.0 |
| clothing trade | 3 | 12 | 81 | 52.9 |
| building trade, ceramics | 2 | 8 | 7 | 4.6 |
| other | 1 | 4 | 8 | 5.2 |
| Total | 25 | 100 | 153 | 100.0 |

may have been St. Nicholas. The originally small-sized Gothic church was extended to the west in the 15th century. In its original form the church was a single-aisled, buttressed Gothic edifice terminating in half of an octagon. Similarly to the church of the Serbs, in had no separate sanctuary.[380]

The still standing Serbian church of the Blessed Virgin is considered to have been the most significant medieval building in Ráckeve. Built in 1487, it is a single-aisled hall-church, terminates in five sides of the octagon, has two Gothic side-chapels in the south and a detached tower whose ground floor is still Gothic. Its sanctuary is narrowed down. The tower and the two side-chapels date from the early 16th century, as shown by the Renaissance doors. Skaricza attributed the building of the church of the Holy Cross, and of the tower of the former church, to Italian builders[381] (Fig. 18).

*(6) Market towns in, and on the fringes of the Great Hungarian Plain*

We have surveyed four settlements which represent different types in terms of their age, owners and economy. The possible similarities between them which can also be detected elsewhere can thus be used for drawing general conclusions. The economy of two of the four towns, Gyöngyös and Miskolc, was based primarily on viticulture. Similarly to the other market towns on the Great Hungarian Plain, Nyírbátor was engaged in animal husbandry and livestock trade, while in Ráckeve the primary branches were grain cultivation and fishing. All four towns can be characterized by a relatively high-level trade (markets), although only Ráckeve was engaged in active long-distance trade. The ratio of craftsmen was the highest in Ráckeve — insofar as the 16th century data can be projected onto earlier conditions. In this one respect the town ranked above the average market towns, but below the free royal towns.

*Aussenhandel Ostmitteleuropas 1450–1650. Die ostmitteleuropäischen Volkswirtschaften in ihren Beziehungen zu Mitteleuropa.* Ed. by I. Bog. Köln–Wien (1971) 354–358.

[376] M. G. Kovachich: *Formulae solennes styli.* Pesthini (1799) 224–225.

[377] A. Kubinyi: Budapest története a későbbi középkorban Buda elestéig (1541-ig) (The late medieval history of Budapest until the fall of Buda in 1541). *Budapest története II.* Ed. by L. Gerevich. Budapest (1973) 57.

[378] Gy. Káldy-Nagy: *Kanuni devri Budin tahrir defteri (1546–1562) (The Tax-Register of the Jalet of Buda from the Hanunis's time: 1541–1562).* Ankara (1971) 85–89.

[379] L. Makkai: Pest megye története (History of Pest county). *Pest megye műemlékei* Vol. II. Ed. by D. Dercsényi. Budapest (1958) 9–10.

[380] *Ibid.,* 15–17.
[381] *Ibid.,* 18–28.

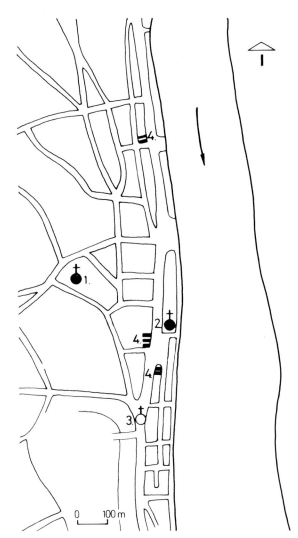

Fig. 18. Ráckeve in the Middle Ages. 1. Church of the Blessed Virgin, 2. St. Nicholas' (?) church, 3. church of the Holy Cross, 4. medieval houses

have settled in Ráckeve since the town's population was overwhelmingly Greek Orthodox. In Miskolc, the hospital may have substituted the monastery. Regarding university graduates, Gyöngyös took the lead (the students numbered less than in the towns proper, but approximately equalled those in the major market towns), Miskolc was a close second, with Nyírbátor following far behind (but still par with the average of the market towns). Ráckeve sent no students to the Latin universities. As for terminology: Gyöngyös and Nyírbátor — the two privately owned manorial towns — were first referred to as villages *(possessiones)* and later as *oppida;* Miskolc, originally a village, first became a town *(civitas)* following the royal takeover, and then an *oppidum;* Ráckeve, established after the resettlement of the royal *civitas* of Keve, also became an *oppidum* following a brief period of village status. In short, despite the different origins, each town had become an *oppidum* by the Late Middle Ages!

Let us now turn to another criterion, namely that of the groundplan and the architecture of these settlements. In terms groundplan, it is the town of Miskolc that offers an abundance of data (based on the historical sources and the archaeological excavations). The relatively late emergence of the still existing grid street pattern must be considered a decisive factor in the town's history. The late 14th century appearance of Miskolc (which differed considerably from that in the 13th century) offers the closest parallel in Hungary to the settlement form typical of the 'Markt's in Upper Austria: the marketplace was the nucleus of the town, and there were no parallel streets. Even though in Miskolc the development of this groundplan (or rather groundplans, in view of the two town parts, the New and the Old Town) can be linked to the replanning of the settlement following the royal takeover in the second half of the 14th century, it nonetheless offers valuable starting points for understanding the groundplan of Gyöngyös. In its primary form, Gyöngyös probably also had a single market street as its nucleus, as has been suggested by local historians. This theory is not contradicted by the fact that from the late 13th century the groundplan of Gyöngyös resembled that of Miskolc. The town of Hajdúböszörmény must have had a similar arrangement: a market street, which later developed into a grid street system, and finally into a 'field-garden' settlement type.[382] In contrast, 14th century Nyírbátor with its two main streets, and Ráckeve with its scattered markets and streets apparently represented a different type. Nyírbátor may also have had a single street as its original nucleus ('Markt'-type), but this is even more difficult to prove than in the case of Gyöngyös. Ráckeve understandably represents a different type.

All in all, there existed a settlement type in, or on the fringes of, the Great Hungarian Plain in the Middle Ages which evolved from a village-like settlement (entitled to hold markets) and which, in terms of its groundplan, resembled the 'Markt's of Upper Austria. These settlements later developed into cross-roads or 'parallel-roads' types or their original groundplan was

This ratio corresponded to that of the average market towns in Gyöngyös and Miskolc (we have no data for Nyírbátor). The three towns differed considerably in terms of the number of crafts — reflecting differentiation. This number was the lowest in Miskolc, although it still corresponded to values obtained for differentiated industrial market towns, and was the highest in Gyöngyös, thus ranking it among the other towns in Hungary. The latter figure may perhaps be traced to the mid-16th century state of the development of the town.

In terms of ownership, Miskolc (from the second half of the 14th century) and Ráckeve were both royal towns, but neither was the centre, or the single town of the estate. The other two towns were manorial or rather secular latifundial market towns, and were also centres of their respective estates. Each of the towns lay along main commercial routes. The monastery of the Mendicant order, considered by Hungarian scholars to be one of the basic criteria to the emergence of a town, was to be found in two of the four towns, but only at a later stage of development. The Mendicant friars could not

[382] Cf. notes 15–16.

146

completely organized (cf. Miskolc). The process discussed in the first section of the present paper — the agglomeration of several small settlements into a unified town (cf. the development of Debrecen, the largest market town on the Great Hungarian Plain) —, should also be taken into consideration here.[383] This appears to have been the case in Nyírbátor, although to a lesser degree as compared with Miskolc, where this agglomeration was established by a royal decree in the second half of the 14th century (Old and New Town, the cotters' streets). Thus, in terms of the late medieval groundplan all the Hungarian towns discussed above differed from the village-like settlements or the Austrian Markt-type towns.

In the reconstruction of the architecture we could rely primarily on the excavations in Miskolc and on the written sources. The erection of stone structures can be confirmed from the 15th century on, even if their number was insignificant until the Turkish occupation. This was presumably the case in Gyöngyös, where only one medieval stone house has survived (though there might have been more), while in newly-founded Ráckeve the stone structures were the rule. This can perhaps be generalized for the settlements on the Great Hungarian Plain. The majority of the houses in Debrecen — where the first multi-storey houses were only erected as late as the 17th century — were built of mud-bricks or had wattle-and-daub walls.[384] The free royal town of Szeged had had more stone structures, but only since the late 15th century.[385] Stone houses and multi-level tunnel-like cellars have also been noted at Pásztó, an *oppidum* west of Gyöngyös near the edge of the Great Hungarian Plain.[386] True enough stone was more readily available on the fringes of the Great Hungarian Plain—in Miskolc, Gyöngyös, Pásztó or Ráckeve than in Debrecen or Szeged—still, the fact that stone houses began to be built at about roughly the same time in Miskolc and Szeged should nonetheless be worth consideration (some scholars are inclined to explain this by the present state of research).

The development of the market towns on the Great Hungarian Plain was obviously a long process. The towns surveyed in the above would suggest that the privileged town-like settlements of the 14th century —which we call market towns —, had their origins in the late 13th century marketplaces and small mercantile centres. Their development had been uninterrupted and, as indicated by the mid-15th century foundation of Ráckeve, the region could have supported more settlements. Disregarding now economic and social factors,[387] let us consider the groundplan and architecture of these

settlements. It is fairly clear that these settlements had a groundplan similar to that of the towns,[388] although the first late medieval stone houses were still only one-storeyed.

The above definitely suggest that the market towns on, and on the fringes of, the Great Hungarian Plain ranked between the town and the village both in terms of economy and architecture, irrespective of the fact that they functioned as towns in the lack of towns proper in the region. By the early 16th century these settlements had all assumed a definitely urban character. This development may have proceeded undisturbed had the Turks not invaded the country (the most densely populated towns in the late 18th century Hungary were still those in the Great Hungarian Plain).[389] Whether the pace of development in these large agrarian settlements would have been faster without the Turks, is a question that cannot be definitely proved.

## SUMMARY

Two types of medieval settlements in the Great Hungarian Plain have been analyzed. The first type — the episcopal and royal towns — can be traced back to the creation of the Hungarian state, while the urbanization of the towns falling into the second category started approximately three centuries later. Ráckeve is still younger: it was settled four hundred years after the foundation of Eger and Vác. There appears to be a marked difference between the two settlement types. The first type includes the free royal towns and the episcopal seats, the population of which consisted of serfs as in the towns of the second group. Nevertheless, the episcopal seats and the free royal towns were definitely more urban in appearance than the market towns. On the other hand, the flourishing of both types can be assigned to the 15th–16th centuries. This period saw the agglomeration of the separate settlements in the first group, and also their economic and social consolidation (cf. Szeged). Still more decisive is the fact that in the 13th–14th centuries a period of stagnation, or even a complete standstill can be noted in the development of the towns in the first group. Accordingly, we can state that there was a temporary lull in the urban development of the towns in the Great Hungarian Plain sometime during the 12th century, which was followed by an upswing in the Late Middle Ages. The stagnation can obviously be linked to the Mongol invasion and to the subsequent settlement of Cumanian tribes, as well as to the changes in the commercial contacts after the occupation of Byzantium in 1204. On the other hand, the

[383] L. Sápi: *Debrecen település- és építéstörténete (Settlement and architectural history of Debrecen)*. Debrecen (1972).

[384] *Ibid.*, 16–19.

[385] Kubinyi (1980) 438.

[386] I. Valter: Műemléki feltárások és helyreállítások Pásztón (Excavation and renovation of monuments in Pásztó). *Műemlékvédelem* 13 (1969) 226–230; I. Valter: Pásztó, a középkori oppidum (Pásztó, a medieval oppidum). *Városépítés* (1976: 1–2) 25–26.

[387] Cf. Gy. Székely: A mezővárosi fejlődés kérdései a XVIII. század végéig (The development of market towns until

the late 18th century). *A Debreceni Déri Múzeum Évkönyve* (1974) 347–370.

[388] Pásztó also had more than one street: I. Valter: Pásztó, a középkori oppidum (Pásztó, a medieval oppidum). *Városépítés* (1976:1–2) 25–26.

[389] L. Makkai: A magyar városfejlődés történetének vázlata (Brief historical outline of the development of towns in Hungary). *Vidéki városaink*. Ed. by J. Borsos. Budapest (1961) 68–70.

upswing of animal husbandry and cattle export, and also of the wine-trade, led to a new wave of urbanization.

However, it should also be noted that only few of the numerous late medieval market towns in, and on the fringes of, the Great Hungarian Plain can be compared with the towns proper. This is also supported by the historical evidence. For example the town of Gyula, which in the Late Middle Ages had an estimated population of 1250 and where 22 crafts were plied, ranked above the market towns of Jánk (population of 410, with 3 crafts) or Apáti (population of 100, with 3 crafts).[390] This again indicates the backwardness of archaeological research concerning the market towns: we still cannot distinguish the markedly urbanized

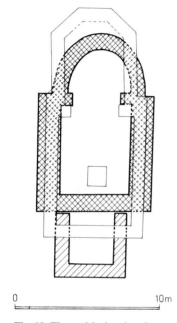

0                              10m

Fig. 19. The parish church at Szer

settlements from the other market towns. The written sources offer us no help in this respect. Still, there is one possibility for a distinction of this kind, which also offers evidence from another point of view.

Art historians have noted that the old churches in the late medieval market towns were regularly enlarged, obviously on account of the economic prosperity and increases in the population.[391] This can clearly be demonstrated in the case of Szeged, Miskolc, Gyöngyös and also Nyírbátor, although its parish church of St. George was erected by the local landlord. The same phenomenon can be noted for the monasteries of the

Mendicant order. Most of these can be assigned to the end of the 15th century, although in some cases (Szeged and Miskolc) their construction took place at an earlier date. It is remarkable that the churches in the towns at issue closely resembled each other.[392] Each had a huge inner space, capable of accommodating a large congregation. The 15th century prosperity of these towns is also reflected by the fact that, besides these churches, each town had other buildings for worship.

It should nevertheless be noted that not all *oppida* had such huge churches. The presence or absence of these buildings can also be considered a criterion in ranking the towns. Accordingly, the market towns with a church of smaller capacity obviously ranked lower in terms of economy. To mention but one example: the excavations conducted on the site of the parish church at Szer, a market town north of Szeged, that was destroyed during the Turkish occupation, have brought to light evidence that the church had been rebuilt and enlarged. The 12th century Romanesque parsonage, a typical village church, was 11.20 metres long and 7.64 metres wide and had a round-arched apse. The western tower was erected in the late 13th century, and the Gothic parts were added to it in the early 14th century. The sanctuary terminated in five sides of an octagon. The rebuilt church was 14.80 metres long and 6.70 metres wide (Fig. 19).[393] Consequently, the church at Szer was not enlarged in the 15th century.

The primary aim of this paper was to point out the significance of archaeology in clarifying the settlement history of the Great Hungarian Plain, and we have also attempted to illustrate general conclusions by citing the most relevant examples.[394]

[390] V. Bácskai: *Magyar mezővárosok a XV. században (Market towns in 15th century Hungary)*. Budapest (1965) 28, 34.

[391] G. Entz: Középkori egyházi emlékek régészeti kutatása (Archaeological investigation of medieval ecclesiastical relics). *RégFüz* II. 14 (1971) 64–66; G. Entz: Gótikus építészetünk településalakító szerepe (The influence of Gothic architecture on settlement forms and settlement patterns). *Építés- és Építészettudomány* 2 (1979) 20–21.

[392] L. Gerevich: A gótika korának művészete (The art of the Gothic). *A magyarországi művészet története* Ed. by L. Fülep. Budapest (1970⁴) 170–173; G. Entz: Baukunst in Ungarn um 1500. *Acta Historiae Artium* 13 (1967) 82–84.

[393] F. Horváth: Szer plébániatemploma és a település középkori története (The parish church at Szer and the medieval history of the settlement). *MFMÉ* (1974–75/1) 347–348. The groundplans of the churches, shown on the same scale in the appendix, clearly indicate that the settlement of Szer was far less significant compared with the other market towns in question which had huge churches.

[394] The Figures were drawn by Zsuzsa Kuczogi. This manuscript was closed in 1981. The ensuing years saw an upswing in the research and historiography of Hungarian towns, and a number of books and studies devoted to towns have been published, including some that discuss the towns surveyed in this study. These are the following: *Szeged története I. A kezdetektől 1686-ig (The history of Szeged I. From prehistory to 1868)*. Ed. by Gy. Kristó. Szeged (1983); *Vác története I. (The history of Vác)*. Ed. by V. Sápi. Szentendre (1983); *Tanulmányok Gyöngyösről (Studies on Gyöngyös)*. Ed. by P. Havassy–P. Kecskés. Gyöngyös (1984); J. Darkó: A mezővárosi fejlődés egy példája: Ráckeve (XV–XVII. század) (A case study for the development of market towns: Ráckeve in the 15th–17th centuries). *Falvak, mezővárosok az Alföldön*. Ed. by L. Novák–L. Selmeczi. Nagykőrös (1986) 343–372. For Nyírbátor see now *Szabolcs-Szatmár megye műemlékei II.* Ed. by G. Entz. Budapest (1987) 133–152. These studies have clarified several minor points, but they have not basically altered the arguments and hypotheses proposed in this study.

# REFERENCES

Bálint, S. (1970–71): Újabb adatok Szeged középkori történetéhez (Contributions to the medieval history of Szeged.) *MFMÉ*, 199–212.

Bálint, S. (1975): *Szeged reneszánsz kori műveltsége (The Renaissance in Szeged)*. Budapest.

Csánki, D. (1890): *Magyarország történeti földrajza a Hunyadiak korában (The historical geography of Hungary in the age of the Hunyadis)*. Vols I—III. Budapest.

Dezséri Bachó, L. (1942): *Gyöngyös története 1526-ig (The history of Gyöngyös until 1526)*. Gyöngyös.

Egli, E. (1962): *Geschichte des Städtebaues II*. Zürich–Stuttgart.

Entz, G.–Szalontai, B. (1969): *Nyírbátor*. Budapest.

Fügedi, E. (1972): Die Ausbreitung der stadtischen Lebensform—Ungarns oppida im 14. Jahrhundert. *Beiträge zur Geschichte der Städte Mitteleuropas II*. Ed. by W. Rausch. Linz/Donau.

Fügedi, E. (1977): *Vár és társadalom a 13–14. századi Magyarországon (Castle and society in 13th–14th century Hungary)*. Budapest.

Györffy, Gy. (1963): *Geographia historica Hungariae tempore stirpis Arpadianae I*. Budapest.

Györffy, Gy. (1977): *István király és műve (King Stephen and his work)*. Budapest.

Györffy, I. (1942): *Magyar nép, magyar föld (Hungarian people, Hungarian soil)*. Budapest.

Horváth, B.–Marjalaki Kiss, L.–Valentiny, K. (1962): *Miskolc*. Budapest.

Kandra, K. (1888): Bakócs-kódex: vagy: Bakócs Tamás egri püspök udvartartási számadó könyve (The Bakócs Codex: the household accounts of Tamás Bakócs, the Bishop of Eger). *Adatok az Egri Egyházmegye történetéhez II*. Eger.

Katzinger, W. (1978): *Die Märkte Oberösterreichs. Eine Studie zu ihren Anfängen im 13. und 14. Jahrhundert*. Forschungen zur Geschichte der Städten und Märkte Österreichs. Linz/Donau.

Komáromy, J. (1957): Beszámoló a miskolci Sötétkapu melletti ásatás eredményeiről (Report on the excavation near the Dark Gate of Miskolc). *HOMÉ* 1, 70–101.

Komáromy, J. (1960): *Adatok Miskolc korai településtörténetéhez (Contributions to the early settlement history of Miskolc)*. Miskolc.

Komáromy, J. (1960a): *A múzeumépület — a középkori scola építéstörténete (The museum building — the architectural history of the medieval scola)*. Miskolc.

Komáromy, J. (1962): *Miskolc élete az Anjouk alatt (Miskolc under the Angevins)*. Miskolc.

Komáromy, J. (1966): Miskolc kezdeti településtörténetének néhány kérdése (The early settlement history of Miskolc). *HOMÉ* 6, 389–406.

Kovács, B. (1965): Eger középkori utcái (The medieval streets of Eger). *EMÉ* 3, 73–92.

Kubinyi, A. (1971): A középkori magyarországi városhálózat hierarhikus térbeli rendjének kérdéséhez (The hierarchic and spatial arrangement of towns in medieval Hungary). *Településtudományi Közlemények* 23, 58–78

Kubinyi, A. (1975): Zur Frage der deutschen Siedlungen im mittleren Teil des Königreichs Ungarn (1200–1541). *Die deutsche Ostsiedlung des Mittelalters als Problem der europäischen Geschichte*. Ed. by W. Schlesinger. Vorträge und Forschungen 18. Sigmaringen, 527–566.

Kubinyi, A. (1977): Einige Fragen zur Entwicklung des Städtenetzes Ungarns im 14–15. Jahrhundert. *Die mittelalterliche Städtebildung im südöstlichen Europa*. Ed. by H. Stoob. Köln–Wien, 164–183.

Kubinyi, A. (1980): Handel und Entwicklung der Städte in der ungarischen Tiefebene im Mittelalter. *Europa Slavica — Europa Orientalis*. Festschrift für H. Ludat zum 70. Geburtstag. Ed. by K. D. Grothusen–K. Zernack. Berlin, 423–444.

László, Gy. (1944): *A honfoglaló magyar nép élete (Life of the Hungarians in the Conquest period)*. Budapest.

Lukcsics, P. (1938): *XV. századi pápák oklevelei (Charters of 15th century popes)*. Vol. II. Budapest.

Magdics, I. (1888): *Diplomatarium Ráczkeviense*. Székesfehérvár.

Major, J. (1966): A magyar városok és városhálózat kialakulásának kezdetei (The emergence of towns and of an urban network in Hungary). *Településtörténeti Közlemények* 18, 48–90.

Maksai, F. (1940): *A középkori Szatmár megye (Szatmár County in the Middle Ages)*. Budapest.

Maksay, F. (1971): *A magyar falu középkori településrendje (Settlement patterns in Hungarian villages in the Middle Ages)*. Budapest.

Marjalaki Kiss, L. (1957): A miskolci főutca topográfiája 1817-ig (The topography of the main street of Miskolc until 1817). *HOMÉ* 1, 102–127.

Marjalaki Kiss, L. (1958): Miskolc régi mellékutcái (The old side-streets of Miskolc). *HOMÉ* 2, 133–153.

Mező, A.–Németh, P. (1972): *Szabolcs-Szatmár megye történeti-etimológiai helységnévtára (Historical-etymological gazetteer of Szabolcs-Szatmár County)*. Nyíregyháza.

Nagy, J. (1978): *Eger története (The history of Eger)*. Budapest.

Németh, P. (1979): Nyírbátor: egy mezőváros a középkorban (Nyírbátor, a medieval market town). *Szabolcs-Szatmári Szemle* 14:3, 41–43.

Pataki, V. (1972): Eger története I. 1000–1526-ig (The history of Eger I. 1000–1526). *HMM* II, 13–17.

Prinz, Gy. (1922): *Magyarország településformái (Settlement forms in Hungary)*. Budapest.

Reizner, J. (1900): *Szeged története (History of Szeged)*. Vols I–IV. Szeged.

Sebestyén, K. Cs. (1938): *Szeged középkori templomai (The medieval churches of Szeged)*. Szeged.

Soós, I. (1975): *Heves megye községei 1867-ig (Settlements of Heves County until 1876)*. Budapest.

Szalontai, B. (1978): Nyírbátor története és középkori cserépedényei (History of Nyirbátor and its medieval pottery). *Szabolcs-Szatmári Szemle* 13:2, 73–94.

Szarka, Gy. (1948): *Vác katolikus intézményei és épületei a török hódítás korában (Catholic institutions and buildings of Vác during the Turkish occupation)*. Vác.

Székely, Gy. (1964): Wallons et italiens en Europe centrale aux XIe–XVIe siècles. *AnnUnivBud* 6, 2–19.

Szendrei, J. (1886–1904): *Miskolc város története és egyetemes helyirata (History and topography of Miskolc)*. Vols I–III. Miskolc.

# ABBREVIATIONS

| | |
|---|---|
| ANRW | Aufstieg und Niedergang der römischen Welt. Berlin. |
| AO | *Anjou-kori okmánytár (Codex diplo-Hungaricus Andegavensis).* Ed. by I. Nagy–Gy. Tasnády Nagy. Vols I–VII. Budapest (1878–1920). |
| AUO | *Árpád-kori új okmánytár (Codex diplomaticus Arpadi continuatus).* Ed. by G. Wenzel. Vols I–XII. Budapest (1860–1874). |
| CD | *Codex diplomaticus Hungariae ecclesiasticus ac civilis.* Ed. by G. Fehér. Vols I–XI. Buda (1829–1944). |
| CIL | Corpus Inscriptionum Latinarum. Berlin. |
| Dl | Hungarian National Archives, pre-Mohács Collection. Budapest. |
| HMM | *Heves Megye Műemlékei (Art monuments of Heves County).* Ed. by D. Dercsényi–P. Voit. Vols I–III. Budapest (1969–1978). |
| MES | *Monumenta ecclesiae Strigoniensis.* Ed. by F. Knauz–C. L. Dedek. Vols I–III. Strigonii [Esztergom] (1874–1882). |
| MGH | *Monumenta Germaniae Historica.* Ed. by G. H. Pertz. Vols I–XXXII. Lipsiae–Hannoverae (1926–1934). |
| MonBp | *Budapest történetének okleveles emlékei (Monumenta diplomatica civitatis Budapest).* Ed. by A. Gárdonyi. Budapest (1936). |
| MRT 2 | I. Éri–M. Kelemen–P. Németh–I. Torma: *Veszprém Megye Régészeti Topográfiája. A veszprémi járás (The Archaeological Site Survey of Veszprém County. The Veszprém district).* Magyarország Régészeti Topográfiája 2. Budapest (1969). |
| MRT 5 | I. Horváth–M. Kelemen–I. Torma: *Komárom Megye Régészeti Topográfiája. Esztergom és a dorogi járás (The Archaeological Site Survey of Komárom County. Esztergom and the Dorog district).* Magyarország Régészeti Topográfiája 5. Budapest (1979). |
| PWRE | Paulys Realencyclopädie der classischen Altertumswissenschaft. Neu begonnen von G. Wissowa. Stuttgart. |
| RegArp | *Az Árpádházi királyok okleveleinek kritikai jegyzéke (Regesta regum stirpis Arpadianae critico-diplomatica).* Ed. by I. Szentpétery. Vols I–II. Budapest (1923–1943). |
| RIU | Die römische Inschriften Ungarns. Budapest. |
| SRH | *Scriptores rerum Hungaricum tempore ducum regumque stirpis Arpadianae gestarum.* Ed. by E. Szentpétery. Vols I–II. Budapest (1937–1938). |
| SzIE | *Emlékkönyv Szent István király halálának kilencszázadik évfordulóján (Memorial volume on the occasion of the 900th anniversary of the death of King St. Stephen).* Ed. by J. Serédi. Vols I–III. Budapest (1938). |
| ZsO | *Zsigmond-kori oklevéltár (Charters from the reign of King Sigismund).* Ed. by E. Mályusz. Vols I–II. Budapest (1951–1958). |

∗

| | |
|---|---|
| ActaArchHung | Acta Archaeologica Academiae Scientiarium Hungaricae, Budapest |
| AnnUnivBud | Annales Universitatis Budapestinensis de Rolando Eötvös nominatae, Budapest |
| AnzÖAW | Anzeiger der Österreichischen Akademie der Wissenschaften, Wien |

| | |
|---|---|
| ArchAustr | Archaeologia Austriaca, Wien |
| ArchÉrt | Archaeologiai Értesítő, Budapest |
| ArchHung | Archaeologia Hungarica, Budapest |
| ArchKözl | Archaeologiai Közlemények, Budapest |
| ArchRozhl | Archaeologické Rozhledy, Prague |
| BAR | British Archaeological Reports, Oxford |
| BJ | Bonner Jahrbücher des Rheinischen Landesmuseums in Bonn und des Vereins von Altertumsfreunden im Rheinlande, Köln |
| BudRég | Budapest Régiségei, Budapest |
| BVbl | Bayerische Vorgeschichtsblätter, München |
| DissPann | Dissertationes Pannonicae, Budapest |
| EMÉ | Az Egri Múzeum Évkönyve, Eger |
| ÉTtK | Értekezések a történeti tudományok köréből, Budapest |
| FolArch | Folia Archaeologica, Budapest |
| HOMÉ | A Herman Ottó Múzeum Évkönyve, Miskolc |
| HOMKözl | A Herman Ottó Múzeum Közleményei, Miskolc |
| IKMK | Az István Király Múzeum Közleményei, Székesfehérvár |
| JÖAI | Jahreshefte des Österreichischen Archäologischen Instituts in Wien, Vienna |
| LevKözl | Levéltári Közlemények, Budapest |
| MFMÉ | A Móra Ferenc Múzeum Évkönyve, Szeged |
| MittArchInst | Mitteilungen des Archäologischen Instituts der ungarischen Akademie der Wissenschaften, Budapest |
| MIÖG | Mitteilungen des Instituts für österreichische Geschichtsforschung, Innsbruck-Graz |
| MTA II OK | A Magyar Tudományos Akadémia Társadalmi-Történeti Osztályának Közleményei, Budapest |
| RégFüz | Régészeti Füzetek, Budapest |